Disorderly Women

Disorderly Women

*Sexual Politics & Evangelicalism
in Revolutionary New England*

SUSAN JUSTER

CORNELL UNIVERSITY PRESS
Ithaca & London

THIS BOOK HAS BEEN SUPPORTED BY A GRANT FROM THE NATIONAL
ENDOWMENT FOR THE HUMANITIES, AN INDEPENDENT FEDERAL AGENCY.

First published 1994 by Cornell University Press.

Printed in the United States of America

⊗ The paper in this book meets the minimum requirements of the
American National Standard for Information Sciences—Permanence of
Paper for Printed Library Materials, ANSI Z39.48-1984.

Library of Congress Cataloging-in-Publication Data

Juster, Susan.
    Disorderly women : sexual politics and Evangelicalism in
  revolutionary New England / Susan Juster.
        p. cm.
    Includes bibliographical references and index.
    ISBN 0-8014-2732-0
    1. Baptist women—New England—History—18th century.
2. Baptists—New England—History—18th century. 3. Sex role—Religious
aspects—Christianity—History of doctrines—18th century.
4. Evangelicalism—New England—History—18th century. 5. New
England—Church history—18th century. I. Title.
BX6239.J87 1994
286'.082—dc20   94-191656

CONTENTS

PREFACE

THOUGH THE MEN AND WOMEN PORTRAYED in this book are distant in time and intellectual orientation, I would hope that they might recognize at least something of themselves in what follows. They would find my reading of their faith in gendered terms strange if not entirely incomprehensible; they would be distinctly uncomfortable with my attempts to place the inner reality of their religious experiences in the context of the larger political struggles of colony and empire; they would reject emphatically any suggestion that their commitment to sexual egalitarianism be judged by the standards of the profane world (including the world of academic feminism). But I would hope that the evocation of the evangelical sense of fellowship as one not bounded by conventional notions of time and space, a fellowship in which saints enjoyed a "glorious Oneness" with one another unmindful of the secular distinctions of wealth, status, and gender which awaited outside the meetinghouse, would strike a familiar chord. The language and cadences of evangelical religion have always struck me as providing a particularly powerful way to understand (indeed to construct) self and community, and I hope that some of the experiential flavor of evangelicalism comes through in this book, despite my efforts to encase it in the categories and analytical structures of gender history.

Throughout this book I have used the case of the Baptists of New England to illustrate the experience of evangelical Protestants more generally. The colony of Rhode Island, that refuge of religious outcasts and scourge of the Puritan establishment, was home to the first Baptist congregations in New England. Though few Baptist communities could be found outside the commercial centers of Newport and Providence in the seventeenth century, by the early eighteenth groups of missionaries from Rhode Island began to cross the border into Connecticut to assist in establishing sister churches. Despite fierce resistance on the part of the Congregational establishment, the Standing Order, these missionaries succeeded in founding a small congregation at Groton in 1704; by 1740, the number of Baptist churches in the entire colony of Connecticut stood only at three. These fledgling societies struggled to survive until the revivals of the First Great Awakening in the 1740s dramatically changed the religious landscape of New England, swelling the ranks of dissenters such as the Baptists. Certainly not all northern evangelicals were Baptists, nor did all Baptists think and act alike in matters of religion. But Baptists were the standard-bearers for the evangelical cause in New England throughout the seventeenth and most of the eighteenth centuries. It was not until the Methodists arrived on the scene in the late eighteenth century that the Baptists' claim to represent the evangelical wing of New England's Puritan heritage was seriously challenged.

By the term "evangelical" I mean both a distinctive theological stance and liturgical style. Evangelicals shared four religious characteristics: an insistence on the primacy of the relationship of the individual to God; lay supremacy within the meetinghouse; unfettered congregational autonomy, in which the local church functioned independently of higher authorities (either ecclesiastical or secular); and a language of religious pietism or emotional fervor. On all four counts, the Baptist community in New England represents perhaps the purest expression of the evangelical mode of worship. By refusing to baptize children and insisting on a full verbal declaration of faith on the part of adult converts who wished to join a church, Baptists remained true to the Puritan notion that religious conversion consisted of the unmediated infusion of God's grace into the individual soul. Once having been immersed in water, the convert reemerged as a new soul, reborn into a community that recognized no relationship save that of the individual with Christ.

The justification for lumping all the various Baptist factions (open and closed communion, Five and Six Principle, Seventh and First Day, General and Particular) into a single group requires some explanation. The collapsing of distinctive strands of the denomination into an undifferentiated community seems to me warranted on several levels. First, as William McLoughlin has stressed in his massive study of New England dissent, Baptists collectively faced a hostile religious establishment committed to their suppression. Even Baptists enjoying the relatively liberal climate of Rhode Island, which placed no legal or political restrictions on worship, considered their fate bound to that of their oppressed neighbors to the south because of their shared status as religious outsiders. Second, all Baptist congregations shared a common set of organizational features which placed ultimate authority in the hands of the laity and severely curtailed the role of the minister, or "elder" as they preferred, who served as a kind of "first among equals." And finally, by the late eighteenth century, decades of united opposition to the legal and political "oppressions" of the Standing Order had effectively muted the distinctive theological and liturgical features of the various Baptist groups. McLoughlin claims that by the time of the American Revolution New England Baptists presented a united front to their ecclesiastical rivals.

To argue that the Baptist churches constituted a coherent community with a consistent world view and institutional structure is not to deny that very real and often violent disagreements existed among open and closed communion, Five and Six Principle, General and Particular Baptists. Yet the extreme sensitivity toward the finer points of doctrine exhibited by many New England Baptists only reaffirms our sense that these people held a common religious ethos. For the cardinal principle of evangelical Protestantism was the ability of lay men and women to interpret scripture for themselves, and the very fractiousness of Baptist church life is testimony to the vitality of the evangelical stress on lay initiative and individual conscience.

I have been helped along the way by scholars of rare insight and wisdom, who have generously shared their time and ideas with me. From the beginning, Kenneth Lockridge has been the ideal adviser—always probing, never intrusive, both friend and critic. The whole enterprise would have been much duller and intellectually pinched if not for his humor and breadth of historical vision. James Turner has read every version of this manuscript, and—in addition to keeping vigilant watch over my tendency to commit various grammatical sins—has contributed his incisive knowledge about the religious and intellectual development of early America and always urged me to place these developments in their transatlantic context. To the members of our junior women's reading group at the University of Michigan, I owe a special debt of thanks: Valerie Kivelson, Susan Johnson, Miriam Bodian, Sueann Caulfield, Liz Faue, Kali Israel, and, especially, Laura Lee Downs have read portions of the manuscript with good humor and healthy criticism. I have been fortunate to work with outstanding graduate students at both the University of California, Santa Barbara, and the University of Michigan from whom I learned more than I imparted: my thanks go to Keith Arbour, Stephen Hum, Catherine Kaplan, Joe LaSala, Erik Seeman, and Keith Zahniser for many hours of stimulating discussion. Others who have read and commented on various portions of the manuscript include Jon Butler, Charles Cohen, Patricia Cline Cohen, Nancy Cott, Stephen Grossbart, David Hall, Carol Karlsen, Linda Kerber, John McKivigan, David Mayfield, Gerry Moran, Teresa Murphy, Mary Beth Norton, George Rawlyk, John Shy, Alan Taylor, Susan Thorne, Maris Vinovskis, and Marilyn

Westerkamp. I thank them all for their generosity and counsel. I consider myself privileged to belong to two enormously exciting and energetic circles of academic scholarship—early American women's history and religious history—and hope that this book will open up new ground for conversation between them.

The staff at several libraries opened their doors and minds to me as I did my research; they made the experience as enjoyable as possible under often difficult circumstances: the Rhode Island Historical Society in Providence, R.I.; the Newport Historical Society in Newport, R.I.; the Connecticut State Library and Connecticut Historical Society, both in Hartford; the John Hay Library, at Brown University in Providence; the Franklin Trask Library at Andover-Newton Theological Seminary, in Newton, Mass.; the Peabody Essex Museum, in Salem, Mass.; the American Baptist Historical Society, in Rochester, N.Y.; and the American Antiquarian Society, in Worcester, Mass. I thank these institutions for permission to quote from their manuscript collections. Special thanks go to the ministers of the Warren Baptist Church and the First Baptist Church of Providence for granting me permission to look at their records, housed respectively at the John Hay Library and the Rhode Island Historical Society.

Financial assistance was provided by the Woodrow Wilson Foundation in the form of a Charlotte Newcombe Fellowship, numerous grants and fellowships from the Rackham Graduate School at the University of Michigan, and a Faculty Career Development Award from the University of California at Santa Barbara to support an additional summer in the archives.

Several portions of this manuscript have previously appeared as articles: parts of Chapters 1 and 4 were published as "Patriarchy Reborn: The Gendering of Authority in the Evangelical Church in Revolutionary New England," *Gender and History* 6 (Winter 1994): 58–81; and Chapter 6 originally appeared in the *American Quarterly* 41 (1989): 34–62.

Finally, I would like to pay special tribute to Peter Agree, my editor at Cornell University Press, for his extraordinary support throughout this whole process. Peter not only encouraged me to send an early version to the press for consideration, but has kept up my spirits at every step of the way as I undertook the tedious task of revision. He has always assured me that this project would become a good book, and I hope he is right.

To David, Jane, and Matt—thanks.

SUSAN JUSTER

Ann Arbor, Michigan

ABBREVIATIONS

Archives

AAS   American Antiquarian Society
ABHS   American Baptist Historical Society
ANTS   Franklin Trask Library, Andover-Newton Theological
              Seminary
CHS   Connecticut Historical Society
CSL   Connecticut State Library
JHL   John Hay Library, Brown University
NHS   Newport Historical Society
OSVL   Old Sturbridge Village Library
PEM   James Duncan Phillips Library, Peabody Essex Museum
RIHS   Rhode Island Historical Society

Journals

ABMMI   *American Baptist Magazine and Missionary Intelligencer*
              (1817–27)
BM   *Baptist Magazine*
CEM   *Connecticut Evangelical Magazine (1800–1807)*
CEMRI   *Connecticut Evangelical Magazine and Religious Intelligencer*
              (1807–15)
MBMMI   *Massachusetts Baptist Missionary Magazine and Intelligencer*
              (1803–16)
MMM   *Massachusetts Missionary Magazine (1803–8)*
RI   *Religious Intelligencer (1816–30)*
WMQ   *William and Mary Quarterly*

Disorderly Women

INTRODUCTION

IN THE SUMMER OF 1803 scandal threatened at the venerable First Baptist Church of Providence. For more than two hours, the congregation listened to wild tales of heresy directed against their minister, Stephen Gano, and several leading brethren in the church. The accuser was Joanna Gano, the wife of the elder, who charged her husband (an avowed freemason) with "worshipping Idols," "perverting the Scriptures," and "holding himself in connection with a Society which in her view was the 'Mystery of Iniquity' and 'in Covenant with Death and agreement with Hell.'" These were "extraordinary charges" indeed, and the church had little choice but to conduct an investigation and give Elder Gano opportunity to clear his name. When the smoke had cleared, it was not Stephen but Joanna Gano who stood convicted of "disorderly conduct." Two weeks later the church excommunicated Mrs. Gano for her "hard and unchristian language and conduct."[1]

Although such church trials were a frequent, if embarrassing, feature of Baptist congregational life throughout the eighteenth and early nineteenth centuries, the incident of Joanna and Stephen Gano departed in significant ways from earlier patterns. Joanna did not speak before the congregation but rather presented written "communications" to the church which her husband, in an extraordinary break with protocol, himself read aloud. That the accused was asked to read his own indictment before the assembled body suggests how contrived the entire trial was. The ritualized presentation of the charges and the pro forma resolution of the controversy through a series of unanimous votes, taken quickly one after another, indicate that the church gave little credence to Mrs. Gano's accusations. This was not a real trial, in which accuser and accused confronted each other in the presence of their peers, but a carefully staged reaffirmation of the church's confidence in their elder.

1. Record Book, First Baptist Church of Providence, 3 August, 9 August, and 15 August 1803, RIHS. I am grateful to the First Baptist Church for permission to use these records.

Joanna's accusations were not simply dismissed; she was in fact ridiculed for her temerity in pursuing the issue. She "complained bitterly of the conduct of several of the Brethren, whom she had called in to deal with her husband and the Masonic Brethren; saying that they had dealt hardly with her, that they had charged her with being under a delusion and with believing a lie; and that they had even said she seemeth to be under a Satanic Influence, etc." Whether the brethren saw her as possessed by demons or merely deluded, they clearly considered her a figure worthy of some contempt, and it was certainly convenient and politically expedient to label her discontents the result of mental derangement rather than to address their substance. The pernicious influence of freemasonry on Christian beliefs was, in fact, a point of contention in many Baptist congregations in the early nineteenth century, and Joanna Gano was not the first member to question publicly the propriety of the clergy's allegiance to this secret society.[2] It was no wild-eyed charge Mrs. Gano flung at her husband but an issue that threatened to upset the Baptist order's precarious social standing.

Married to a prominent and respected religious leader, well educated and highly articulate, Joanna Gano is hardly a typical figure. Her travails speak little to the experience of the thousands of humble, semiliterate Baptist women who filled the rough meetinghouses of rural New England each Sunday. Yet her exclusion from the First Baptist congregation in Providence underscores a crisis in gender relations which reverberated throughout the evangelical community in the late eighteenth century. An unlikely rebel, Joanna represents a strain of female discontent that has remained largely hidden from public view both then and now. It would be easy to dismiss her complaints as the rantings of a spiteful wife, evidence of a domestic rather than a religious tragedy, but to do so would be a mistake. In laying the blame for her estrangement from her husband and the church solely at her feet, the Providence Baptist Church signaled the intention of the larger evangelical community both to distance itself from the "disorderly" women who disrupted congregational life and to reassert its solidarity as a united household. It is significant that Joanna's failings as a Sister in Christ were largely the failures of an errant wife, for by the late eighteenth century the church had become an extension of the domestic sphere. Her sin was that of disobedience: disobedience of her husband and of the church.

Evangelical women had not always been so bound by the dictates of

2. See, for example, the records of the Second Baptist Church of Ashford for 24 January 1829 and 15 April 1831, in which several members were disciplined for being "friendly" to free masons. Record Book, vol. 1, CSL.

domestic fealty. Like marginal religious groups everywhere, the fledgling Baptist community of the late seventeenth and early eighteenth centuries had its fair share of spirited, articulate, and determined women believers. This robust tradition of female piety was further invigorated by the revivals of the First Great Awakening in the 1740s, which broke the bounds of Puritan orthodoxy in ways that had important implications for women. Rejecting the typological equation of the church with the family, revivalists sought to construct a new vision of the covenant, a vision which harkened back to the primitive church when the first apostles left family and friends behind to bond in spiritual fellowship. David Hall has evoked this sense of otherness in his description of the original vision of the Puritan emigrants: "Bounded by a special sense of time, bounded by the rituals that occurred uniquely in this place, the members of the gathered church affirmed in covenanting with one another that the 'church' was wholly different from the 'world.'"[3] Yet this vision of an otherworldly community had been slowly eroded by the "instinctive tribalism" that, in the words of Increase Mather, sought to cast the "lines of Election . . . through the loyns of godly parents."[4] The orthodox Puritan view of the church as a miniature family, originally understood in allegorical terms, had become too much of a social reality for evangelical New Lights. Only grace, they believed, should bind saints to one another.

Such a transcendental view of the power of grace flowed easily into an affirmation of the spiritual equality of souls before God. Hence the evangelical insistence that men and women, rich and poor, lettered and ignorant, were as capable of discerning spiritual truth as were ordained ministers. Hence—and here we come to the crux of the matter—the relative egalitarianism of the evangelical polity in matters of church governance in the mid-eighteenth century. For most of the eighteenth century, Baptist women enjoyed unprecedented access to the formal channels of authority within the church. The sexual egalitarianism implicit in evangelical faith, with its emphasis on individual rebirth and its undifferentiated sense of community, translated into a sharing of power between the sexes in the internal governance of the church. Until the late eighteenth century women along with

3. David D. Hall, *Worlds of Wonder, Days of Judgment: Popular Religious Belief in Early New England* (Cambridge, Mass., 1990), p. 117.

4. The Mather quote and the phrase "instinctive tribalism" are taken from Hall, pp. 152, 154. On Puritan tribalism, see Edmund Morgan, *The Puritan Family: Religion and Domestic Relations in Seventeenth-Century New England*, rev. ed. (1944; New York, 1966), chap. 7; and Gerald Moran, "Religious Renewal, Puritan Tribalism, and the Family in Seventeenth-Century Milford, Connecticut," *WMQ*, 3d ser., 36 (1979): 236–54.

men participated in all the major decisions of collective governance, from electing and dismissing pastors to admitting new members and excluding backsliding ones. We find women communicants asserting themselves theologically in the often fractious debates over the nature of conversion and qualifications for church membership and challenging with their lay brethren the periodic attempts of the Baptist clergy to enlarge their sphere of authority.

The accommodation of women at the very center of religious life in the evangelical community in the mid-eighteenth century highlights the extent to which evangelical religion itself was perceived to be "feminine." What women communicants shared with their dissenting brethren was, above all, their marginality within broader Puritan culture. In the words of one contemporary critic, revivals appealed to "old women of both Sexes."[5] Amy Schrager Lang has made the suggestive comment that, as a heuristic category for the dispossessed, the "feminine" should be taken to include not only women but all those social groups that occupied the margins of colonial New England—the poor, transient, young, and unfree. This equation of marginality with femininity was enhanced, Lang argues, in the First Great Awakening. "For all the attention paid by historians to the new male convert during the Great Awakening, it may be more useful, finally, to regard these converts as so many more 'women' constrained not by their sex but by the conditions attending their lives in the 1740s." Because the "feminine" religious language of the Awakening (which elevated the heart over the head) seemed to remove the experience of grace from the bonds of law and place it in the realm of affection, the entire theological underpinnings of Puritanism were placed at risk. Not "visible signs" such as wealth or social status or familial position mattered in the crucial task of identifying the regenerate, but rather the state of one's heart.[6]

Lang's insight is key to understanding why the evangelical community initially welcomed women into its ranks and accorded them political privileges not available in Congregational churches. As fellow travelers in the crusade to revitalize a moribund faith, evangelical men and women both positioned themselves outside the dominant religious culture and—more important—celebrated their otherworldly status as a sign of divine grace. Constantly exhorting one another to "come out and be ye separate," to reject the bonds of family, neighborhood, and society, mid-eighteenth-century evangelicals constructed a model of community on the ideal of *communitas*

5. "Extracts from Interleaved Almanacs of Nathan Bowen, Marblehead, 1742–1799," *Essex Institute Historical Collections* 91 (1955): 170. I am grateful to Erik Seeman for this reference.

6. Amy Schrager Lang, *Prophetic Woman: Anne Hutchinson and the Problem of Dissent in the Literature of New England* (Berkeley, Calif., 1987), pp. 105–6.

(to borrow an anthropological phrase). The essence of true community is that "glorious Oneness" that evangelical congregations sought to forge in their congregations, "a flowing from *I* to *Thou*" (in Martin Buber's terms) which signaled the breakdown of old barriers and the creation of a new community undifferentiated by conventional social categories.[7]

To suggest that such a vision of community was gendered is not to say that eighteenth-century evangelicals necessarily thought in terms of "feminine" and "masculine" when they contrasted the sacred to the profane. Certainly they did not speak in the language of gender but rather in the neutral idiom of the Spirit, which, after all, by its very nature transcended earthly categories. Nonetheless, the qualities that defined the evangelical faith—its emotionalism, sensuality, and above all its porous sense of self—were qualities that to the eighteenth-century mind were distinctly female. The sexual undercurrent of evangelical language converted saints into "brides" of Christ who shared an erotic as well as spiritual union with the divine bridegroom.[8] But the feminine nature of evangelical religion goes much deeper than its sexualized tropes and sensuous imagery. Converts not only assumed particular female roles like those of wife and lover but shared in the essential instability of the female character. To early modern theorists woman was a creature of passion, emotionally as well as intellectually unstable. As an early modern proverb put it, "women are in churches, saints: abroad, angels: at home, devils: at windows, sirens: at doors, magpies: and in gardens, goats."[9] Woman's protean character made her particularly susceptible to manipulation by those of stronger will and superior understanding.

Such was the contemporary understanding of evangelical religion as well, which could appear both divine and demonic at the same time. The speed with which manifestations of grace (the physical convulsions, wild cries, and distorted features of the converted) could degenerate into crude displays of carnal excess suggests how porous was the line between God's handiwork and the devil's. And straddling the line was "woman," that "liminal crea-

---

7. The phrase "glorious Oneness" is from *The Diary of Isaac Backus*, ed. William McLoughlin (Providence, R.I., 1979), 1:233. Buber's phrase is quoted in Victor Turner, *The Ritual Process: Structure and Anti-Structure* (Chicago, 1969), p. 127.

8. David Leverenz, *The Language of Puritan Feeling: An Exploration in Literature, Psychology, and Social History* (New Brunswick, N.J., 1980); Donald Maltz, "The Bride of Christ Is Filled with His Spirit," in *Women in Ritual and Symbolic Roles*, ed. Judith Hoch-Smith and Anita Spring (New York, 1978); Margaret Masson, "The Typology of the Female as a Model for the Regenerate: Puritan Preaching, 1690–1730," *Signs: A Journal of Women in Culture and Society* 2 (1976): 304–15; and Philip Greven, *The Protestant Temperament: Patterns of Child-Rearing, Religious Experience, and the Self in Early America* (New York, 1980).

9. Quoted in Peter Brown, *The Body and Society: Men, Women, and Sexual Renunciation in Early Christianity* (New York, 1988), p. 153.

ture" (in Phyllis Mack's words) who occupied the interstices of early modern epistemological categories: nature/culture, feeling/reason, sacred/profane. Mack has noted astutely that religious dissenters in the seventeenth and eighteenth centuries could hardly avoid the derogatory label of "feminine," for the soul itself had come to be defined as largely female. Any tradition that elevated the soul to the pinnacle of religious experience, that made experience the sine qua non of spiritual authority, invariably bore the stigma of debased femininity. Like the female sex with which it was associated, the soul was thought to inhabit the dual worlds of the natural and supernatural, indeed to mediate between the two as the believer progressed from sin to redemption.[10]

The feminine nature of evangelical religion helps us understand not only the privileged place of women within the early church but also why the Baptist community would retreat from such a position in the late eighteenth century, when its marginality within American religious culture came to be seen as a liability rather than as a sign of grace. In the half-century following the Awakening, women's position within the evangelical church underwent a dramatic reappraisal as the Baptist churches in New England transformed themselves from (in classic sociological terminology) a sect to a denomination. Baptists experienced spectacular growth in the second half of the century and achieved a corresponding measure of legitimacy in the eyes of the Standing Order of New England Congregationalism.[11] Beginning with the establishment of a college to train prospective ministers and the formation of the first regional association of Baptist churches in the 1760s, the Baptist order began to refashion its sense of self and its mission. What had once been a true community of saints became transformed into a society of churchgoers.

This new concern for legitimacy was fueled in part by the involvement of

10. Phyllis Mack, *Visionary Women: Ecstatic Prophecy in Seventeenth-Century England* (Berkeley, Calif., 1992), pp. 24–44. On the disorder of women in early modern culture, see Natalie Zemon Davis, "Women on Top," in her *Society and Culture in Early Modern France* (Stanford, Calif., 1965), pp. 124–51; and Lyndal Roper, "Will and Honor: Sex, Words, and Power in Augsburg Criminal Trials," *Radical History Review* 43 (1989): 45–71. On the instability of the female subject in English Renaissance literature and culture, see Catherine Belsey, *The Subject of Tragedy: Identity and Difference in Renaissance Drama* (New York, 1985), part 2. See Mack, *Visionary Women*, and Denise Riley, *Am I That Name? Feminism and the Category of "Women" in History* (Minneapolis, 1988), for a discussion of the gendered nature of the soul in early modern thought.

11. By 1740, fourteen Baptist churches had been established in Rhode Island, including large congregations in Newport and Providence, with another eleven Baptist churches scattered throughout Massachusetts and Connecticut. For a detailed account of the institutional growth of the northern Baptists, see William McLoughlin, *New England Dissent, 1630–1833: The Baptists and the Separation of Church and State* (Cambridge, Mass., 1971).

the evangelical leadership in the revolutionary movement of the late eighteenth century. Retreating from its steadfastly apolitical stance of the 1740s and 50s, the Baptist clergy began in the late eighteenth century to demonstrate a new political consciousness that put a sectarian gloss on the imperial crisis of the 1760s and 1770s. Drawing parallels between the struggle of the American colonies to free themselves from a tyrannical imperial master and the struggles of religious dissenters against the oppressions of the established Congregational church, evangelicals threw their support behind the patriot cause. Issuing patriotic calls to arms through political broadsides and pamphlets, serving as militia chaplains in the Continental army, and bringing the patriot message to the thousands of rural New Englanders who gathered in meetinghouses on Sunday mornings, the Baptist clergy assumed a prominent moral authority during the revolutionary crisis that signaled their political coming of age.[12]

As the evangelical church thus moved from the periphery to the center of religious and political life in New England, its relationship with its female members became more problematic. The feminine nature of the church became a cause for concern among the evangelical leadership because the marginality of the church was now, for the first time, seen as a sign of weakness rather than strength. A politically vigorous and socially respectable religious society needed a more masculine image, and hence we see the emergence of patriarchal language and structures in Baptist churches after 1780. References to the church as a "household" ruled by "father" figures and to God as a "parent" who punishes disobedient "children" and rewards filial piety become more commonplace in the last decades of the century. The role and authority of the pastor (who increasingly adopted the title of "reverend" rather than "elder") assumed new heights, and many aspects of church governance were delegated for the first time away from the collective membership to standing committees composed exclusively of men. In the process, women were effectively disenfranchised from church politics and their voices ignored or silenced. Those who did attempt to speak out against their marginality found themselves, like Joanna Gano, disowned for "disorderly conduct," a popular phrase.

By 1780 or so, "disorder" in general had become a synonym for femininity.

12. Patricia Bonomi, *Under the Cope of Heaven: Religion, Society, and Politics in Colonial America* (New York, 1986); Harry Stout, *The New England Soul: Preaching and Religious Culture in Colonial New England* (New York, 1986); Donald Weber, *Rhetoric and History in Revolutionary New England* (New York, 1988). William McLoughlin has been the foremost authority on the role of the Baptist clergy in the Revolution; see his essays in *Soul Liberty: The Baptists' Struggle in New England, 1630–1833* (Hanover, N.H., 1991) and his monumental *New England Dissent*.

Not only were individual women excluded from church communion for a variety of offenses having to do with disorderly speech and conduct (slander, lying, fornication, lascivious carriage) but feminine qualities in general came to define the very essence of sin. The process by which sin became a gendered construct was a subtle one, occurring largely beneath and between the lines of the official church records. "Dissimulation," for example, was a key element in the evangelical understanding of disorder and manifested itself in a variety of guises in the late eighteenth century—from women who spread false rumors about their neighbors' private affairs to men who tried to deceive their customers and defraud their creditors. The general motif of dissimulation can be found throughout church discipline records, but on closer examination the peculiarly female quality of dissimulation is apparent. The strong association of women with certain categories of sin, most notably slander and bearing false witness, lent a feminine cast to other categories of transgression which were not gender-specific. Once "dissimulation" was redefined as an inherently feminine vice, men who practiced deceit became, to paraphrase Amy Lang, "so many women" in the eyes of the evangelical church. This process of transference is most striking in the case of men who joined the Baptist church during the revivals of the early nineteenth century; as unreliable and suspect soldiers in the evangelical cause, recent converts (male and female alike) were more prone to be disciplined for sins that, in the larger population of church members, devolved specifically on women.

The relationship between the semiotics and the politics of gender, between the rhetorical strategy of defining disorder in gendered terms after the Revolution and the marginalization of women within the evangelical church, is elusive and difficult to document. It was certainly not direct. There is always a danger in assuming that the ideological configuration of gender opposition—what is meant by the terms "masculine" and "feminine" as a means of organizing social perception—has a direct bearing on the way individual men and women live and relate to one another. But, as feminist scholarship has made abundantly clear, we must be careful not to confuse masculine/feminine with male/female. "The former are a set of symbolic references, the latter physical persons, and though there is a relationship between them, they are not the same," Joan Scott cautions.[13] The difficulty lies in determining exactly what that relationship should look like. Where

13. Joan Scott, "Language and Working-Class History," in her *Gender and the Politics of History* (New York, 1988), p. 63. In this book I have tried to remain true to contemporary understandings of "masculine" and "feminine" in Anglo-American culture in the eighteenth and early nineteenth centuries rather than assume an essential, ahistorical set of meanings.

do individuals form their notions of "masculine" and "feminine"? One answer points to the body and sexuality, to the gender-specific experiences of birth, lactation, menstruation, ejaculation. Historians of religion have been acutely aware of the power of body representations, specifically those relating to sexuality, in generating the language and images through which people imagine their faith (Christ as "Spermidote," the church as nursing mother, the saint as receptive womb for the "seed" of grace).[14] "We are more than culture. We are Body," Caroline Walker Bynum has written in a somewhat defiant assertion of the integral relationship between human sexuality and cultural practices, including and most especially religion.[15] Early modern political theorists, too, used metaphors of body to describe the power of the state (the king's "two bodies," the magical royal "touch" that cured disease) and invoked images of disease and pathology when state and society broke down. From the Renaissance on, the "high" discourses of philosophy, statecraft, theology and law were conducted primarily in the idiom of the body.[16]

"Body," however, is not a fixed biological reality but an imaginative construct, one whose gendered nature has, moreover, only recently emerged as the defining characteristic of the self.[17] In this book I have located the source of ideologies of gender more in the realm of political struggle than in the realm of bodily experience, however mediated notions of "masculine" and

14. For examples of sexualized imagery in Puritan writings, see Walter Hughes, "'Meat out of the Eater': Panic and Desire in American Puritan Poetry," in *Engendering Men: The Question of Male Feminist Criticism*, ed. Joseph A. Boone and Michael Cadden (New York, 1990); Margaret Masson, "The Typology of the Female as a Model for the Regenerate: Puritan Preaching, 1690–1730," *Signs* 2 (1976): 304–15.

15. Caroline Walker Bynum, *Fragmentation and Redemption: Essays on Gender and the Human Body in Medieval Religion* (New York, 1992), p. 20. See also her "The Body of Christ in the Later Middle Ages: A Reply to Leo Steinberg," *Renaissance Quarterly* 39 (1986), and "Bodily Miracles and the Resurrection of the Body in the High Middle Ages," in *Belief in History: Innovative Approaches to European and American Religion*, ed. Thomas Kselman (South Bend, Ind., 1991). The starting point for many religious historians is the work of Mary Douglas on the relation between body symbols and cosmology; see her discussion of the continual exchange of meanings between the physical and the social body, *Natural Symbols: Explorations in Cosmology* (London, 1970), pp. 65–81.

16. Ernst H. Kantorowicz, *The King's Two Bodies: A Study in Medieval Political Theology* (Princeton, N.J., 1957); Marc Bloch, *The Royal Touch: Sacred Monarchy and Scrofula in England and France*, trans. J. E. Anderson (London, 1973). See Peter Stallybrass and Allon White, *The Politics and Poetics of Transgression* (Ithaca, 1986), for a discussion of the role of body images in cultural discourse which draws on Mikhail Bakhtin's influential paradigm of the aesthetic and political relation between the "classical" and the "grotesque" body; Bakhtin, *Rabelais and His World*, trans. Helene Iswolsky (Bloomington, Ind., 1984).

17. See Thomas Laqueur, *Making Sex: Body and Gender from the Greeks to Freud* (Cambridge, Mass., 1990).

"feminine" are by the physical parameters of one's sexual identity. Early modern discourse was deeply concerned with the proper order of things, and a hierarchy of nature dictated the organization of the social world into its constituent and interlocking parts (including categories of gender). In this cosmology masculine was to feminine as strong was to weak, public to private, rational to expressive, material to spiritual, universal to particular.[18] Such oppositions were never merely ideological, however, but were always deeply implicated in the political battles of the early modern era which pitted the will and resources of the universalizing modern state (strong, public, rational, material) against the dense thicket of particular alliances (weak, private, expressive, spiritual) that defined the medieval past. One of the underlying themes of this book is that the modern nation-state in its various incarnations, including republican America, was quintessentially masculine in its conception of power, in the myths it told about its origins, and in its representation of "otherness"—what it was not, and what it most feared it would become.

For all its attention to individual women and their struggles with the evangelical church, then, this is as much a story about political discourse and its deeply gendered structure. The politics of language has never been absent from our narratives of women's history, although it has often played only a muted role. By identifying relations of power, rather than the boundaries between men's and women's "spheres" as the primary object of study, women's historians are beginning to attach the study of gender relations to the larger questions of how power is construed and exercised. Unlike earlier scholars who uncritically accepted the basic premise of the "separate spheres" paradigm which declared politics off limits for women and their chroniclers, historians such as Linda Kerber and Mary Beth Norton situate changes in gender norms squarely within the framework of politics (broadly conceived as both language and structure).

This book contributes to this project by examining women's changing role within the church and the adoption of a newly gendered model of authority by the evangelical community as inseparable components of the democratization of evangelical religion (components entirely absent from recent celebratory renditions of the same process).[19] Coincident with the

18. See, in particular, Michel Foucault, *The Order of Things: An Archaeology of the Human Sciences* (New York, 1970), and *The History of Sexuality: An Introduction*, trans. Robert Hurley (New York, 1985).

19. See Nathan O. Hatch, *The Democratization of American Christianity* (New Haven, Conn., 1989); Gordon S. Wood, "Evangelical America and Early Mormonism," *New York History* 61 (October 1980): 359–86; and Wood, *The Radicalism of the American Revolution* (New York, 1992).

evangelical clergy's embrace of revolutionary politics, an older model of authority premised on the organic unity of the body of saints gave way to a newer model predicated on the hierarchical layering of individual interests. The story of the evangelical church's transformation from a community of saints to a society of churchgoers is, in part, a retelling of one of the major stories of early American history: the evolution of political ideology away from the consensual model of republican virtue to the mechanical model of democratic self-interest. What I hope to show is that this broad transformation of political culture was enacted not only on the level of political organization but also on the ideological terrain of gender.

The risk in analyzing the political and ideological roots of gender symbolism at such a high level of abstraction is that gender may appear an entirely empty category, an epistemological system of differentiation which hovers above the contingencies of lived experience.[20] I have tried in this book to move constantly back and forth between these two levels of analysis—the symbolic and the political, to see how the changing ideological construction of gender within the evangelical community during the revolutionary era disrupted the balance of power between the sexes within that community. Late-eighteenth-century evangelicals did not merely jettison an older religious vocabulary of *communitas* in favor of a more secular language of society by redefining this older tradition as "female," but they took active measures to rid the church of those flesh-and-blood women who were seen to be the bearers of this tradition. Women and their ineradicable femaleness became a metaphor for disorder in the revolutionary era, but they were a living metaphor whose presence could not be erased by a simple act of linguistic displacement.

The revolutionary era has proved a particularly fruitful context for examining the relationship of gender to politics, of language to power.[21] Women's slide into marginality within the evangelical church prefigured the success of the American Revolution in aligning political and patriarchal authority in the form of the manly citizen. The Revolution did not create the legal and

20. For an illuminating exchange over this tendency to reify the category of gender, see Laura Lee Downs, "If 'Woman' Is Just an Empty Category, Then Why Am I Afraid to Walk Alone at Night? Identity Politics Meets the Postmodern Subject," *Comparative Studies in Society and History* 35 (April 1993): 414–37, Joan Scott's reply, "The Tip of the Volcano," and Downs's "Reply to Joan Scott," pp. 438–51.

21. As Nancy Cott noted in a forum on gender in the early republic, "In the era of democratic revolutions the language of politics was changed significantly; new words had to be invented to express new concepts. We ought to pay attention insofar as gender organization is implicated in these changes in the language of politics." Cott et al., "Beyond Roles, Beyond Spheres: Thinking about Gender in the Early Republic," *WMQ* 46 (July 1989): 567.

political disabilities under which American women suffered well into the nineteenth century (and even ameliorated some of them), but it threw into bold relief the disjuncture between men who enjoyed the "natural rights" of life, liberty, and property and women whose domestic labor and fealty were suborned in order to secure these rights. Female dependency and male independence were yoked together in republican visions of the political family, a bind that was particularly galling for evangelical women who had once shared a "glorious Oneness" with their dissenting brethren.

The moral of the story is not that the colonial period constituted a kind of golden age for American women and the Revolution a biblical fall. True, in one critical area—radical religion—women enjoyed relatively full access to the formal channels of authority (with the important exception of the pastorate) for most of the eighteenth century. And true, such broad political powers were abruptly canceled after the Revolution as the evangelical church masculinized its polity and its mission. Just as American women in general were not included under the political category of citizen in the early republic, so Baptist women in New England were no longer considered citizens of the church but rather dependents in a household ruled by men.[22] But however vital and empowering evangelical religion was for colonial women, it offered but a slender reed upon which to build a more egalitarian vision of society. Equality in the eyes of the Lord has never meant equality outside the religious community; the term "equality" itself is probably misleading when applied to things of the Spirit, for it smacks of the kind of earthly considerations evangelicals eagerly left behind when they assembled in their congregations. Indeed, the very ground on which notions of spiritual equality were nourished made translation into secular terms difficult if not impossible. For evangelical women drew strength and purpose from a

22. The relevant literature is too vast to be covered here, but for exponents of the "golden age" thesis see Mary Ryan, *Womanhood in America* (New York, 1975); Roger Thompson, *Women in Stuart England and America: A Comparative Study* (New York, 1974); and Gerda Lerner, "The Lady and the Mill Girl: Changes in the Status of Women in the Age of Jackson," *Mid-Continent American Studies Journal* 10 (1969): 5–15. Cornelia Dayton's study of women and the law in eighteenth-century Connecticut narrates a path for colonial women from integration to marginality over the course of the century similar to the story told here; see her "Women before the Bar: Gender, Law, and Society in Connecticut, 1710–1790," Ph.D. diss., Princeton University, 1986. Those who disagree with this interpretation include Lyle Koehler, *A Search for Power: The "Weaker Sex" in 17th-Century New England* (New York, 1980); Mary Beth Norton, "The Evolution of White Women's Experience in Early America," *American Historical Review* 89 (1984): 593–619; Carol F. Karlsen, *The Devil in the Shape of a Woman: Witchcraft in Colonial New England* (New York, 1987); and Christine Heyrman, *Commerce and Culture: The Maritime Communities of Colonial New England* (New York, 1984). Norton, especially, in *Liberty's Daughters: The Revolutionary Experience of American Women, 1750–1800* (Boston, 1980), presents the American Revolution as a decisive victory for women, a defining moment in the search for ultimate political and legal equality.

faith that equated piety with humility, marginality with godliness—attributes that signified powerlessness to the world beyond the walls of the meetinghouse.[23] Whatever power Baptist women possessed was the power of the weak: a paradox that unraveled in the revolutionary crisis of the late-eighteenth century, leaving evangelical women to bear alone the burden of dependency as men assumed their place in the governing structures of the new republic.[24]

23. For a less pessimistic reading of the Puritan tendency to equate piety with female humility, see Amanda Porterfield, *Female Piety in Puritan New England: The Emergence of Religious Humanism* (New York, 1992).

24. See Elizabeth Janeway, *Powers of the Weak* (New York, 1981), and Albert Memmi *Dependence* (Boston, 1984), for discussions of how early modern concepts of dependency envisioned a realm of voluntary subordination rather than coerced subjection; as Joan R. Gundersen points out, this definition of dependency underwent significant alteration in the revolutionary crisis of the late eighteenth century as American men struggling to free themselves from their own political dependency as colonial subjects stripped the term of its voluntary associations and rewrote independence as a male prerogative. Gundersen, "Independence, Citizenship, and the American Revolution," *Signs* 13 (1987): 59–77.

CHAPTER ONE

"BREAKING" THE SABBATH

The Evangelical Challenge in the Great Awakening

WHEN THE PURITANS FIRST ENCOUNTERED (in Robert Cushman's memorable phrase) the "vast and empty chaos" that to them was New England, they set out to consecrate the land they had taken from the native inhabitants.[1] Harkening back to an almost medieval conception of the sacred, the first settlements in colonial New England made palpable a vision of community which sought redemption in the land. The fabled "City upon a Hill" was to be no mere religious abstraction, an allegorical rendering of an essentially theological vision, but the material shape of Puritanism itself.

True iconoclasts in their rejection of the ritualized features of orthodox Protestantism, Puritans created new icons of their own.[2] No icon was more powerful, more generative of symbolic meaning, than land itself. Settling the land they called a "remote, rocky, barren, bushy, wild-woody wilderness" meant more to the first émigrés than clearing the brush, felling trees, planting crops, or even driving away the heathenish natives; it meant converting that land into sacred space in the same way that individual souls were converted by the grace of God.[3] The peculiar land policies of the first half-

---

1. Robert Cushman, "Reasons and Considerations Touching the Lawfulness of Removing out of England into the Parts of America," in *Remarkable Providences: Readings on Early American History*, ed. John Demos, 2d ed. (Boston, 1991), p. 7.

2. For a discerning discussion of Puritan iconoclasm and the re-creation of new icons in the New World, see Ann Kibbey, *The Interpretation of Material Shapes in Puritanism: A Study of Rhetoric, Prejudice, and Violence* (New York, 1986). For a very different treatment of a similar theme, see E. Brooks Holifield's essay on the re-creation of rituals within New England Puritanism; "Peace, Conflict, and Ritual in Puritan Congregations," *Journal of Interdisciplinary History* 23 (1993): 551–70.

3. See Edward Johnson, *Johnson's Wonder-Working Providence, 1628–1651*, as quoted in John Frederick Martin, *Profits in the Wilderness: Entrepreneurship and the Founding of New England*

century of settlement created a landscape in which ownership and cultivation went hand in hand. Until 1675 only collective ownership was allowed by Puritan authorities, and title carried with it the obligation to improve the land for human habitation. Absentee ownership was forbidden, although occasionally tolerated when it advanced the greater goal of bringing all of New England under Christian cultivation.[4] The obsession with improving the land (as with improving one's time) can be traced to the symbolic associations of the wilderness with idleness, corruption, and chaos; in short, with evil. The wilderness was rhetorically likened to the empty desolation of souls, both in need of regeneration through "planting" the seed of Christ. Yet, as John Frederick Martin stresses, "the wilderness was not only a metaphor for waste; it *was* a wasteland."[5] And such an empty wasteland was an affront to God and the spiritual ambitions of his people.

The solution was to "plant" towns. The New England town was to be, in ideal form, the physical embodiment of the community of "visible saints," and among first-generation Puritans the founding of a church and founding of a town were virtually synonymous events. The territorial nature of the Puritan church collapsed the social into the sacred in ways that medieval Catholics might have found familiar. Despite their efforts to smash the old icons of medieval Christendom, from holy statues to church architecture, Puritans inherited a deep and abiding attachment to the notion of sacred space, which they attempted to literalize in the wilderness of the New World.

The conflation of the physical and spiritual qualities of objects (whether of towns or churches) was a consequence of the act of transplantation itself, as old forms were discarded or reshaped in response to new needs. In the process of removing out of the Old World and into the New, Puritans invested signs and symbols that had purely allegorical significance in English culture with material shape. Thus the symbolic passage from the old to the new self through the experience of conversion became literalized in the very act of migration, while the metaphor of "visible saints" assumed concrete form in the rituals of admission adopted by Puritan churches. In

---

Towns in the Seventeenth Century (Chapel Hill, N.C., 1991), p. 112; see also John Stilgoe, *Common Landscape of America, 1580 to 1845* (New Haven, Conn., 1985), pp. 43–58, for a discussion of how Puritans envisioned enclosed communities of self-generating holiness in explicit contrast to the impermanent settlement patterns of Native Americans.

4. For a thorough discussion of Puritan land policies, see Martin, *Profits in the Wilderness.* Martin's study provides an important corrective to the prevailing interpretation of New England Puritans as anticommercial and antiexpansionist.

5. Ibid., p. 116.

similar fashion, the trope of female sanctity which was so central to Puritan rhetoric on both sides of the Atlantic became literalized in New England in the form of the pious wife and mother, as did the biblical injunction to "honor thy mother and father." And, as Ann Kibbey has argued, iconoclastic violence against the symbols of orthodox corruption became in the New World actual violence against flesh-and-blood opponents—Native Americans and witches.[6] To "convert" the profane into the sacred, it seems, was no longer an ontological problem but a material one in Puritan New England.

Such a literal enactment of the twin processes of cultivation and conversion held sway until the late seventeenth century. The reintroduction of allegory into the Puritan landscape assumed a variety of shapes. Religious innovations such as the Half-Way Covenant (1662) broke the bond between conversion and church membership, while what E. Brooks Holifield has called the "sacramental renaissance" of the late seventeenth century placed new emphasis on the ritual elements of Puritan worship.[7] Economic developments such as the spread of commerce and credit, increased land speculation, and the use of paper money helped break the landed spine of the Puritan social order. Political developments including the loss of the Massachusetts Bay charter and the creation of the Dominion of New England (1686) and the new charter of 1691 destroyed the autonomy of the Puritan commonwealths and made authority contingent on royal favor. In all these cases, what had once been a *literal* relationship became an increasingly *symbolic* one: symbolic rebirth (baptism) replaced literal rebirth (conversion) as the standard of church membership after 1662; economic value was increasingly determined by symbolic forms of capital such as paper money rather than by the concrete possession of land; and political authority was now the secondary reflection of power that resided elsewhere, in the figure of the king.

Within the Puritan church itself, a similar process was occurring. Once the Half-Way Covenant was adopted, the notion of a church of visible saints was seriously compromised, fatally so in the eyes of some. Other corruptions soon followed. The "open communion" policy of Solomon Stoddard in the Connecticut River valley, in which the doors of his church were thrown

6. Patricia Caldwell, *The Puritan Conversion Narrative: The Beginnings of American Expression* (New York, 1983); Charles Lloyd Cohen, *God's Caress: The Psychology of Puritan Religious Expression* (New York, 1986); Amanda Porterfield, *Female Piety in Puritan New England: The Emergence of Religious Humanism* (New York, 1992); and Kibbey, *Interpretation of Material Shapes*.

7. Robert Pope, *The Half-Way Covenant: Church Membership in Puritan New England* (Princeton, N.J., 1969); E. Brooks Holifield, *The Covenant Sealed: The Development of Puritan Sacramental Theology in Old and New England, 1570–1720* (New Haven, Conn., 1974), 197–224.

open to all who exhibited the proper moral character regardless of spiritual status, was a logical extension of the notion of "half-way" membership. The territorial autonomy of local congregations was undercut by the growing presence of ministerial consociations in the early eighteenth century which supervised the internal discipline of churches and set qualifications for aspiring clergy. Perhaps of most immediate concern to lay men and women was the increasing formalism of the sermon. The "Word" as it was preached seemed to emanate less from God himself and more from the head of the minister. More and more laity began to feel that the literal meaning of the original Puritan mission was in danger of disappearing under the accumulated weight of these symbolic innovations.[8]

The response of disaffected Puritans was an upswelling of religious fervor which historians have labeled the "Great Awakening." The mass revivalism touched off in 1739 by the British evangelist George Whitefield's grand tour of the American colonies has occasioned as much controversy now as it did then. Jon Butler's dismissal of the Awakening as interpretive fiction notwithstanding, most historians agree that *something* significant happened in the late 1730s and 1740s which changed the face of Puritan religion for better or worse. Whether initiated by the clergy or the laity, whether a sign of religious declension or vigor, whether rooted in social dislocations or in the effusions of the Holy Spirit, the revivals touched thousands of New Englanders who believed life in the Spirit to be the only life worth living.[9]

Despite manifold disagreements, a common vocabulary connects the many histories of the Awakening, most of which have concentrated on

8. On the growing institutional presence and professionalism of the established churches in the eighteenth century, see Patricia Bonomi, *Under the Cope of Heaven: Religion, Society, and Politics in Colonial America* (New York, 1986); Jon Butler, *Awash in a Sea of Faith: Christianizing the American People* (Cambridge, Mass., 1990); and John Corrigan, *The Prism of Piety: Catholick Congregational Clergy at the Beginning of the Enlightenment* (New York, 1991).

9. The literature on the Great Awakening is vast and growing, but some of the works I have found most helpful include: Harry Stout, *The Divine Dramatist: George Whitefield and the Rise of Modern Evangelicalism* (Grand Rapids, Mich., 1991); Marilyn Westerkamp, *The Triumph of the Laity: Scots-Irish Piety and the Great Awakening, 1625–1760* (New York, 1988); Richard Bushman, *From Puritan to Yankee: Character and the Social Order in Connecticut, 1690–1765* (Cambridge, Mass., 1967); Michael Crawford, *Seasons of Grace: Colonial New England's Revival Tradition in Its British Context* (New York, 1991); Christine Heyrman, *Commerce and Culture: The Maritime Communities of Colonial Massachusetts, 1690–1750* (New York, 1984); and Rhys Isaac, "The Evangelical Revolt: The Nature of the Baptists' Challenge to the Traditional Order in Virginia, 1765–1775," *WMQ*, 3d ser., 31 (1974): 345–68. Jon Butler has raised important questions about the usefulness of subsuming the scope and variety of eighteenth-century revivalism under a single rubric, but for historians of New England the concept of a "Great Awakening" is still a valid (if overworked) analytical tool. Butler, "Enthusiasm Described and Decried: The Great Awakening as Interpretive Fiction," *Journal of American History* 69 (1982): 305–25.

studying the phenomenon in a single locale.[10] The metaphors that contemporaries (both friends and foes) used to describe the movement evoke above all *motion*—revivals are "waves," "fires," "impulses," "pulsations," spiritual "eruptions" that "sweep over," "ignite," "rush in upon," or "engulf" a community. As the revival made its way over the colonial landscape, the hardhearted were moved to tears by the sensibility of their own sinfulness, the godly moved to celebrate each new conversion as a triumph of the Spirit over the flesh, and entire communities moved to renew their covenant vows with God. But more than this, the site of worship itself was often moved, out of the meetinghouse and into the surrounding fields and meadows of New England. Just as sinners found themselves cut off from the comfortable and secure existence they had enjoyed in their profane lives, so religion itself was uprooted from its secure moorings in the Puritan notion of sacred space.

The sheer *movement* of revived religion which relentlessly forced the stony fields and stern countenances of rural New England to yield to the Spirit has lent the historiography of the Awakening a distinctive cadence, in which metaphorical flights of fancy seem to overwhelm sober judgment. We may have exaggerated the Awakening's force as a watershed in the history of Puritan religion, but it is an easy mistake to make, given the overblown rhetoric of the participants themselves. And it is, I think, important to heed the hyperbolic quality of the religious discourse surrounding the Awakening, for it reveals the true cultural significance of the movement to eighteenth-century Americans. Renewal was to come not through the traditional sites of Puritan worship, the church and family, but through a radical rupturing of the notion of sacred space. Whereas the first generations of Puritans had collapsed the social into the sacred in their covenanted churches, eighteenth-century evangelicals wished to dissolve the social altogether by exploding the nexus of church and community. No physical barriers were to impede the movement of the Spirit as it passed from soul to soul, church to church, town to town.

Rhys Isaac has made the strongest case for the argument that the evangelical revival posed a fundamental challenge to established patterns of authority and association which would decisively alter the cultural landscape

10. John M. Bumsted, "Revivalism and Separatism in New England: The First Society of Norwich, Connecticut, as a Case Study," *WMQ*, 3d ser., 24 (1967): 588–612; John W. Jeffries, "The Separation in the Canterbury Congregational Church: Religion, Family, and Politics in a Connecticut Town," *New England Quarterly* 52 (1979): 522–49; Gerald F. Moran, "Conditions of Religious Conversion in the First Society of Norwich, Connecticut, 1718–1744," *Journal of Social History* 5 (1972): 331–43; Peter Onuf, "New Lights in New London: A Group Portrait of the Separatists," *WMQ*, 3d ser., 37 (1980): 627–43; James Walsh, "The Great Awakening in the First Congregational Church of Woodbury, Connecticut," *WMQ*, 3d ser., 28 (1971): 543–62.

of colonial America. In the ragged congregations gathered by the Baptists in back-country Virginia, no social distinctions were recognized, in defiance of Anglican gentry culture. Rich and poor, men and women, black and white all communed together in the presence of the Lord, often without a minister.[11] But this insight into the countercultural nature of Baptist worship misses the most radical feature of revival religion, its insistence that a church—*any* church—could not define the boundaries of the sacred community. Only the immediate presence of the Spirit of God, however fleeting, signified community.

In minimizing the importance of structure—including the physical structure of the meetinghouse—evangelicals embraced a vision of community which anthropologists would recognize as liminal. Liminality refers to that floating state of being in which all rules have been overturned; temporarily suspended between the world one has left behind and the world one must join, individuals undergoing liminal rites of passage experience a profound sense of freedom from social conventions and indeed from society itself. In a liminal state, true community or *communitas* can take place; to quote Martin Buber, "[*Communitas*] is the being no longer side by side (and, one might add, above and below) but *with* one another of a multiple of persons. And this multitude, though it moves toward one goal, yet experiences everywhere a turning to, a dynamic facing of, the others, a flowing from *I* to *Thou*."[12] For evangelicals, such a deep sense of fellow-feeling naturally followed upon the alienating experience of conversion. After undergoing a process of radical individualization, converts often felt as if the experience of grace had initiated them into a kind of brotherhood of saints which transcended all earthly ties. Though he "knew none of 'em personally," the

11. See Rhys Isaac, *The Transformation of Virginia, 1740–1790* (Chapel Hill, N.C., 1982).

12. Quoted in Victor Turner, *The Ritual Process: Structure and Anti-Structure* (Chicago, 1969), p. 127. See Arnold Van Gennep, *The Rites of Passage*, trans. Monika Vizedom and Gabriella Caffee (Chicago, 1960), for a discussion of liminal rites of passage. The foremost authority on the evangelical experience in Maritime Canada similarly uses the term "*communitas*" to describe the deep sense of fellow-feeling which united saints; see Geroge Rawlyk, *The Canada Fire: Radical Evangelicalism in British North America from 1775 to 1812* (Kingston, Ont., 1994), passim. Henry Abelove's description of early Methodism also highlights the sense of uncanny "oneness" which bound congregations together, although he cites Sigmund Freud rather than Turner as his theoretical authority. Abelove, *The Evangelist of Desire: John Wesley and the Methodists* (Stanford, Calif., 1990), pp. 45–48. For a discussion of adolescent rites of passage which draws on the concept of liminality, see Karen Halttunen, *Confidence Men and Painted Women: A Study of Middle-Class Culture in America, 1830–1870* (New Haven, Conn., 1982). Perhaps the closest historical analogy to the anthropological theory of social liminality is the experience of carnival in preindustrial European societies, in which the existing order is "turned upside down" for a brief moment before being reasserted. For descriptions of carnival, see Natalie Zemon Davis' essays in her *Society and Culture in Early Modern France* (Stanford, Calif., 1975); and Peter Burke, *Popular Culture in Early Modern Europe* (London, 1978).

renowned Baptist minister Isaac Backus felt moved to open his heart and soul to the crowd that had gathered to hear him speak. "I knew not of their being Such a people as this in the World," he marveled, and "scarce one of 'em ever heard of there being such a Creature as I in the world."[13] The intense communion of those who had previously been entire strangers to one another was cause indeed for wonder. "They felt all as one, as if they had been made up all into one man, all drinked into one Spirit and oneness," Nathan Cole, a Connecticut farmer, wrote in 1758. Dreaming one day of a meeting of saints, he recounted how in his vision, "I heard such melodious singing that it ravished my Soul. . . . I could hear every voice clear and distinct at the same time; and yet hear them all at once and no hindrance at all, every tongue begins the note as one and Ends as one." Such visions were not the mere delusion of sleep. "I am no stranger to the saints having communion with one another when they are some miles apart," Cole insisted.[14]

Visions, however, cannot last forever. Dreamers awake, and the heat of the revival inevitably cools in time. The very notion of liminality, as anthropologists use the term, signifies a transient state, one that necessarily gives way to a renewal of structure. As so many scholars have pointed out, the radical egalitarianism implicit in the revival was confined largely to the fringes of evangelical culture, a tantalizing but ultimately untenable vision of an alternative religious community. Revival seasons were just that—seasons—in which conventional religious structures were overturned for a brief moment before being reasserted in somewhat altered form. The evangelical revival was thus premised on an inherently unstable concept of the sacred, one that elevated the ephemeral over the concrete. It is difficult to imagine a more fragile definition of community, and evangelical men and women struggled throughout the eighteenth century to find a middle ground between revival and survival.

The quest for a middle ground placed evangelicals squarely on gendered territory. The liminal nature of evangelical worship signaled its inherently feminine quality; as Phyllis Mack has argued for the early modern period, "Womanhood stood to contemporaries as an emblem of timelessness, of an eternal and repetitive reality quite outside the ordered march of history." In pedagogical and religious discourse of the seventeenth and eighteenth cen-

13. *The Diary of Isaac Backus*, ed. William McLoughlin (Providence, R.I., 1979), 1:12–13.

14. Michael J. Crawford, "The Spiritual Travels of Nathan Cole," *WMQ*, 3d ser., 33 (1976): 106–10. The paradoxical quality of evangelical faith, which combined an intensely individualistic model of conversion with a deep sense of community, is described by Isaac in *The Transformation of Virginia*, pp. 170–71.

turies, women were commonly portrayed as "liminal creatures inhabiting a no-man's land of natural and spiritual forces that had nothing to do with culture."[15] The "no-man's land" that the feminine signified was precisely the spiritual state that evangelicals aspired to, and in their embrace of *communitas* they constituted themselves as a female force in an otherwise masculine religious universe. The instability inherent in the evangelical concept of the sacred was thus the instability of women writ large. To be sure, evangelicals would have rejected such a gendered reading of their ethos; if anything, they believed they were resurrecting the androgynous nature of the early apostolic church in which, to echo the biblical passage, "there was neither slave nor free, male nor female." Yet to their contemporaries, especially those who opposed the excesses of the revival, such an androgynous vision was inescapably gendered female. For at bottom, androgyny—that nebulous world of sexual identity in which the masculine and feminine are dissolved into an undifferentiated whole—is a supremely liminal state, and that was the great paradox. The very attempt to efface sexual boundaries placed one squarely in the feminine realm of flux and dissolution. In the process, evangelicals came dangerously close to recreating the "vast and empty chaos" the Puritans thought they had left behind when they converted wilderness into sacred space.

"To Turn Things Topsy Turvy": Order and Disorder in the Evangelical Revival

"Religious man thirsts for *being*," Mircea Eliade has observed. When he encounters space that is "uncosmicized because unconsecrated," he experiences a profound sense of alienation; "he feels emptied of his entire substance, as if he were dissolving in chaos."[16] Many orthodox Puritans felt that they had indeed strayed into such an evil place when they came face to face with the evangelical revival. The "uncosmicized" space of the revival was an affront to orthodox notions of hierarchy, structure, and authority. The deepest sources of religious authority in Puritan New England—the learned clergy, the incorporated church, the hierarchical arrangement of communi-

---

15. Phyllis Mack, *Visionary Women: Ecstatic Prophecy in Seventeenth-Century England* (Berkeley, Calif., 1992), p. 24; see, in general, pp. 24–32 for a discussion of early modern views of women and femininity. Victor Turner also associates women with liminality, with the generation of *communitas*; see his *Process, Performance and Pilgrimage: A Study in Comparative Symbology* (New Delhi, 1979), pp. 104–5, and *Ritual Process*, pp. 99–105.

16. Mircea Eliade, *The Sacred and the Profane* (New York, 1957), p. 64.

cants in the meetinghouse—were challenged by revivalists who spurned sacred for profane space, structure for chaos. Both literally and figuratively, the revivals of the Great Awakening threatened to "break" the Sabbath.

In fact, the Great Awakening can be understood, in J. B. Jackson's terms, as a "conflict between two different attitudes toward time and space." Against the conservative belief of orthodox Puritans in a fixed cosmology, in which time and space were consecrated in the act of public worship in the meetinghouse, the dissenters sought "a private sudden sanctity" that was indifferent to structured space.[17] As the deep Puritan commitment to land attests, any attack on the notion of sacred space was also an attack on the entire social and political order, a bold attempt to introduce what contemporaries saw as "Anarchy and Confusion" into the peaceable kingdoms of New England—the ultimate sin.[18] Opponents of the revival went so far as to ascribe to the revivalists' agitations the breakdown of all civil as well as religious authority: the New Lights, charged Isaac Stiles, were "ever & anon for change of Government, and thence are raising a Dust, making a Bustle, and endeavouring to Overset the Government; to turn things *topsy turvy*, and bring all into Convulsion."[19] When we look more closely at the words and actions of radical New Lights, we can begin to understand why stalwart Puritan divines reacted with such alarm.

The rejection of orthodox uses of space was a self-conscious strategy of such revivalists as Ebenezer Frothingham who proudly declared their indifference to traditional places of worship. In a pamphlet published in 1750, Frothingham set forth the articles of faith and liturgical practices of the Separates, who had broken away from the orthodox Congregational churches during the Awakening to found more pure and "primitive" societies for religious worship: "It is not any Meeting Place or House, that is appointed by Man only, that makes God's House; No! for what makes a Place to be God's House, is his special, spiritual Presence; and where his Children meet, under the Divine Influence of his blessed Spirit, for social and Spiritual Worship, whether it be a public Meeting-House, or a private House, or the open Wilderness."[20] In disregarding the formal sites of public

17. J. B. Jackson, "The Sacred Grove in America," in his *The Necessity for Ruins and Other Topics* (Amherst, Mass., 1980), p. 82.

18. John Thomson, "The Government of the Church of Christ," (1740), in *The Great Awakening: Documents Illustrating the Crisis and Its Consequences*, ed. Alan Heimert and Perry Miller (New York: 1967), p. 26.

19. Isaac Stiles, "Looking-Glass for Changelings," in Heimert and Miller, *The Great Awakening*, p. 311.

20. Ebenezer Frothingham, "The Articles of Faith and Practice, with the Covenant, That is

worship set apart and consecrated by the religious establishment, the revivalists explicitly rejected the nexus of church and town which was the backbone of the corporate Puritan communities carved out of the American wilderness in the seventeenth century.

In makeshift meetinghouses, in private homes, in fields and groves and cleared spaces of any kind, the preachers of the Great Awakening moved the act of worship from formal sites designated by the authorities to undifferentiated, previously profane space in a radical break with the past. Excerpts from the British evangelist John Cennick's journals, published in the evangelical magazine *The Weekly History*, attest to the ingenuity of revivalist preachers in finding places where worship would not be molested by scoffers and jesters. "When the Church was done," Cennick reported in a 1741 issue, "I went out into the Green (which was about half a Mile off) and to about 2000 I preached . . . [then] I went about 3 Miles distant to the *New-School at Brinkworth*. . . . I went near the Walls of it, and on a low Part of the Same, I knelt down and pray'd." Another day, he continued, "I was in the Parish of *Lineham*, at a Place call'd Preston, in our Brother Smith's house, but that being too Small for the Congregation, we went into his Hay-barkin, or Yard." The next day, because of the threat of disruption from zealous opponents, Cennick was forced to move his pulpit "out of the Green into a Neighbour's field just by."[21] Subsequent issues of the magazine describe the evangelist preaching "under some Willow-trees in the Common before the *Poor-house*" and on a bench "under an Apple-Tree."[22] Cennick's willingness to use any available space to impart his message enraged the orthodox clergy, one of whom reportedly told him, "*if you will Preach in the House you may; but you shall not Preach anywhere else!*" "How envious is the old Serpent against Field Preaching!" was Cennick's response.[23]

While Cennick and other traveling evangelists faced much stiffer persecution in England than in New England, their colonial counterparts likewise preferred to preach in unstructured spaces despite the greater accessibility of standing pulpits. Time and again in his diary, Separate minister Isaac Backus noted in passing, "Preached in the Afternoon to Some number of People under the Shadey Trees."[24] Indifferent to *where* they preached, the

---

confessed by Separate Churches," in *The Great Awakening: Documents on the Revival of Religion, 1740–1745*, ed. Richard Bushman (New York, 1970), p. 108.

21. *Weekly History*, 12 September 1741, 1:2–4.
22. Ibid., 19 September 1741, 1:2–3.
23. Ibid., 26 September 1741, 1:4.
24. *Diary of Isaac Backus*, 1:92.

revivalists' only concern was that their efforts be infused with the energy of divine grace. George Whitefield, in fact, deliberately shunned the church in favor of open fields as the most efficacious place to reach inattentive souls. After his tour of Philadelphia, he wrote in his journal, "Great numbers of the inhabitants would have built me immediately a very large church, if I would have consented; but the Lord, I am persuaded, would have his Gospel preached in the fields; and building a church would, I fear, insensibly lead the people into bigotry, and make them place the Church again, as they have done for a long time, in the church walls."[25] No building erected and dedicated by men could contain the spirit of God, which—in a common Awakening metaphor—was free to wander without restraint throughout the land alighting upon and awakening the souls of New England's impious. Proudly, in 1784, the Seventh Day Baptist Church of Newport affirmed their commitment to the undifferentiated presence of God in the world in a letter to an errant member: "we Lay as Little Stress upon those Distinctions as any Society in the Land we believe that god is to be worshipped in Spirit and in truth and where he is so worshipped in Sincerity and uprightness to heart that worship he will accept whether it be in a House Dedicated to his Service or not or if it be in a field."[26]

Not only the institutional authority incarnated in the physical building of the meetinghouse, but also the hierarchical ordering of the community embodied in the seating arrangements within, was disrupted by the revivalists' practice of open-field preaching. The levels of stratification (age, wealth, and gender) inscribed in the seating arrangements of seventeenth-century Puritan meetinghouses were abandoned in the mass, unstructured gatherings of the revival; young and old, men and women, rich and poor, educated and unlettered stood side by side in undifferentiated space. The preacher himself, as Harry Stout points out, entered into a new relationship with his auditors in such a promiscuous setting. "Immensely significant was the itinerant's unfamiliarity with his audience and his lack of personal connection to local authority figures. The itinerant speaker—neither employed by nor in authority over a particular congregation—was freed to establish a special rapport with his audience that dramatically altered the flow of authority in public communications."[27]

25. "Extracts from George Whitefield's *Journals*," in Bushman, *The Great Awakening*, p. 27. Harry Stout identifies Whitefield's open-field preaching as his signature badge among revivalist preachers of the eighteenth century; see *The Divine Dramatist*, esp. chap. 5.

26. Letter to a member requesting dismission to the Presbyterian church, 20 April 1784, Record Book of Seventh Day Baptist Church of Newport, NHS.

27. Harry Stout, *The New England Soul: Preaching and Religious Culture in Colonial New England* (New York, 1986), p. 193. See Robert J. Dinkin, "Seating the Meetinghouse in Early

Within the meetinghouses of New Light ministers a similar restructuring of the internal space of the assembly was taking place which likewise
undermined traditional notions of hierarchy. Ministers anxious to further
the awakening of their audience no longer stationed themselves at a fixed
pulpit (usually elevated above the congregation), but ventured into the assembly to exhort sinners to repent. As one historian describes it, "a configuration that was based on lines and perpendiculars that represented and
acknowledged the community's moral hierarchy of values, was replaced [in
the Great Awakening] by one of flow and circularity, as ministers and converted laymen moved through the space, alternately exhorting or comforting the assembly. This patterning of sacred space was to become a permanent feature of Protestant evangelical revivals."[28] Under such promiscuous
mingling of pastors and laity, the principle of social hierarchy in all spheres
of association was endangered. "When Men strive so hard to dissolve the
solemn Tye of the sacred Relation between Ministers and People under the
Notion of Liberty," threatened an antirevivalist pamphlet, "why may not
they plead for the same Liberty in other Relations?"[29]

The practice of worshiping in open fields and its attendant assault on the
principle of hierarchy was but one part of a feature of the Awakening far
more pernicious in the eyes of its opposers: the rise and spread of itinerant
preachers not attached to any particular parish who went from town to town
delivering their messages wherever and whenever they could, occasionally
without the permission of and in direct opposition to the ordained minister
in residence. A sympathetic description of that "Grand Itinerant" Whitefield's tour through New England in 1741 recounted how the Standing ministers refused to allow the evangelist into their meetinghouses. "We lead our
People to the Crouded Assemblies, but the Church Ministers warn'd their
People against hearing him. The Day he arrived he preached in our House to
Five-thousand Hearers. He saw such Alienation in the Church Ministers to
his Doctrine and Way that he never ask'd the Liberty of their Houses."[30]
Forbidden the pulpits of the standing churches, Whitefield was forced to

---

Massachusetts," in *Material Life in America, 1600–1860*, ed. Robert St. George (Boston, 1988), pp.
407–18; John Demos, "Old Age in Early New England," in *The American Family in Socio-Historical
Perspective*, ed. M. Gordon (New York, 1983), pp. 269–305; and David Hackett Fisher, *Growing Old
in America* (New York, 1977), pp. 38–40, for descriptions of the seating arrangements in the Puritan
meetinghouse.

28. Clarke Garrett, *Spirit Possession and Popular Religion: From the Camisards to the Shakers*
(Baltimore, 1987), p. 113.

29. "A Short Reply to Mr. Whitefield's Letter," 1741, in Heimert and Miller, *The Great
Awakening*, p. 141.

30. *Weekly History*, 27 June 1741, I:3.

adopt an itinerant style of evangelical preaching which was copied by his American followers. Whitefield's invasion of Boston brought a loud outcry of condemnation from Harvard College, which in a protest published in 1744 condemned the itinerants who "have thrust themselves into Towns and Parishes, to the Destruction of all Peace and Order," and charged Whitefield himself with endangering the "very Being of these Churches of Christ."[31] Like open-air worship, the practice of itinerancy challenged the political principle of the territorial church. Thus it is not surprising that the establishment perceived the itinerants' disregard of territorial boundaries as an attack on the very foundations of the Puritan political order. The "Wonderful, Wandering Spirit" of the revival, charged its opposers, "above all hates rules and good order, or *bounds and limits.*"[32]

Indeed, the general assembly of Connecticut judged the danger of political anarchy to be so great that it quickly passed laws restricting the practice of itinerancy in an attempt to contain the spread of the revival movement. The Act of 1742 declared that "any *Foreigner* or *Stranger*" who attempted to preach or exhort publicly without permission from the settled ministers was to "be sent (as a *vagrant* Person) by Warrant . . . out of the Bounds of this Colony."[33] Itinerants were thus to be "warned out" in the same way that other undesirables were warned out by town authorities intent on preserving the moral unity of the community. To be labeled a "vagrant" was to be placed beyond the pale of the covenant that defined membership in the town or church. Revivalist preachers were truly "Strangers" in their own land whose unconventional practices, moreover, opened the tight-knit corporate communities of New England to the scrutiny and ridicule of other outsiders. "The Controversy . . . being noised abroad in the Land," wrote an indignant Old Light minister in 1751, "has drawn on Us the Censure of Multitudes, who before this were great Strangers to Us."[34] Strangers within,

31. "The Testimony of Harvard College against George Whitefield," in Heimert and Miller, *The Great Awakening*, pp. 341, 352.

32. "The Wonderful, Wandering Spirit," in Heimert and Miller, *The Great Awakening*, p. 148, emphasis mine.

33. "An Act for Regulating Abuses and Correcting Disorders in Ecclesiastical Affairs," 1742, in Bushman, *The Great Awakening*, pp. 58–60. Thirty years later, the Warren Association of Baptist Churches, an organization formed to further the interests of the Baptist order in New England, adopted a similar policy of warning church members against allowing "vagrant" or "stragling" itinerants into their meetinghouses in almost identical terms. It repeated this warning periodically, as the Association apparently learned a valauble lesson from "the disorders . . . introduced into churches by vagrant persons who pretend to ye sacred office of ye ministry," disorders that had occurred a generation earlier. Letters from Warren Association, 9 September and 27 August 1772, Backus Papers, Box 9, ANTS.

34. John Bass, "A True Narrative of an Unhappy Contention in the Church of Ashford," in Heimert and Miller, *The Great Awakening*, p. 466. Stout has suggested that the distinctive feature

the New Light preachers made common cause with strangers without—or so it seemed to a frightened orthodoxy.

The New Lights also challenged previous notions of sacred time. Their practice of holding services at irregular and unpredictable times was one element in this new sense of time. Rather than taking place promptly at a specified hour of the morning of the Sabbath, revival meetings were often held spontaneously, at any time of day or night, on any day of the week. The Reverend Jonathan Parson's account of the revival at Lyme recalled that "Sabbaths alone wou'd not suffice for hearing Sermons, but greater Numbers still urg'd for frequent Lectures. I was well pleas'd to observe such a flocking to the Windows, and a hearing Ear became general; and therefore I readily consented, upon the Request of the People, to preach as often as I coul'd, besides the stated Exercises of the Sabbath."[35] The Reverend James Robe, in his narrative of the revival he conducted in his congregation, likewise observed "an uncommon earnest Inclination in the People of all Sorts to hear the Word of God" and resolved "to have the Word *more frequently* preached to them while they were so pressing and eager to attend unto it."[36] By holding services at unconsecrated times, the revivalist preachers opened the way for greater lay participation in the movement. More people found their way to attend worship services that not only took place at more convenient locations (such as private homes or neighboring fields), but at more convenient and frequent times as well. The established order of the services itself was disrupted as well, as enthusiastic preachers often continued speaking long past the accustomed time and eager listeners compelled the extension of religious exercises well beyond the stated hour.

The clearest manifestation of this transformation of the notion of sacred time, however, was a change in the morphology of conversion from that of a gradual, protracted, and progressively induced phenomenon to that of a sudden "circumcision of the heart," to use David Lovejoy's telling phrase.[37] The phenomenon of "new birth" associated in particular with the Whitefieldian tradition was very different from Puritan conversion. No longer a state to be achieved through slow and methodical instruction in the ways

---

of the revivals of the Great Awakening was precisely its extralocal character; as word of revivals in one town "filled the neighboring towns with talk," the fire of religious enthusiasm spread. Stout, *New England Soul*, p. 188.

35. "Account of the Revival at Lyme," *Christian History* (1741), 1:198.

36. *Christian History* (1743), 1:38.

37. David S. Lovejoy, *Religious Enthusiasm in the New World: Heresy to Revolution* (Cambridge, Mass., 1985), pp. 181–82. See also Jerald C. Brauer, "Conversion: From Puritanism to Revivalism," *Journal of Religion* 58 (1978): 227–43. Jackson also stresses the importance of a compressed model of conversion in undermining traditional notions of time and space. Jackson, "The Sacred Grove," pp. 82–83.

and means of grace, a lifetime process of edification and regeneration, religious conversion became, to the revivalists, a powerful moment of sublime
fusion with God, a gift that could be neither predicted nor produced by
human means. This compression of the act of conversion into a single
moment (a moment existing outside of time) was one of the most unsettling
aspects of New Light theology to conservative divines, for it seemingly
negated the importance of the ministry in guiding their congregations in the
quest for grace.

One New Light described the process of conviction in violent terms:
"The [Spirit] sometimes [convicts sinners] more *suddenly*; and by a more
forceable Impression, filling the Soul with the greatest Agony & Distress,
from the most lively Views of his aggravated Sins, and of the amazing
Wrath of God. This alarms all the Powers and Passions of the Soul, and
pricks the poor Sinner *to the Heart*."[38] An Old Light critic described the
Whitefieldian conversion as "an *absolute, immediate, instantaneous* Work—
darted in upon us like a Flash of Lightning . . . changing the *whole* man into
a *new Creature*, in the twinkling of an eye or a *Moment* of time."[39] Another
minister complained that the revivalists believed "that this Work of Conversion or the New Birth is sudden and instantaneous and wrought by an
irresistible Degree of God's Grace and Power. . . . For they say, that as the
Work of Creation was wrought in an Instant . . . so our second Creation,
likewise, must be an instantaneous Work."[40] New Light converts could
pinpoint the exact time of their conversions: Isaac Backus noted with pride
in his journal that he was reborn at the age of seventeen years and seven
months.[41]

"Loose, General, *and* Indefinite *Words*":
 The Problem of Language

These epiphanies were wrought by a new "Word" preached in a new way by
traveling evangelists. Hannah Heaton, a Connecticut farm woman, recalled
her own reaction to a fiery sermon she attended in 1741 at the age of twenty.
As "the power of god come down," she wrote in wonderment, "my knees

38. Jonathan Dickinson, "The Witness of the Spirit" (1740), in Heimert and Miller, *The Great Awakening*, pp. 101–2.

39. Alexander Garden, "Regeneration and the Testimony of the Spirit," in Heimert and Miller, *The Great Awakening*, p. 59.

40. Samuel Quincy, "The Nature and Necessity of Regeneration," in Heimert and Miller, *The Great Awakening*, pp. 488–89.

41. *The Diary of Isaac Backus*, App. 1, 3:1526.

smote together . . . it seemd to me i was a sinking down in to hell i thot the floor i stood on gave way and i was iust a going but then i began to resign and as i resigned my distress began to go off till i was perfectly easy quiet and calm . . . it seemed as if i had a new soul & body both."[42] The raw and emotional language with which many converts described their experiences of grace echoed the raw language coming from the pulpits. As part of their assault on traditional religious practice, evangelicals invested speech with the power both to destroy old patterns of existence and to create new ones. Speech in fact became the primary medium through which a new order was asserted. Donald Weber notes that during such moments of cultural upheaval as in religious revivals "language acquires what anthropologists call a subjunctive mood or tense; meanings become unmoored from fixed references, discourse is multivalent." From this perspective, Weber argues, such features of the Awakening as James Davenport's infamous book-burning incident can be viewed as "a cultural crisis centered on the meaning, nature, and spiritual efficacy of the spoken word."[43]

Critics of the revival movement, like subsequent historians, laid particular stress on the often indiscriminate and incendiary use of emotionally charged words by itinerant preachers as a measure of the anarchic tendency of the movement. Charles Chauncy sharply criticized Jonathan Edwards' use of "*loose, general,* and *indefinite* Words, which People may put a Meaning to, just as they are led by their Imaginations."[44] Chauncy seemed obsessed by the linguistic indecencies of the New Lights, and he returned again and again to this theme in his polemical writings against the movement. The Awakening, he protested in 1743, "loosed Men's Tongues to utter such Language as would not be seemly, even in those who profess no Sense of GOD."[45] What so enraged Chauncy was the indeterminate meaning carried by the revivalists' words and the potential for subversion such ambiguity implied. "The word as it was preached in the fields and pulpits of New England," Amy Lang asserts, was "a new word. . . . What was at issue was the authority of both word and speaker, and the two were closely linked."[46] Orthodox protests against such New Light innovations as the delivery of

42. "Experiences or Spiritual Exercises of Hannah heaton" (1741), photocopy of original ms., CHS.

43. Donald Weber, *Rhetoric and History in Revolutionary New England* (New York, 1988), pp. 13 and 22.

44. Quoted in Amy Schrager Lang, *Prophetic Women: Anne Hutchinson and the Problem of Dissent in the Literature of New England* (Berkeley, Calif., 1987), p. 101.

45. Chauncy, "Seasonable Thoughts on the State of Religion," in Heimert and Miller, *The Great Awakening,* p. 296.

46. Lang, *Prophetic Women,* pp. 74–75.

extemporaneous, unprepared sermons and the promiscuous practice of allowing lay men and—even worse—lay women to exhort and pray aloud at
prayer meetings, concealed an underlying concern (as Lang suggests) that
the fundamental relationship between word and meaning was being irrevocably severed in the revivalists' deliberate disregard of rhetorical conventions. And their distaste for the impropriety of such unstructured and loose
speech stemmed directly from their fear that the authority of the clergy was
itself at stake.

Describing Gilbert Tennent's preaching, Chauncy noted in disgust that
it "was in the *extemporaneous* Way, with much Noise and little Connection."[47] George Whitefield was the progenitor of a new style of preaching
which departed radically from the standard practice of delivering prepared
sermons from written notes. In order to catch the spirit of the times before it
passed, revivalist preachers shunned the study and trusted to holy inspira-
tion when they exhorted the faithful. The itinerants of the Great Awakening adopted what Weber has called the "fragmentary style of the Awakening
pulpit," a kind of "sermonic shorthand characterized by fragmentary syntax,
vertical catalogues, and incantatory phrases."[48] The shift from fully penned,
closely read orations to sermons delivered from notes carried a political as
well as a rhetorical significance; the fragmentary style itself was a sign of the
social marginality of the evangelical clergy, linguistic confirmation of their
outsider status.

This overstepping of conventional boundaries by unprincipled young
preachers in hot pursuit of public acclaim was one thing; the deliberate
encouragement and sponsoring of unlicensed exhorting by lay men and
women of all stripes was even worse. "It is impossible to relate the convulsions into which the whole Country is thrown by a set of Enthusiasts that
strole about harangueing the admiring Vulgar in *extempore* nonsense," wrote
an outraged Charles Brockwell, the Anglican rector at Salem, "nor is it
confined to these only, for Men, Women, Children, Servants & Negroes are
now become (as they phrase it) Exhorters."[49] Charles Chauncy was especially incensed at the practice of allowing lay women to speak publicly: "the
encouraging WOMEN, yea GIRLS to speak in the assemblies for religious

47. Chauncy, "A Letter from a Gentleman in Boston to Mr. George Wishard," in Bushman,
The Great Awakening, p. 118.
48. Weber, *Rhetoric and History*, p. 11. See also David Lovejoy, "'Desperate Enthusiasm': Early
Signs of American Radicalism," in *The Origins of Anglo-American Radicalism*, ed. Margaret Jacob
and James Jacob (Boston, Mass., 1984), pp. 216–17, for a discussion of extemporaneous preaching.
49. Quoted in C. C. Goen, *Revivalism and Separatism in New England, 1740–1800; Strict
Congregationalists and Separate Baptists in the Great Awakening* (New Haven, Conn., 1962), p. 30.

worship is a plain breach of that *commandment of the LORD*, where it is said, *Let your WOMEN keep silence in the churches.*[50] The propriety of women's right to a public voice in the church was an especially sensitive issue for early-eighteenth-century Puritan communities. In the early years of Puritan settlement, women as well as men were expected to deliver verbal accounts of God's labors with their souls in order to be admitted to full membership in the church. Gradually, beginning in the mid-seventeenth century, however, women were increasingly confined to delivering their professions of faith in private to the minister, who would then report on its acceptability to the larger body of church members. Whether this change in policy was instituted out of deference to women's more sensitive and delicate natures, as Puritan divines claimed, or in response to women's increasingly vocal defiance of established church doctrines and practices (as some historians of women argue), is a matter of some dispute.[51] In either case, Puritan congregations were no longer accustomed to hearing women speak in public meetings as a matter of course, and the reemergence of female voices as lay exhorters and preachers during the Great Awakening must have seemed an ominous departure indeed.

Lang notes that the unsilencing of feminine voices in the Awakening entailed more than the occasional appearance of women preachers. She sees in the new rhetoric of emotional release and "heart over head" expounded in the revivalists' sermons the emergence of a distinctly "feminine" language of religious affection which would come to characterize evangelical discourse for the remainder of the eighteenth century.[52] Furthermore, she argues, the theological innovations of the New Lights, which repudiated visible signs of grace, reinforced the typological equation of sanctification with femininity. If public (i.e., male) attributes such as wealth and status no longer signified election, then male converts had little choice but to assume a feminine posture in order to be saved. Converts of both sexes thus spoke in a feminine

50. Chauncy, "Enthusiasm Described," p. 241.

51. See in particular Mary Maples Dunn's article "Saints and Sisters: Congregational and Quaker Women in the Early Colonial Period," *American Quarterly* 30 (1978): 582–601, for an account of women's gradual displacement from the arena of public debate over doctrinal issues in the mid-seventeenth century. See also Carol Karlsen, *The Devil in the Shape of a Woman: Witchcraft in Colonial New England* (New York, 1987), for a discussion of attempts to silence women's voices in the dissenting movements that periodically rocked New England in the seventeenth century.

52. Other historians have similarly characterized the language of evangelicalism as feminine or feminizing; see Philip Greven, *The Protestant Temperament: Patterns of Child-Rearing, Religious Experience, and the Self in Early America* (New York, 1977), pp. 124–40; and Barbara Eaton, "Women, Religion, and the Family: Revivalism as an Indicator of Social Change in Early New England," Ph.D. diss., University of California–Berkeley, 1975.

voice, and the language of affection became the dominant dialect of evangelical discourse.

The abrupt severing of the traditional links between visible and invisible signs in evangelical theology forced a new understanding of conversion and its verbal expression. The conversion act had always been, in Ann Kibbey's words, a "linguistic event" in that it entailed a spoken declaration of faith evaluated by a congregation of auditors. "Not only did speech generate conversion," Kibbey writes, but "the hearer's religious experience was itself a linguistic event. . . . Puritans generally believed that only spoken words, and spontaneous speech at that, could produce conversions."[53] Yet only after 1740 did the linguistic dimensions of this act take on such heightened significance. For without the conventional supports of external signs to rely on, an individual's conversion could be judged only by its spoken relation. Words thus took on an unprecedented importance in the critical process of distinguishing false from true conversion, the wheat from the chaff. The implication is that disorderly speech could literally lead to disorderly conversions. Not surprisingly, Old Light Puritans reacted with dismay and foreboding to the verbal excesses of the revivalists and their followers, for what was at stake was the ability of the churches to gather the saints out of the profane world.

Revivalist preachers were well aware of the potential of their new rhetorical style for inducing sudden conversions; indeed, they cultivated the skill. A letter to George Whitefield describing a revival in Lyme attributed the religious awakening in that town to a particularly fiery sermon: "[I]n the midst of this Sermon the Spirit of God fell upon the Assembly with great Power, and rode forth with Majesty upon the Word of Truth. In a Minutes Time the People were seemingly as much affected as if a thousand Arrows had been shot in among them."[54] Given the enormous power of the revivalist message, New Light ministers were careful to denounce the unprincipled use of such a potent weapon in the wrong hands. The revival in Lyme, the chronicler continued, was accompanied by the appearance of several "Strangers" who attempted to manipulate the revivalists' words to their own ends. "There came a Young Man to my House (to me an intire Stranger)," he wrote, who claimed to be "encouraged to the Work of the Ministry" by

---

53. Kibbey, *Interpretation of Material Shapes*, pp. 6–8. John Owen King III, in *The Iron of Melancholy: Structures of Spiritual Conversion in America from the Puritan Conscience to Victorian Neurosis* (Middletown, Conn., 1983), also argues that the language of conversion cannot be separated from the act itself; they were, in Puritan eyes, one and the same thing. Even more than King, Cohen stresses the verbal nature of the conversion experience, the essence of which, he argues, was contained not in written texts (as King would suggest) but in "the hearts, tongues, ears, and minds of a living community." Cohen, *God's Caress*, p. 19, n.37.

54. *Weekly History* 1 (24 April 1742):1.

Whitefield himself. But despite his pretensions, "it is easy to perceive by the Incoherence of his Discourse, that he is defective in Common Sense; he is full of Words, but very confused and inconsistent; he has got many of Mr. Whitefield's phrases, but uses them very impertinently."[55] Such "Incoherence" was, after all, precisely what opponents had warned would result from the revivalists' use of indeterminate speech. The subversive power of speech can also be glimpsed in an anecdote submitted to the *Weekly History* by a reader in Boston: "A Gentleman, being a great hater of Religion and especially Mr. Whitefield's Preaching, one Day as he was walking his Room he thought he heard Mr. Whitefield: He stood some time very pensive about it; and hearing him, as he thought, conclude his Prayer and begin his Sermon, he thought the Voice was in another Room: he went to see who was there and found one of his Negroes preaching." The Negro, he continued, "had the very Phrases of Mr. Whitefield."[56] If a black servant was capable of mimicking the language of the itinerants, what was to prevent an unscrupulous servant of the devil from assuming the voice of a minister of God? So charged the antirevivalists, and the New Light preachers were often hard pressed to counter the accusation.

It is important to recognize the degree to which the evangelical community was largely a community of language rather than of people or space.[57] If grace was not actually created by language (and Ann Kibbey, for one, suggests that it was), it was nonetheless cultivated, communicated, and celebrated by the words of preachers and converts. Evangelicals may not have agreed on all the essentials of doctrine, or worshiped together in the same buildings, or shared a common social or cultural location, but they all spoke the same language. Once the physical parameters of the sacred community had been exploded and the social nexus of conversion broken, only language

55. Ibid., p. 3.
56. Ibid. 1 (17 October 1741):3–4.
57. I am indebted to the work of Stephen Hum and Catherine Kaplan and the other graduate students in my Early American History Seminar at the University of Michigan for their insights into the ways language can be used to construct a sense of community among socially or politically marginal groups. Hum's study of free blacks in postrevolutionary Philadelphia pinpoints the language of evangelicalism as the primary means by which a community was achieved out of the shards of racial and class hostility, and Kaplan's work on the literary community of Federalist writers and politicians in the early 1800s reveals how the language of gender was used both to create a sense of fraternity and to repel the political and linguistic challenges of the emerging democratic majority. See their unpublished seminar papers "The Language of Mercy: The Uses and Misuses of Evangelical Language for Philadelphia's Free Black Community in the Early Republic," and "Language, Sex, and Gender in the *Port Folio*." A particularly insightful study of the role of language in early-nineteenth-century Methodism is Russell E. Richey, *Early American Methodism* (Bloomington, Ind., 1991).

remained as the glue that bound converts together. Indeed, language was the means by which revivalists broke through the physical and social barriers of orthodox Puritanism in order to allow a new kind of community to emerge, as well as the material embodiment of that community. Language was thus both the means and the end of evangelical fellowship. In this respect, eighteenth-century evangelicals exhibited the same sensibility toward language that Robert St. George has found in seventeenth-century Massachusetts. Like first-generation Puritans, the Awakeners invested verbal and written language with a power, far beyond what modern men and women might expect, to distort and subvert the social order.[58]

This point should not be exaggerated; like revivals themselves, spoken words are evanescent things. Although the "said" of speech may have lasting material consequences, as St. George and Walter Ong argue, words themselves dissolve into ephemera once uttered. The parallels are revealing, for like speech, revival seasons could not outlast the moment of their enactment and were usually followed by a sedate return to older patterns of worship. Furthermore, the deliberate unmooring of the "Word" from its scholarly foundation by revivalist preachers was partly a chimera. Revivalist preachers were hardly the wild-eyed illiterates their critics made them out to be. Most had some degree of college training, and many went on to assume traditional pastoral responsibilities after the intoxicating moment of the revival had passed. But, as recent studies of popular religion have made abundantly clear, the message lay men and women received from these revivalist leaders was not necessarily the message intended.[59] The radical posturing of these preachers, however much it remained simple posturing, was taken to heart by lay men and women who saw in the fiery countenances of their preachers the very image of the Holy Spirit. And, as we shall see, some of these

58. Robert St. George's analysis of "heated speech" in New England court records argues that to colonial Americans "speech seemed inherently more mysterious, dangerous, and 'real' than it does today. . . . Although modern language theory maintains words to be arbitrary signs and merely referential, seventeenth-century speakers believed that the uttering of the word itself could result in actual physical destruction." St. George, "'Heated Speech' and Literacy in Seventeenth-Century New England," in *Seventeenth-Century New England: A Conference Held by the Colonial Society of Massachusetts*, ed. David Hall and David Grayson Allen (Boston, 1984), pp. 279, 301. The physicality of speech is a distinguishing characteristic of oral-aural cultures, according to Walter Ong, in which "saying evil things of another is thought to bring him direct physical harm." Ong, *The Presence of the Word: Some Prolegomena for Cultural and Religious History* (New Haven, Conn., 1967), p. 113. Ong sees the eighteenth century as the critical era in the shift from an oral to a literate culture, a shift that fundamentally transformed the relationship of men to words; see pp. 69–73. Kibbey goes further than this, claiming that not only did words have material effects but they had material shape as well. Kibbey, *Interpretation of Material Shapes*.

59. David D. Hall, *Worlds of Wonder, Days of Judgment: Popular Religious Belief in Early New England* (Cambridge, Mass., 1989).

converts refused to retreat from the evangelical message of spiritual egalitarianism, even after the fires of revival had burnt themselves out.

From "Holy Kisses" to "Brutish Lust": Sexual Disorder in the Great Awakening

Central to the disorders perpetrated by some unprincipled revivalists and their deluded converts was the inversion of sexual mores which seemed to follow close on the heels of the Holy Spirit as it blazed a path across New England. At its most extreme, the revivalist message of spiritual individualism seemed to many Old Lights to sanction a kind of sexual anarchy which was predicated on an antinomian disregard for legal restraints of any kind. The revival, Charles Chauncy protested, "has made strong attempts to destroy all property, to make all things common, *wives* as well as *goods*. It has promoted faction and contention; filled the state oftentimes with confusion, and the state sometimes with general disorder."[60] In Chauncy's eyes, sexual disorder was but one part of the general breakdown in social and political order occasioned by the excesses of the awakening.

The "perfectionist" movement of the 1740s and 1750s, in which some radical New Lights believed themselves to be entirely free of sin, was characterized by a blatant disregard for conventional sexual boundaries, including that of marriage.[61] Several notorious cases of spouse-swapping and sexual promiscuity resulting from the perfectionist strain of the Awakening were brought to light and publicly denounced in Isaac Backus's *History of New England*. The perfectionist spirit "soon carried them [the Separates] into knavery in temporal dealings, intemperance, and what not":

> About the beginning of 1748, some people in Cumberland [Rhode Island] advanced the opinion, that if a saint found that he or she had not been married to the person that was made for them, they were not held by legal bonds from a right now to take their true mate, if they saw who it was. Hereupon an only child of a rich father, not living comfortably with her husband, ventured to reject him, and to lodge with another man. . . . [Her father] said he did not believe there was any harm in it, for they lay with the bible between them. But to his sorrow and shame, his daughter proved to be with child by her new companion; and her husband obtained a legal divorce from her.

60. Chauncy, "Enthusiasm Described," p. 243.
61. William McLoughlin, "Free Love, Immortalism, and Perfectionism in Cumberland, Rhode Island, 1748–1768," *Rhode Island History* 33 (1974): 67–86.

Separates in nearby Easton and Norton followed the example set by their misguided neighbors: "And near the close of 1749, a number of people in Easton and Norton . . . met by a place of water, and one would baptize another, and then he the next; so that about twenty persons were dipped, by four or five administrators among themselves. Parting from their lawful wives and husbands, and taking of others, immediately followed; until some bastard children were born among them, with many other abominations."[62] According to his account, the repudiation of sexual bonds followed "immediately" upon the ritual of baptism which was the cornerstone of evangelical religion.

Celebrated as these cases were at the time, they nonetheless represented extreme instances of the potential for sexual libertinism implicit in the more individualistic rhetoric of the Awakening. Even in the absence of any hard evidence that religious enthusiasm was breeding sexual licentiousness, Jonathan Edwards and other preachers repeatedly cautioned against the "counterfeit of love" which threatened to turn "holy kisses" into "unclean and brutish lust."[63] And in fact such cases may reflect more the fears of orthodox critics of the movement than actual instances of promiscuity. The commonplace metaphor comparing itinerant preachers with harlots and seducers in antirevivalist diatribes—Chauncy described Whitefield, for example, as "running from Place to Place" arousing the passions of young girls—speaks to the close connection between sexual anarchy and religious dissent in the Puritan world.[64] The rhetorical relationship between sexual disorder and heresy was a long-standing one in American Puritanism, for those most threatening of all protest movements (antinomianism, Quakerism, witchcraft) were routinely denounced as sexually deviant. In fact, in one historian's words, "sexual excess was more disturbing to the Puritan mind as a *sign* of disorder in the world, a world which God might, in anger, forsake. God's absence in a society predicated on religion, was more threatening than punishment."[65] The rhetorical construction of religious radicalism as sex-

---

62. Isaac Backus, *A History of New England, with Particular Reference to the Denomination of Christians Called Baptists*, 2d ed. (Newtown, Mass., 1871), 2:185–86, 209.

63. Quoted in Lovejoy, "'Desperate Enthusiasm,'" p. 218.

64. Chauncy, "A Letter from a Gentleman in Boston," p. 117.

65. Kathleen Verduin, "'Our Cursed Natures': Sexuality and the Puritan Conscience," *New England Quarterly* 56 (1983): 229. For other examples of this rhetorical coupling of sexual and religious disorder, see Karlsen, *The Devil in the Shape of a Woman*, on the close link between the persecution of women as witches and their association with religious dissent. Carla Pestana's examination of Puritan prosecution of Quakers in seventeenth-century Massachusetts likewise exposes the sexual content of Puritan fears of Quaker influence, in which the danger posed by religious dissent was explicitly couched in sexual terms. Pestana, "The City upon the Hill under Siege: Puritan Perceptions of the Quaker Threat to Massachusetts Bay, 1656–1661," *New England*

ually aberrant tainted mainstream revivalist preachers like Backus himself as well as the radicals they so pointedly condemned. An outraged Backus wrote in his diary in 1748: "Sometimes the World would tell that I had a Wife and 2 or 3 Children up in the Countery; at other times they would say that I had Bastards in this or that place. And when I went a Journey to see my friends in the Summer, some Boldly asserted that there was a girl or two with Child by me here so that I would never dare to come back again."[66]

Not only the revivalists themselves, but the nature of the religious services they conducted, seemed to their opponents to conduce to a generally sexualized climate that was subversive of proper religious sentiments. The emphasis on the emotional release of conversion, often expressed in physical convulsions and ecstatic cries, was singled out by many opposers of the revival as a particularly contemptible aspect of the new theology. Samuel Blair's "faithful" narrative of a revival of religion in New-Londonderry recalled the orgiastic antics of the awakened. "Several would be overcome and fainting; others deeply sobbing, hardly able to contain, others crying in a most dolorous Manner, many others more silently Weeping. . . . And sometimes the Soul Exercises of some (tho' comparatively but very few) would so far affect their Bodies, as to occasion some strange unusual Bodily Motions." Blair described the physical sensations experienced by converts in the moment of conversion in terms which approximated sexual release: "they felt, perhaps, a quivering over come them . . . or a Faintness, thought they saw their Hearts full of some nautious Filthiness, or . . . felt a heavy Weight and Load at their Hearts, or felt the Weight again taken off, and a pleasant Warmness arising from their Hearts."[67] Jonathan Parsons' account of a revival at Lyme strikes a similar chord. As the "Joynts of their Loyns were Loosed," several men swooned and young women were "thrown into Hysterick Fits."[68] As any eighteenth-century reader would know, the reference to hysterical women was unmistakably an allusion to the implicitly sexualized nature of the conversion experience.[69]

Quarterly 56 (1983): 323–53. And the persistent attempts of Puritan divines and later chroniclers to associate Antinomianism with a corrupt and deformed sexual nature, manifest in the supposed monster-births of Anne Hutchinson and several of her female followers, proved an enduring narrative strategy through the entire colonial period; see Lang, *Prophetic Women*.

66. *The Diary of Isaac Backus*, 1:35.

67. Samuel Blair, "A Short and Faithful Narrative of the Late Remarkable Revival of Religion in New-Londonderry" (1744), in Bushman, *The Great Awakening*, pp. 73–76.

68. "Account of the Revival at Lyme," *Christian History* (1744) 2:125–26.

69. Christine Heyrman argues that "the swooning and screaming of women at revival gatherings . . . points to a sublimation of suppressed physical passion in religious ecstasy." This strong sexual undercurrent of religious excitement was especially noticeable among women converts. See her *Commerce and Culture*, pp. 383–84.

The setting in which the conversion experience took place is also described in the literature of the Great Awakening in terms that carried sexual overtones. William Henry Williams' study of American Methodism—a later stage of the Awakening in the South—argues that encounters between itinerant circuit riders and their (largely) female audiences took place in a "sensually charged atmosphere": "The itinerants' passionate pleas for changed hearts were heard in candle-lit barns or in bucolic settings under shade trees besides meandering brooks and creeks, as well as in the simplicity of newly completed Methodist meetinghouses. The combination of the young itinerant, his fervent message, and the romantic setting stirred emotions in female hearts which were a mixture of the sacred and profane."[70] The exposure of susceptible female hearts to the romantic gestures of young and unprincipled preachers led inevitably, opponents charged, to sexual promiscuity: "it must be owned that some of the crying or roaring Women among us have brought forth something that may be both seen and felt."[71]

From Communitas to Church:
The Fraternity of Saints

Images of sexual disorder resonated so deeply in the polemical literature surrounding the Awakening precisely because the image of the evangelical church itself was constructed not on the model of the family (the archetype for the established Congregational church) but rather on the model of fraternity.[72] Deliberately eschewing the hierarchical elements of the orthodox church (from the raised pulpit to the formalized seating arrangements within the meetinghouse), the evangelical churches that emerged out of the Awakening adopted the rituals and symbols of what Rhys Isaac has called "cohesive brotherhood."[73] The title "reverend" or "pastor" was replaced by

70. William Henry Williams, *The Garden of American Methodism: The Delmarva Penninsula, 1769–1820* (Wilmington, Del., 1984), p. 129.

71. Unattributed remark quoted in the Introduction to Heimert and Miller, *The Great Awakening*, p. xxviii.

72. Note Carole Pateman's warning about using the term "fraternity" to denote community in a general sense: "The general acceptance that 'fraternity' is no more than a way of talking about the bonds of community illustrates how deeply patriarchal conceptions structure our political theory and practice." Pateman, *The Disorder of Women: Democracy, Feminism, and Political Theory* (Stanford, Calif., 1989), p. 41. Pateman is of course correct; my use of the term "fraternity" to describe the sense of *communitas* around which the structure of the evangelical church was organized is meant to highlight the egalitarian, nonhierarchical nature of the church and reflects the lack of an adequate, nongendered, substitute.

73. Isaac, *The Transformation of Virginia*, pp. 163–67.

the far more egalitarian term "elder." Communicants called each other "brother" and "sister" and enjoined on one another a long list of mutual obligations and reciprocities in their covenant vows. Among the Baptists, only adult men and women were admitted into fellowship, a direct repudiation of the entire "covenant theology" of Puritan New England which had come to rest on a tribal understanding of the church as an extended family by the mid-eighteenth century.[74]

Evangelicals did consider themselves a "family" united by the bond of grace, but they were nonetheless a peculiar family—one in which parental authority was reserved for God alone and earthly domestic ties were irrelevant. In a revealing case, a council of Separate churches convened in 1751 investigated the "wantonness" of one Ebenezer Titus who was accused of "Promiscuous dancing of men and women and Kissing his wife—not in token of her Being his Wife but in token of his Felloship with another man in his Wanton dancing with her."[75] Here the sexual relationship of husband and wife was extended to embrace the fellowship of male saints and their shared passion for women. Such unorthodox readings of evangelical "fellowship" were condemned by church leaders, but the persistent confusions among lay men and women about the proper boundaries between sexual and spiritual communion suggest the extent to which such boundaries were called into question by evangelical practices.

Evangelicals constantly exhorted one another in their sermons and public addresses to "come out and be ye separate," to renounce the bonds of natural family and society and join together in an otherworldly community of saints. In place of such natural domestic ties, evangelicals cultivated a "spirit of adoption" which allowed spiritual relationships to supercede earthly ones.[76] As one enthusiast wrote in praise of the "Grand Itinerant" George Whitefield, "*Strolling and Vagabond Orphans*, without *Father* and without *Mother*, without *Purse* and without *Friend*, he seeks out, picks up, and adopts into his Family."[77] In this context, it is no wonder that the sexual antics of the "perfectionists" who spurned matrimonial ties as easily as orthodox minis-

74. Philip Gura has linked the Baptists' rejection of infant baptism to an assault on the entire theological edifice of the covenant; see *A Glimpse of Sion's Glory: Puritan Radicalism in New England, 1620–1660* (Middletown, Conn., 1983), pp. 94–95.

75. "A Copy of what the Council of the Lord did, Rehoboth, May 8th, 1751," Backus Papers, ANTS.

76. As Isaac Backus wrote in his diary in 1750, "the Lord gave Sweet inlargement . . . to Come as a Child to a father and tell him all my wants and open my very heart to him. I think I han't had So much of a spirit of adoption For this Long time: O that I were always like a Little Child." *The Diary of Isaac Backus*, 1:97.

77. "Some Accounts of Reverend Whitefield," *Christian History* (1745), 2:373.

ters generated such widespread anxiety. As one aspiring New Light minister declared bluntly, "[A]ll the fleshly humain tye that was Betwene Man & Wife Parants & Children was from the Devil."[78]

The strain of having to choose between one's natural family and one's spiritual family could at times be painful. One woman wrote plaintively of the intolerable pressure she felt at having to make such a choice. When admonished by the First Baptist Church of Middleborough for her absence from meeting, Relief Hooper explained, "I should Be glad if I could have the Liberty But I must Brake up my famely if I come I must not Returne Back again my Husband Drives one way and my Brethren another and my triles are great I have no Desier to Brak Covnant with my Brethern." The church was not moved by her predicament. "Tho' we would ever avoid any just occasion of offence to any & particularly between husbands & wives," they replied, "yet when husbands commands interfers with Christs authority we ought to obey God rather than man." Such advice was not always easy to take, but evangelicals remained resolute in their insistence that ultimate obedience was owed to God, not man.[79]

"*Ravished* with the discoveries of *another World*," converts had little use for the conventional distinctions of this world.[80] Accounts of the revival published in the *Christian History* all stress the universalizing tendency of the revival; as the editor, Thomas Prince, described the scene in Boston, "Old and Young, Parents and Children, Masters and Servants, High and Low, Rich and Poor together, [are] gathering and passing as *Clouds* in our Streets."[81] Jonathan Edwards praised the revival in Northampton, Mas-

78. Letter from Church at Suffield to Church at East Windsor, 5 January 1753, Canterbury Separate Papers, vol. 1, CSL. A story that may be more apocryphal than true was related by Isaac Backus in his *History of New England* (2:175), which links revivalist preaching to attempts to destroy natural family relations. In visiting Elder Thomas Marsh, the pastor of Canterbury, who had been jailed in 1746 for preaching without a license, Backus noted that Marsh had been placed beneath the cell of a physician who had been arrested for "giving a single woman a potion to destroy the fruit of her womb, which destroyed her own life." The juxtaposition of the evils of itinerant preaching with the evils of abortion illustrates how radical religion and disordered families were linked in the eyes of the authorities.

79. Letter from Relief Hooper to the Middleborough Church, 30 June 1774, and the church's reply; Backus Papers, Box 10, ANTS. Isaac Backus' diary records many instances of confrontations between pious members (mostly women) and their enraged spouses; in June 1752 Phebe Fobes's husband Abner stormed into Backus's church and was "dreadfully enraged" to find his wife communing there. Two months later, another man "came out and open raged at his wife for her religion." *The Diary of Isaac Backus*, 1:224 and 236.

80. "Account of Revival at Lyme West Parish," *Christian History* (1744), 1:108.

81. Thomas Prince, "Account of Revival of Religion at Boston," *Christian History* (1745), 3:382.

sachusetts, "on account of the *Universality* of it, affecting all sorts, sober and vicious, high and low, rich and poor, wise and unwise."[82] Such a transcendental view of the power of grace easily translated into an affirmation of the spiritual equality of souls before God.

From the evangelical insistence on the equality of all souls came the relative egalitarianism of the evangelical polity in matters of church governance in the mid-eighteenth century. For not only did evangelical women share in the spiritual fruits of New Light theology, but they reaped more tangible benefits as well. Baptist women participated on an equal footing with Baptist men in choosing ministers and administering church discipline. With the important exception of the pastorate, women were thus granted a formal role in the organizational structure of the evangelical church far beyond what was available to them in orthodox societies. Such a sharing of power would not have been possible without a prior repudiation of the familial model of the church.

The records of the earliest Baptist churches are sparse, and often incomplete. It is difficult to document with any precision the exact role of women in the internal governance of these churches, but the available evidence suggests it was considerable. When the First Baptist Church of Groton met in 1756 to choose a new pastor, both men and women consented to the selection of Timothy Wightman.[83] Ancient rituals such as the washing of feet or imposition of hands were often contested practices in Baptist churches, and women participated along with men in these vital debates. When the issue of washing of feet came up in the Tiverton Baptist Church in 1779, "a motion was made to know the minds of the Brethren and Sisters respecting the Practice of washing of feet whereupon Some manifested that they thought it was their duty to Practice it and it was Left for further Consideration."[84] In Newport and Providence, Baptist women had long voted to admit new members and elect deacons. Although no formal policy was ever adopted on the subject, it was clear to the renowned Congregational minister Ezra Stiles that Baptist women participated on an equal footing with men in all the major decisions of church governance—in contrast to women in his own denomination. When consulted by a bewildered Baptist deacon on the subject, Stiles reviewed the recent history of several Baptist churches and concluded, "On the whole:—it appears plaine to me,

82. *Christian History* (1744), 2:125.
83. Record Book, First Baptist Church of Groton, 20 May 1756, CSL.
84. Record Book, First Baptist Church of Tiverton, 7 February 1779, RIHS.

that it is a Usage & practiced Principle among the Baptists of this Colony . . . to admit the Sisters to equal Votes in the Chh meetings, & this by
Lifting Up of Hands."[85]

But the most important evidence on this score is negative; in contrast to
the later eighteenth century, when churches explicitly recorded that "men"
and the "brethren" voted to call a new pastor or admit new members,
records from the early and mid-century note that "the church" or "the
members" undertook such decisions. The absence of gender-specific language in church records is of course hardly conclusive evidence that women
participated in church business, but when combined with scattered references to actual instances in which women's votes were recorded, it suggests
that church governance was a shared responsibility for evangelical men and
women.

That responsibility extended to the most sensitive area of all, the right to a
public voice. In 1754 a lay Baptist offered a spirited defense of women's right
to speak in church which illustrates the lengths to which some evangelicals
were willing to go in defiance of conventional injunctions on women's public
role. At a council in Suffield called to inquire into the issue, Brother Benjamin Kent set forth an elaborate exegesis of key biblical passages to support
his contention:

> What God said to Adam (when he called after him in the Garden) he
> said to Eve etc. and that when the apostle saith that the woman shall not
> speak in the Chh & usorp authority over the man he saith the man there
> meant is Christ, and the woman the Chh; and where the apostle saith Let
> her ask her Husband etc. he saith the woman there is Human Reason,
> and the man is faith; and where the apostle saith Adam was first formed
> and then Eve etc. He saith that Adam there means Christ, and Eve the
> Chh.[86]

Here Kent explicitly rejects the use of familial metaphors to describe the
relationship between a church and its minister, or between male and female
members. The church is not to be considered a household but rather the
feminine principle incarnate; the labels "husband" and "wife" do not indi-

---

85. *The Literary Diary of Ezra Stiles*, ed. Franklin B. Dexter (New York, 1801), 1:145–47. In this
passage of the diary Stiles recorded several occasions on which women voted in Baptist churches,
including the controversial decision of the Second Baptist Church of Newport to retain Elder
Nicholas Eyres in 1750; the election of deacons; and the admission of James Manning to the First
Baptist Church of Providence in the 1760s.

86. Result of Council at Suffield, Canterbury Separate Papers, 9 December 1754, Larned
Collection, CSL.

cate a familial relationship of dominance and subordination but rather the abstract concepts of "faith" and "Human Reason." Thus the opposition between husbands and wives posited in the Bible becomes, in this reading, not a metaphor for the unequal relation of women to men in the visible world (as it would be for later evangelicals) but an affirmation of eternally recurring principles. Such an ingenious reading of scripture would have been considered the worst kind of sophistry in the early nineteenth century, but it suggests the uncompromising refusal of mid-eighteenth-century evangelicals to incorporate worldly distinctions (including that of gender) into their communal ethos.

Not all evangelicals were willing to go this far. The council of Baptist churches called to hear Kent's petition rejected his "horable way of perverting the scriptures" and reaffirmed the church's position that "it plainly appears that God dealth with them [Adam and Eve] distinctly in the different denomination of man & woman, Husband and wife and Charged the man with sin in hearkening to the voice of his wife in suffering her to speak & usorp over the man."[87] Appeals to extrachurch councils were usually anathema to Baptist churches, but such action was warranted in this case because the issue at stake was nothing less than the evangelical principle of sexual egalitarianism taken to its logical conclusion. In contrast to the decision of the Suffield council, the Philadelphia Baptist Association grudgingly accorded women some space to speak in 1746: "A woman may, at least, make a brother a mouth to ask leave to speak, if not ask it herself; and a time of hearing is to be allowed." Yet, they warned, women "ought not to open the floodgate of speech in an imperious, tumultuous, masterly manner."[88] The "tumult" of women's voices clearly disturbed more conservative ministers such as Isaac Backus, who recalled a day when three female exhorters from Sturbridge, Massachusetts, visited his congregation and "were much overcome, and Spake much Publickly. I fear a great Part of it was wood hay and Stuble, though I hope there was some true wheats."[89] However discomfited Backus was by their unruly appearance, he nonetheless allowed the exhorters to speak. The record on this highly sensitive issue is decidedly mixed, and the dissension sparked by women's assumption of a public voice illustrates both the potential and the limitations of the evangelical commitment to shared governance.

87. Ibid.
88. *Minutes of the Philadelphia Baptist Association, 1707 to 1807* (Philadelphia, 1851), p. 53. I thank Jon Butler for directing me to this episode.
89. *The Diary of Isaac Backus*, 1:90.

Eighteenth-century evangelicals were a contentious lot. Emboldened by a theology that stressed the primacy of the individual in the quest for grace, energized by the stiff opposition of orthodox Puritans who derided their motives and ridiculed their piety, evangelical men and women stretched the bounds of Puritan ecclesiology in their search for the pure faith. From book-burning to itinerant preaching, the rituals and rhetoric of the First Great Awakening marked out new boundaries for religious experience.

A close reading of the religious discourse of the Great Awakening reveals its preoccupation with anarchy—the breaking of those spatial, temporal, linguistic, and sexual boundaries that served to define and confine the spiritual life of orthodox Puritans. By holding worship services out-of-doors and extending the frequency of prayer sessions, allowing lay men and even women to preach, and embracing an extemporaneous, unstructured sermon style, the itinerant preachers who brought the revival to town after town flirted dangerously with that "uncosmicized space" so feared by religious man. The potential for such practices to produce chaos rather than conversion was not ignored by the revivalists. Enamored as they were of creative disorder (their continued stress on the unmediated conversion experience is the best example), they knew how artificial and impermanent any truths but God's are. A religious ethos that constantly skirts the edge of liminality is a fragile and perhaps untenable one, and we find evangelicals in the post-Awakening years striving to come to terms with the radical implications of their faith.

Yet the underside of anarchy was the liberation that followed from the breaking of old patterns of religious worship, and women reaped considerable benefits (both symbolic and real) from the egalitarian impulse in evangelical religion. The deceptively simple statements found in the church records—the "church" voted to call Elder Smith to the pastoral office, the "members" gathered to "discourse" with Sister Lucy Stone about her "evil conversation," the "church as a body" withdrew fellowship from Brother John Smith—conceal what was in fact a significant widening of women's sphere of authority within the church.

Even more than the opportunities afforded for church governance, however, evangelical religion offered women a faith that explicitly embraced feminine qualities. From its emotional rhetoric to its ecstatic conversions, evangelical religion embodied what to eighteenth-century New Englanders were distinctly female traits. Puritans viewed religious enthusiasm, and the "affections" it aroused, as both disruptive and redemptive, susceptible to manipulation by Satan as well as by Christ. One could never be sure, warned Old Light ministers, that the "enthusiastical" excesses of the Elect were the work of the Spirit and not the snares of the devil. The danger of religious enthusiasm lay in its potential for arousing the passions, for unleashing the sensuality that lay hidden in every carnal being. Beneath the antirevivalist attack on revived religion as overly sensuous was a long-standing rhetorical tradition that equated passion with femininity. The underlying typology on which the image of the revival was based was the dual nature of the feminine as both chaotic/dangerous and powerful/regenerative. Women's inordinate lust and uncontrollable passions were the very essence of social and political disorder to early modern pedagogues, and in promoting a faith that gave free rein to the "affections," the Awakeners presented a female face to orthodox religious culture.[90] In this context, Lang's comment that revival converts were "so many women" hints at a broader truth, that revived religion itself was inherently "feminine." However awkward such a feminine posture would become in later years, in the mid-eighteenth century evangelical religion did not shun the more female aspects of its piety just as it did not bar women from exercising their full rights as members of the body politic.

90. Karlsen, *The Devil in the Shape of a Woman*; Natalie Zemon Davis, "Women on Top," in her *Society and Culture in Early Modern France* (Stanford, Calif., 1965), pp. 124–51; and Verduin, "'Our Cursed Natures.'" For a recent discussion of the ambivalence of Puritan ministers to religious "affections," see John Corrigan, *The Prism of Piety: Catholick Congregational Clergy at the Beginning of the Enlightenment* (New York, 1991).

CHAPTER TWO

"ALL THINGS ARE BECOME NEW"

The Conversion Experience

AT THE HEART OF THE EVANGELICAL FAITH was the experience of religious conversion. More than any other ritual, conversion embodied the individualistic message of the Great Awakening. What Patricia Bonomi calls the "defiant individualism" of New Light pietists can be seen in Isaac Backus' description of conversion as a man looking at the sun; while the sun shines for all men, at the moment of conversion "its rays appear to point as directly to us as if there was not another person in the whole world for it to shine upon."[1] Alone before God, the sinner stood naked, stripped of all conventional attributes, from sex to caste. "In Christ, there is neither Jew nor Greek, slave nor free, male nor female," insists the scripture, and evangelicals heeded the word.

Such a resolutely individualistic position was not so much a radical departure from orthodox patterns as a return to earlier ways. Orthodox Puritans had moved gradually away from the pure church ideal in the late

---

1. Patricia Bonomi, in *Under the Cope of Heaven: Religion, Society, and Politics in Colonial America* (New York, 1986), p. 159. The Backus quotation is in William McLoughlin, *New England Dissent, 1630–1833: The Baptists and the Separation of Church and State* (Cambridge, Mass., 1971), 1:357. For other studies stressing the individualist nature of the conversion experience, see Jerald Brauer, "Conversion from Puritanism to Revivalism," *Journal of Religion* 58 (1978): 241; Charles Lloyd Cohen, *God's Caress: The Psychology of Puritan Religious Experience* (New York, 1986), p. 274. On the other hand, Barbara Epstein locates in the collective experience of the revival the communal essence of religious conversion during the Awakening, which she argues represented a shift from the individual model of conversion in orthodox Puritan thinking. Although she is right in emphasizing the collective nature of revivals, in which many sinners were first awakened, a person more often experienced the moment of conversion in the privacy of one's chamber or alone in a field than in the midst of an aroused congregation. See her *Politics of Domesticity: Women, Evangelism, and Temperance in Nineteenth-Century America* (Middletown, Conn., 1981), p. 11.

seventeenth and eighteenth centuries in widening the definition of the Elect to include not only those who had undergone intense personal crises but also those who through the ties of family and kinship had some sort of prior claim to election. In protest against this encroaching tribalism evangelical Protestants deliberately renounced any measure of spiritual status beyond that of a direct and immediate encounter with God. By refusing to recognize the validity of infant baptisms, the Baptist church took the evangelical ideal to its logical extreme in insisting that family ties played a minimal role in the critical task of nurturing and harvesting godly souls; only the unmediated confrontation between God and the adult sinner could produce conversion. The Baptists' rejection of infant baptism was, as William McLoughlin has pointed out, nothing less than an abandonment of the traditional covenant theology of New England.[2]

Placed beyond the bounds of family or covenant, the act of conversion became an event rather than a process. No longer conceived of as a life-long process of acquiring sufficient knowledge about one's self and the nature of divine justice (from parents or ministers), conversion in the revivals of the 1740s became an actual (at times physical) encounter between the soul of the sinner and an angry God. God and his archenemy, Satan, became very real figures in the conversion narratives of the Great Awakening, where they lend these texts a vivid theatrical quality not found in early-eighteenth-century narratives. As representations of God and the devil became more literal, the sinner himself became more of an actor in the drama of salvation. This is not to suggest that humans were endowed with greater agency in the attainment of individual salvation in revivalist theology, which remained rigidly Calvinist in its insistence on the irresistible and unmerited quality of grace, but rather that evangelical converts appear less as undifferentiated pawns in God's overarching plan for the world than as real men and women struggling to come to terms with the authoritarian demands of their faith.

The anatomy of conversion was subtly altered as well as condensed in the Great Awakening. Under both the orthodox and the revivalist models, the sinner normally experienced five stages in the conversion process: awakening, in which he or she first became aware of the need for salvation; conviction, in which the innate corruptness of man and the sinful quality of the sinner's profane life is brought home; a period of reform, in which the sinner tries in vain to effect salvation through external works such as reading the

2. McLoughlin, *New England Dissent*, 1:427. For discussions of the tribal nature of Puritanism, see Edmund Morgan, *Visible Saints: The History of a Puritan Idea* (New York, 1963), and Gerald F. Moran, "Religious Renewal, Puritan Tribalism, and the Family in Seventeenth-Century Milford, Connecticut," *WMQ*, 3d ser., 36 (1979): 236–54.

Bible, attending services, and living a moral life; despair at the utter inability of one's own efforts to reach salvation and submission to the necessity for total dependence on the will of a gracious God; and finally conversion, which could be achieved in a single moment or over a period of time extending for months or even years. In this final stage, the range of emotions felt by the newly regenerate ranged from intense joy and exultation to quiet confidence and serenity of mind.[3]

This model was largely left intact by the revivals of the mid-eighteenth century, but subtle shifts of emphasis are apparent at different stages of the process, and these signal a new understanding of both the psychology of sin and of the relationship of God to man. In particular, the period of conviction was given heightened emphasis in revivalist preaching, as New Light ministers sought to impress on their congregations the horrors of hell and the terror of eternal damnation. Sermons such as Jonathan Edwards' famous "Sinners in the Hands of an Angry God" were calculated to arouse the deepest fears of abandonment and helplessness among a people who faced the arbitrariness of death and the fragility of human ties in their daily lives. The intense preoccupation of eighteenth-century men and women with death and disease (which persisted in spite of a relatively favorable demographic climate) and the fear of arbitrary and unpredictable natural disasters portending divine displeasure and retribution were recurrent themes in evangelical writings.[4] Sudden deaths and natural calamities were not new to the eighteenth century, of course, but revivalist preachers consciously exploited the association of such ominous signs with an ever-growing uneasiness among New Englanders about their own spiritual state and the health of their communities.[5]

3. For a description of the morphology of conversion in seventeenth-century Puritan culture, see Morgan, *Visible Saints*; Cohen, *God's Caress*; Norman Pettit, *The Heart Prepared: Grace and Conversion in Puritan Spiritual Life* (New Haven, Conn., 1966); and Charles Hambrick-Stowe, *The Practice of Piety: Puritan Devotional Discipline in Seventeenth-Century New England* (Chapel Hill, N.C., 1982).

4. For a discussion of the perception and the reality of death and mortality in colonial America, see Maris A. Vinovskis, "Angel's Heads and Weeping Willows: Death in Early America," in *Studies in American Historical Demography*, ed. Maris A. Vinovskis (New York, 1979), pp. 181–210.

5. One study of the conversion experience in the Great Awakening found an overwhelming concern with death and damnation in the narratives of men and women converts, which the author attributes largely to the inescapable presence of a harsh and unpredictable natural environment. See Epstein, *The Politics of Domesticity*, pp. 16–21. David Stannard, on the other hand, finds a more benign attitude toward death and dying in the spiritual writings and material artifacts of post-Awakening New Englanders; see *The Puritan Way of Death: A Study in Religion, Culture, and Social Change* (New York, 1977), pp. 146–61.

This pervasive sense of unease in revivalist literature has made it tempting to view the Great Awakening as the by-product of increasing tensions within the social and economic life of New England towns. Since Richard Bushman first located the seeds of religious fervor in the accumulated feelings of guilt engendered by a rapidly expanding social order and the shift toward a market economy, historians have teased the available records for evidence of the social origins of revived religion.[6] But environmental explanations of the heightened concern with themes of death and damnation in the conversion narratives of the Great Awakening are insufficient in and of themselves to explain these fears. However great the disruptions caused by the shift from an agricultural to a commercial economy (and the parameters and timing of this shift are by no means clear), however pervasive the threat of epidemic disease and natural disasters such as the earthquakes that rocked New England in 1727 and again in 1755, the social and physical environment within which the Awakening took shape did not differ markedly from that which shaped late-seventeenth-century Puritanism.[7] The *psychological* environment was, however, very different. A new awareness of human subjectivity which placed individual man as errant sinner in an almost confrontational encounter with a very real savior, unbuffered by social context or group covenant, gave rise to a new psychology of sin and conversion.

The new psychology of conversion marked this experience as a profoundly liminal event, a rite of passage in anthropological terms. A deep alienation from one's prior self or condition is followed by an existential state of limbo in which old values and structures are discarded, ultimately leading to a new level of being in which structure and values are reaffirmed, albeit in a transformed state. The radical separation between the old, unregenerate state and the new, transformed one which occurs in the process of conversion is summed up in Jonathan Edwards' famous statement that the converted are truly "new men, new creatures; new, not only within, but without;

---

6. Richard Bushman, *From Puritan to Yankee: Character and the Social Order in Connecticut, 1690–1765* (New York, 1967). Christine Heyrman similarly links the growth of religious piety in the 1740s in two Massachusetts seaports to changes in the commercial economies and social structures of these communities, albeit in ways that were profoundly conservative rather than liberating. See her *Commerce and Culture: The Maritime Communities of Colonial Massachusetts, 1690–1750* (New York, 1984).

7. The analytical confusion surrounding the timing and nature of the transition from an agricultural to a commercial economy in colonial New England is illustrated by the tendency of historians of witchcraft to ascribe the Salem witch craze of 1692 to precisely the same kinds of social and economic tensions presumed to have initiated the Great Awakening fifty years later. The best example of the socioeconomic interpretation of the Salem trials is Paul Boyer and Stephen Nissenbaum's classic, *Salem Possessed: The Social Origins of Witchcraft* (Cambridge, Mass., 1974).

they are sanctified throughout, in spirit, soul and body; old things are passed
away, all things are become new; they have new hearts, and new eyes, new
ears, new tongues, new hands, new feet . . . a new conversation and practice;
and they walk in newness of life, and continue to do so to the end of life."[8]
Reversal is the controlling motif of the conversion story, as in other rites of
passage; dead souls become reborn, and attributes of the sinner's persona are
inverted in the sacred state.

We should pause, however, before adopting too uncritically the anthropological model of liminality, which stresses the universal presence of liminality in human societies. Caroline Walker Bynum, in particular, has questioned the appropriateness of the liminal model to the conversion stories of
both sexes, arguing that theories of liminality are themselves gender biased.
Stories of reversal, she claims, are more common in male conversion narratives than in female ones.

> Turner's ideas [of liminality] describe the stories and symbols of men
> better than those of women. Women's stories insofar as they can be
> discerned behind the tales told by male biographers are in fact less pro-
> cessual than men's; they don't have turning points. And when women
> recount their own lives, the themes are less climax, conversion, reintegra-
> tion, and triumph, the liminality of reversal or elevation, than conti-
> nuity. . . . So that one either has to see the woman's religious stance as
> permanently liminal or as never quite becoming so.[9]

In the accounts she has studied, medieval male saints tended to describe
their converted state as a feminized one, drawing from the rhetorical tradition that equated saints to brides. Men thus had to undergo a reversal of
sexual identity in order to be reborn. Women saints, on the other hand,

8. Quoted in Philip Greven, *The Protestant Temperament: Patterns of Child-Rearing, Religious
Experience, and the Self in Early America* (New York, 1977), p. 62.

9. Caroline Walker Bynum, "Women's Stories, Women's Symbols: A Critique of Victor
Turner's Theory of Liminality," in *Anthropology and the Study of Religion*, ed. Robert L. Moore and
Frank E. Reynolds (Chicago, 1984), p. 108. Bynum's conclusion that women's religious stance can be
seen as "permanently liminal" is consistent with the work of anthropologists who see in the
feminine principle the eternal expression of liminality or *communitas* in preindustrial societies.
Mary Douglas, for instance, links the concept of pollution—defined as "that which cannot be
clearly classified in terms of traditional criteria of classification, or falls between classificatory
boundaries"—with the blood of women released in menstruation and childbearing. See the discussion of Douglas' work in Victor Turner, *The Ritual Process: Structure and Anti-Structure* (Chicago,
1969), p. 109. For Bynum, however, the association of women with liminality is not an intrinsic,
cognitive feature of medieval society but rather the result of a specific historical process whereby
male elites articulated an ideology of feminine structurelessness to serve their own (largely political)
interests.

rarely assumed a male persona after conversion. Rather, they preferred to describe themselves as female (i.e., brides) or as truly androgynous (that is, gender*less*).

The gendered nature of the liminality model in Bynum's analysis extends beyond the specific content of male and female stories of the self, however; the entire medieval discourse on piety reveals a gender ideology that placed women outside the bounds of conventional social experience. Not only do the lives of individual male saints revolve around the theme of reversal, but male religious theorists used images of reversal to express the ideal of spiritual perfection. Chief among these images, Bynum argues, was "woman"— as being and as symbol. Woman (virgin, bride, mother) was the prevailing image not only for the regenerate but for all those who were outside the social structure. The opposition between the religious and secular order thus took on a gendered quality of its own, as masculinity was equated with profane status and femininity with the divine. Within this oppositional structure, theories of liminality are inevitably male-centered. The need for release from structure which liminal episodes represent is more acute for those in positions of authority, those for whom structure functions to empower. "The problem seems to be that the dichotomy of structure and chaos, from which liminality or *communitas* is a release, is a special issue for elites, for those who in a special sense *are* the structure. A model which focuses on this need for release as *the* ultimate socio-psychological need may best fit the experience of elites."[10] Women writers, on the other hand, "say less about gender, make less use of dichotomous gender images, speak less of gender reversal, and place more emphasis on interior motivation and continuity of self. . . . It is men who develop conceptions of gender, whereas women develop conceptions of humanity."[11] Women's structural subordination within secular medieval society leads them, in this argument, to downplay gender dichotomies and embrace a more universalistic model of religious experience.

Bynum's work is enormously useful in directing our attention to the close link between the sociology of gender and its semiotic expression in religious literature. But even more important, it alerts us to the gender-specific nature of ideologies of gender, that men and women may hold very different conceptions of what it means to be masculine and feminine and how these qualities are or are not inscribed in social experience. Sensitivity toward and

10. Bynum, "Women's Stories, Women's Symbols," pp. 110, 118.

11. Caroline Walker Bynum, "'And Woman His Humanity: Female Imagery in the Religious Writing of the Late Middle Ages," in *Gender and Religion: On the Complexity of Symbols*, ed. Caroline Walker Bynum et al. (Boston, 1986), pp. 261–62.

consciousness of gender distinctions, she suggests, are the product of one's position within the prevailing structures of authority, and the proclivity of medieval women saints to assume an androgynous or genderless persona is indicative of their marginal status in a male-dominated world.

What did conversion mean for men and women in colonial New England? Can we speak of a male and a female model of conversion corresponding to the distinction between reversal and continuity uncovered by Bynum in medieval texts? Or did the relative equality of men and women within the eighteenth-century evangelical church contribute to a blurring of even the subtlest gender distinctions in the conversion experience? Were evangelical women able, in short, to escape if not transcend the constraints of gender through the experience of grace? Historians have probed the accounts of religious conversion left by men and women for evidence that evangelicals practiced what they preached. What they have found is that evangelical men and women largely spoke in "one tongue" in describing their experiences of grace. It is, as Charles Cohen and Barbara Epstein have argued, often difficult to determine the sex of the author if no signature is provided in the manuscript. Differences in social role inevitably surface in these texts, Cohen concedes: "The strength energized by conversion did flow into separate behaviors. What a woman endeavored with her spiritual strength differed from what a man did." Nonetheless, he agrees with Epstein that there is no discernible difference in the emotional tone or psychological content of male and female conversion narratives.[12]

Other scholars attribute this leveling of sexual distinctions in religious conversion to a particular discursive tradition rather than to the egalitarian nature of evangelical religion. Noting the pervasiveness of images of the saint as bride or wife in sermon literature, Philip Greven and Margaret Masson argue that the rhetorical demand that all saints—male and female— assume the feminine posture of vessels to be impregnated with the seed of God resulted in a uniformly feminized sense of self among evangelicals. "By becoming brides of Christ," Greven writes, "evangelical men found them-

---

12. Cohen, *God's Caress*, pp. 222–23; Epstein, *Politics of Domesticity*, p. 14. Epstein argues that the lack of gender distinctions exhibited by mid-eighteenth-century conversion accounts derives from the "rough equality of the sexes" in New England which was fostered by "common participation in a household economy that was to a large extent independent of the market, and also by the near-frontier conditions of life," pp. 21 and 31; see also p. 31 n.48. Epstein's position is reminiscent of the "golden age" thesis first put forward by Gerda Lerner that men and women, though hardly equal, enjoyed a rough comraderie born of shared responsibilities in rural colonial New England; see the literature cited in the Introduction, n.22.

selves able and willing to assume the passive role, and the symbolic identity of a woman, in relation to their Savior."[13] Masson also sees a blurring of gender roles as the inevitable consequence of the sexual imagery of Puritan religious writing.[14] In the end, both argue that the conversion experience, because conceived in terms of sexual union, contributed to a leveling of gender distinctions in Puritan society by promoting a model of conversion which was essentially the same for both sexes.

My reading of the conversion literature of the Great Awakening suggests a model of the regenerate somewhere in between the gendered medieval saint and the androgynous Puritan saint. Rather than men's and women's stories diverging along paths marked out by their unequal social status, with men seeking release from the burdens of power while women retreated into marginality, the accounts written by New England men and women share a basic similitude that reflects the rough equality of the sexes within the evangelical community. Yet men and women saints did not speak entirely with "one tongue"; the more sensual elements in the conversion experience are accented in women's stories, while men apparently found comfort in the ritualized forms of collective worship. These distinctions, however subtle, confirm Bynum's insight that liminality often functions differently in male and female stories of religious conversion. We need to pay close attention to how men and women perceived the boundaries that constrained them before we can understand how the experience of conversion helped transcend these boundaries.

"I was born in a land of Light": Conversion before the Awakening

Before we examine the Awakening conversion experience, however, a brief survey of some conversion accounts from the 1720s will help highlight the ways in which the later narratives differ in tone and content. It is perhaps misleading to characterize these earlier texts as conversion narratives at all, because few describe before-and-after periods separated by a discernible conversion experience. Recorded on the occasion of an applicant's request to

13. Greven, *Protestant Temperament,* p. 125.

14. Margaret W. Masson, "The Typology of the Female as a Model for the Regenerate: Puritan Preaching, 1690–1730," *Signs* 2 (1976): 304–15. Masson has a much more benign view of the consequences of such a "feminizing" of religious experience than does Greven, arguing that Puritan hostility toward women was mitigated by the recognition among male saints that they must become more like women in order to achieve salvation.

be admitted into full membership in a particular church, these accounts resemble more a declaration of faith, in which the prospective communicant affirms his or her creed for the benefit of the congregation. Affirmations of doctrinal purity rather than personal regeneration, these spoken declarations of faith reveal a communal understanding of church membership rooted in family ties rather than in individual experience.

In 1728, Jonathan Pearson stood before the Second Church of Christ in Lynn, Massachusetts, and delivered the following testimony in fulfillment of the requirements of admission into the church: "I was Shapen in Iniquity and In Sin did my Mother conceive me but I thank God that I was born in a land of Light wherein the Way of Salvation by John 1, Christ is revealed to the Sinful Children of Man—and that it pleased God to cast my lot in religious familys where I was called upon to early piety."[15] Like her fellow communicant, Abigail Hodgman gave praise to God that "I was born and brought up In a Land of Light and under the Ministry of the Word where the doctrine of God is opened."[16] Jeremiah Eaton gave credit to "the good Education and Instruction I've had from my parents & that I was given up by them to him in Baptism."[17] John Comer, elder of the First Baptist Church in Newport, began his diary by praising God for "granting my birth in a land of gospel light where I was favoured with a religious education, having each of my grandmothers, viz. Mrs. Elinor Comer and Mrs. Mary Pittom, noted among the godly for eminent and exemplary piety."[18] These conventional gestures to the benefits of a gospel education, infant baptism at the hands of godly parents, and residence in a "Land of Light" testify to the importance of family and community in the preparation of souls for the responsibilities of church membership in pre-Awakening New England.[19] For these saints, admission into church membership involved a reaffirmation of baptismal vows rather than an assertion of individual piety. "I promise to God a new Life," Jonathan Pearson's account concluded, "and renew

15. Relation of Jonathan Pearson, 7 January 1728, Testimonials of faith relating to the Second Church of Lynn, PEM.

16. Relation of Abigail Hodgman, 31 December 1727, ibid.

17. Relation of Jeremiah Eaton, 7 January 1728, ibid.

18. *The Diary of John Comer*, ed. C. E. Barrows and J. W. Willmarth, *Collections of Rhode Island Historical Society* 8 (1893): 15.

19. On the importance of family in preparing the younger generation to receive grace in seventeenth-century New England, see Edmund S. Morgan, *The Puritan Family: Religion and Domestic Relations in Seventeenth-Century New England* (New York, 1966), pp. 174–86; and Gerald F. Moran and Maris A. Vinovskis, "The Puritan Family and Religion: A Critical Reappraisal," *WMQ*, 3d ser., 39 (1982): 35–36.

my baptismal vows and obligations which my parents layd me under In my tender years."

After duly noting the advantages bestowed on them from youth through pious parents and an accommodating religious climate, converts in the pre-Awakening period proceeded to narrate the particular providential occurrences that had contributed to their awakening and conviction of sin. "To the best of my remembrance," John Comer wrote,

> the Providence that first stir'd me up was the surprising death of a little lad about my age, his name was William Thomas, who was playing marvils near the Old North Meeting House, Boston, and a cart laden passing by, a marvil rolling under the cart he stept to get it, the horse starting run the wheel over his head and brake it so that his brains came out and he died. . . . O how my soul seemed at that time when mine eyes affected my heart wonderfully. I thought, were it my case to lie so bruised and broken, and to have my soul fly into the world of spirits, how would it be? I was lost in myself.[20]

Comer's religious awakening was completed by the smallpox epidemic that swept his native Boston in 1721, further alerting him to the precarious state of his own soul. From the point at which he abandoned his profane life to take up the calling of a minister, Comer's diary is a continuous catalogue of the providences provided by God for the rousing of a lethargic and inattentive people. Storms, diseases, earthquakes, accidental deaths, and inexplicable disasters of all kinds provide a recurring motif for the working out of God's divine plan on earth.[21]

Abigail Strong of the East Windsor church was awakened by "a mental distemper" that made her "very much afraid that I should die," as some of her neighbors had.[22] Jonathan Pearson was brought under conviction first by the sudden death of his mother and a young acquaintance, though his concerns were sharply increased by "the late amazing Earth-quake" that "Layd open my Neglect before me." Along with Pearson, seven women and one other man made public confessions of faith before the Second Church

20. *The Diary of John Comer*, pp. 17–18.

21. See for example Comer's description of the death by lightning of one Deborah Grinman at Narragansett two days after "she dreamed that a woman lay dead in ye same spot she was struck down in. She told her sister of it under great surprise, and that she was kill'd with thunder. In ye morning of ye day in which she was kill'd 'twas very clear, but she apprehended it would be a fatal day." *The Diary of John Comer*, p. 54.

22. Relation of Abigail Strong, 14 September 1725, in Kenneth P. Minkema, "The East Windsor Conversion Narratives, 1700–1725," *Connecticut Historical Society Bulletin* 51 (1985): 54.

of Lynn following the devastating earthquake of 1727; many credited the earthquake with first alerting them to their natural, sinful condition.[23] "It has pleased God," declared Elizabeth Aburn, "by the late terrible & surprising Earth-quake to awaken me and fix such Impressions on me as I desire may not be worn of[f]."

Once awakened to their precarious state, pre-Awakening converts were brought to acknowledge the various sins they had committed in their profane lives. Rather than list specific misdeeds or rebellious acts, sinners were more likely to confess the innate corruptness of their nature under original sin. Fully one-half of the accounts from the 1720s mention natural sin as the primary offence of which they were cognizant, while only one man referred to a specific act of rebellion against God (in this case, disobedience to his parents). Mrs. Mary Bassett of Martha's Vineyard confessed: "I Sinned more in one day in my own thoughts, than all the world was ever guilty of before me. No Sin I could think of but I was guilty of it And I could think of nothing else, but Sin & Sorrow It Seemed to flow over me like mountains of Lead. . . . Every Day new Sins & new Sorrows would fill my thoughts. Adams sins imputed to me, a corrupt natur[e] dwelling in me, & 50 years Spent in one continued act of Sin."[24] Frances Bancroft of East Windsor thought she was "so vile a creature, and so polluted with sin that [I] could not but wonder that God should bare any regard to [me]," though she could not recall any particular transgression that would warrant so harsh a judgment.[25]

The absence of references to actual behavior, aside from the formulaic expressions of regret for a life misspent "hardened in sin," indicates the relatively abstract nature of the relationship between God and man revealed in the pre-Awakening narratives. As the sinner is but a single representative of the larger family of humankind embodied in the Adamic legend, so the figure of Christ is but a manifestation of some larger divine force. In these texts, God appears less as an anthropomorphic figure with human qualities and attributes than as a force acting through natural phenomena.

The impersonal quality of divine intercession in pre-Awakening accounts recedes in narratives of conversion dating from the 1740s, as familial images of God replace providential occurrences as the instrument of religious awakening. God as father and Jesus as lover become the dominant meta-

23. Testimonials of faith relating to the Second Church of Lynn, 1727–28, PEM.

24. "A Brief Account of the dealings of God with Mary Bassett of Marthas Vineyard," 1728, Backus Papers, Box 6, ANTS.

25. Relation of Frances Bancroft, 8 June 1722, in "The East Windsor Conversion Narratives," p. 48.

phors of the deity in the narratives of revival converts. The counterpart to the personification of the figures of God and Jesus was the emergence of Satan as a palpable adversary who appeared in visions that were often painfully real to sinners under conviction. Cohen has argued that, in seventeenth-century Puritan accounts, the role of the devil was downplayed. "Most impulses to sin, the accounts record, proceed spontaneously from the individual. . . . The real adversary is not Satan, but oneself."[26] By the eighteenth century, however, as Murray Murphey concludes, conversion involved "interaction with God, Christ, and the Holy Spirit [and, by extension, Satan] conceived as real persons; these were *inter*psychic relationships, not *intra*psychic ones."[27] Evangelical men and women created new personas for themselves out of the shards of these psychic encounters.[28]

"Swallowed up in God": The New Birth

The most famous account of religious conversion from the First Great Awakening in New England begins, "I was born Feb 15th 1711 and born again octo 1741."[29] Nathan Cole, a Connecticut farmer and radical pietist, recorded in his journal an extraordinarily detailed account of his awakening under the preaching of George Whitefield in the first year of Whitefield's American tour. As a description of the lay response to the revivalists' mes-

26. Cohen, *God's Caress*, p. 218. In a sample of 78 conversion accounts, Cohen counts only 21 references to Satan (14 in male accounts, 7 in female ones); p. 222 n.79.

27. Murray G. Murphey, "The Psychodynamics of Puritan Conversion," *American Quarterly* 31 (1979): 137.

28. This chapter draws on an analysis of over 100 accounts of religious conversion dating from the 1740s, 1750s, and 1760s that exist in manuscript form in the records of several New Light churches (including 30 accounts written by men, 68 by women, and 8 jointly by husband/wife couples). The two largest collections of narratives from the mid-eighteenth century are those recorded by John Cleaveland of Massachusetts for the Chebacco parish of which he was minister, located in the John Cleaveland Papers, James Duncan Phillips Library, Peabody Essex Museum, Salem, Massachusetts; and those found in the Sturbridge Congregational Society Papers, in the private possession of the society's clerk, Sturbridge, Mass. The former collection consists of 52 accounts, 37 female and 15 male; the later contains 37 accounts, 20 female, 9 male, and 8 husband/wife couples. Epstein's chapter on religious conversion in the eighteenth century in her *Politics of Domesticity* also draws primarily on these two collections, but she mistakenly labels the Sturbridge accounts as belonging to the Baptist Society in the town rather than the Congregational. I am indebted to Richard Rabinowitz for his generosity in providing photocopies of the Sturbridge accounts from his own personal files, as the original records were not available to me. In addition to these two collections, scattered accounts are contained in the Backus Papers, ANTS; and several more have been published.

29. Quoted in Michael J. Crawford, "The Spiritual Travels of Nathan Cole," *WMQ*, 3d ser., 33 (1976): 92.

sage, Cole's account is unsurpassed. As a personal journey through the psychic regions of despair, terror, and ultimately resignation and release, it is a classic New Light statement on the morphology of the conversion experience. In this first line we can see the New Light understanding of conversion as an act of rebirth that takes place in a single moment rather than over a lifetime.

Cole first heard Whitefield preach at Middletown in 1740, along with an estimated three or four thousand eager listeners. When he heard that the celebrated evangelist was to speak that afternoon, "I dropt my tool that I had in my hand and ran home to my wife telling her to make ready quickly to go and hear Mr Whitefield preach at Middletown, then run to my pasture for my horse with all my might; fearing that I should be too late. . . . We improved every moment to get along as if we were fleeing for our lives." Under the influence of revivalist preaching, Cole began to doubt his own spiritual status. "I began to think that I was not Elected, and that God made some for heaven and me for hell. . . . My heart then rose against God exceedingly, for his making me for hell." A period of almost two years of black despair and "hardness of heart" followed for Cole, who could not shake off his convictions. During these dark years, Cole struggled daily with an unrelenting and merciless God before finally yielding to the scriptural dictate of unconditional submission.

> God appeared unto me and made me Skringe: before whose face the heavens and the earth fled away; and I was Shrinked into Nothing; I knew not whether I was in the body or out, I seemed to hang in open Air before God, and he seemed to Speak to me in an angry and Sovereign way what won't you trust your Soul with God; My heart answered O yes, yes, yes; before I could stir my tongue or lips, And then He seemed to speak again, and say, may not God make one Vessel to honour and an other to dishonour and not let you know it; My heart answered again O yes, yes before I cou'd stir my tongue or lips. . . . When God appeared to me everything vanished and was gone in the twinkling of an Eye, as quick as A flash of lightning; But when God disappeared or in some measure withdrew, everything was in its place again, and I was on my Bed. My heart was broken; my burden was fallen of my mind; I was set free, my distress was gone, and I was filled with a pineing desire to see Christs own words in the Bible.

After he awoke from this vision, Cole said, "my heart and Soul were filled as full as they Could hold with Joy and sorrow; now I perfectly felt truth; now my heart talked with God; now every thing praised God; the trees, the stone, the walls of the house and everything I could set my eyes on, they all

praised God. . . . I was swallowed up in God." Echoing Jonathan Edwards'
words, Cole rejoiced that "now I saw with new eyes; all things become new,
A new God; new thoughts and new heart."[30]

All the key ingredients of the evangelical conversion model are present in
Cole's account. God appears "in the twinkling of an Eye, as quick as A flash
of lightning" to the doubting sinner, whose distress is then lifted immediately. The effect of this complete transformation of the soul is literally a
new birth—Cole felt as if he were "swallowed up in God" and, when he
emerged, he "saw with new eyes" and had "new thoughts and [a] new heart."
Cole himself initially doubted the validity of this kind of conversion experience. On confiding his vision to his doctor (who assured him: "That is what
I call Conversion") Cole at first was reluctant to accept the doctor's counsel:
"[His words] made me start, what thought I, is this Conversion . . . I do not
know; this is a new way I never thought of being Converted so; I had laid
out a way in my mind how I should be converted if ever I was, but this is a
way I never though[t] of before."[31] Cole rightly recognized the novelty of
the evangelical model with its emphasis on spontaneous, immediate conversion. Other New Light converts expressed similar confusion about the true
nature of conversion. Hannah Heaton, a farm woman from Connecticut,
confessed in her journal that she "could not think what conversion was unles
it was this & i fancied it was i thot a person must be in a sort of trance and be
carried to heaven and see wonders there and then be brought back again."[32]
However confused about the nature of the conversion experience, Cole and
Heaton would have agreed with the confident assertion of one New Light
minister that "Christians generally know the time of their conversion."[33]

In his doubts about the legitimacy of his conversion, Cole was especially
vulnerable to the stratagems of Satan to dissuade him from his newfound
faith. In the year following his conversion, Cole recounted several close
encounters with the devil which nearly drove him to suicide.

> Well Satan comes upon me and says there is one way to know quick;
> destroy your self says he and you will soon know; for if you be converted
> you will certainly be saved; and if not you never will be converted, there-
> fore destroy your self and you will know at once; I told him I will not on
> no account; but he follow'd me day after day and week after week for

30. Ibid., pp. 92–93, 96, 97.
31. Ibid., p. 98.
32. "The Spiritual Exercises of Hannah heaton" (1740–90), photocopy of manuscript journal,
CHS.
33. "Diary of Rev. Eleazer Wheelock," *Historical Magazine*, 2d ser., 5 (1869): 239. I am grateful
to Erik Seeman for directing me to this source.

about three months with this horrible temptation. . . . he still followed me very Close and as I was alone here and there about my fields, he would say come this is a good opportunity now.

Cole was able to escape the snares of the devil on this occasion, but his wife was not so fortunate. Laboring under "great fears that she had never entered that strait gate of Conversion," Nathan's wife was "so far borne down with it that she was at her wits end while she was talking about it so that she screamed out three or four times as loud as she could which surpriz'd me, and she said it will fall on me, I said what will fall, she said a great Cloud, I said it won't, She screamed out and said it will, it will, it is close to my head now, a great black Cloud." In the ensuing battle with Satan over his wife's soul, Cole took upon himself the task of disputing with his archenemy, since, as he wrote, "I knew his voice." Cole's wife remained a semi-invalid for most of her life as a result of this and other bruising encounters with the forces of darkness. Her conversion was in effect aborted by her inability fully to recover her senses, and Cole's diary records the strain her mental instability imposed on their marriage.[34]

For both Nathan Cole and his less fortunate wife, the devil was a very real adversary who appeared in a variety of guises to tempt the unwary sinner. Yet the fact that the intrusions of Satan were so much more debilitating for Cole's wife than for himself suggests that women may have been peculiarly susceptible to the devil's lures. In fact, with the exception of Cole's account, the most vivid descriptions of death-defying battles with Satan occur in women's narratives. Moreover, three times as many women as men mentioned their terror of death and damnation as the catalyst for their convictions of sin, further underscoring the vulnerability of the female psyche to the devil's insinuations. Hannah Heaton had many such encounters with Satan, including an especially devastating one at the time of her father's death, when she engaged in a dialogue with the devil over a period of several days. Like Cole, Heaton was driven by the suggestions of the devil to contemplate suicide:

> now it began to be whispered in my ear it is too late too late you had better hang your self and when i see a convenient place how it would strike me i was a fraid to go alone to pray for fear i should see the devil once when i was on the ground away a lone at prayer trying to give up all to christ in great distress of soul i thot i felt the devil twitch my cloaths i iumpt up and run in fixed with terror.[35]

34. "The Spiritual Travels of Nathan Cole," pp. 101, 104–5.
35. "The Spiritual Exercises of Hannah heaton," CHS.

Writing of Heaton's diary, Barbara Lacey argues that "Deity and devil were vividly alive in her mind. . . . In these experiences, Satan was a disembodied voice, sending thoughts into her mind that engaged her in a self-contained dialectical argument."[36] The physicality of Heaton's description, however— "i felt the devil twitch my cloaths"—argues for a more embodied perception of the devil than Lacey suggests. Satan did appear in Heaton's dreams and visions as a disembodied voice, but he also tormented her physically at times.[37]

The diary of another Great Awakening convert, Susanna Anthony, is richly laced with explicit descriptions of Satan and his stratagems which, though dismissed at times as fanciful delusions, nonetheless presented very real obstacles in her journey toward God. That "cursed fiend," the devil, was suffered by God to "vex [her] soul" by implanting thoughts of suicide in her mind. Such blasphemous thoughts, Anthony wrote, were especially distressing: "I thought these were the product of my own heart; that it was from the enmity of my nature against God, and not from satan, that they did proceed. This added vastly to my distress: for I thought myself one of the worst of monsters; and often wished that I might be annihilated." At other times, however, Satan "assaulted" her bodily: "I seemed as one really possessed of the devil. For, when at secret prayer, I was so surprised, hurried, and distracted, as to start right up, and run about, not knowing what I did, or why I did it; only that satan seemed to have had full power of me." On another occasion, under the devil's prompting she felt she had "twisted every bone out of its place: and have often since wondered that I never disjointed a bone when, through the violence of my distress, I wrung my hands, twisted every joint, and strained every nerve; biting my flesh; gnashing my teeth; throwing myself on the floor." Such episodes of bodily torment contradict Anthony's own assertion that her conversion was free from the kind of "sordid notions of vital religion on which some persons of wild imagination have laid great stress," such as hearing voices and being transported by visions of heaven and hell. "Satan was never permitted to present

---

36. Barbara E. Lacey, "The World of Hannah Heaton: The Autobiography of an Eighteenth-Century Connecticut Farm Woman," *WMQ*, 3d ser., 45 (1988): 285.

37. Heaton's diary contains many references to dreams that she clearly interpreted as prophetic visions. In one, she dreamed: "i was by the side of a great mountain and there was a hollow or cave in the mountain methot i see it full of burning flames like a glowing oven methot i see a man in it which i very well knew and the devil in the shape of a great snake all on a flame with his sting out run violently at the man and seemed to aim at the mans mouth i knew he was a wicked profane man so i awoke with a great sence of the dreadful s[t]ate of the wicked and wrastled with god in prayer." "The Spiritual Exercises of Hannah heaton," CHS. In this dream sequence, we can see again the vividness with which Satan was present in her spiritual dramas.

anything to my bodily eyes or ears," she proudly claimed; "My fancy or imagination was never carried away."[38] Her effort to distance herself from the more enthusiastic elements of the Great Awakening, which came under such approbation in antirevivalist writings, reveal just how radical and unsettling the evangelical emphasis on the unmediated conversion experience was for orthodox Puritans.

Why were women saints in particular so tormented by the devil? The emergence of gender distinctions at key points in the conversion process is one of the intriguing aspects of Awakening spiritual autobiographies, despite a recent claim that the experience of grace "submerged the peculiarities of gender,"[39] in Charles Cohen's phrase. Evangelical men and women together may have assumed an ever more dynamic role in the psychological confrontation between the self and an "other" which constituted the essence of the conversion experience, but distinctions of gender (however subtle) can be detected in the way this confrontation was enacted. In the kind of cosmic script enacted by pre-Awakening New Englanders, "man" in a generic sense did battle with the force of God unleashed in nature. In the clash of wills which constituted the conversion experience after the Awakening, sinners appear more as human beings with real social and physical characteristics. The element of personal distress engendered by the unmediated confrontations with deity and devil around which these narratives revolve was often more severe for women converts than for men; likewise, the rapture with which saints embraced a saving Christ was greater for women. It is not so much that women's accounts display a qualitatively different understanding of conversion, but rather that they seemed to have absorbed more intensely the changing dynamics of the conversion experience which affected both sexes after the Awakening. The Awakening model of conversion, with its stress on the psychic interplay between sinner, God, and devil, was embraced more fully by female than by male evangelicals.

"To be Encirckled in those Blessed Arms": Images of God and Christ

The raw visions of the power of Satan to invade the souls and bodies of sinners that we saw in women's narratives were counterbalanced by an equally palpable conception of Christ as personal savior. A figure as powerful and

---

38. Samuel Hopkins, ed., *The Life and Character of Miss Susanna Anthony* (London, 1803), pp. 20, 23–24.

39. Cohen, *God's Caress*, p. 223.

interventionist as the devil appears in these accounts could be checked only by a deity whose personal hold on the affections and allegiance of the regenerate was equally tenacious. Only after 1740 does God appear in these narratives as a humanlike figure capable of inspiring both love and fear.[40]

Hannah Heaton described her first vision of God under the experience of grace as that of a loving and compassionate savior.

> soon after meeting began the power of god came down many were crying out the other side of the room what shall i do to be saved i was imme-diately moved to press through the multitude and went to them a great melting of soul come up on me i wept bitterly and pleaded hard for mercy mercy. . . . it seemd i was a sinking down in to hell: thot the flor i stood on gave way and i was just a going but then i began to resign and as i resined my distress began to go of till i was perfectly easy quiet and calm. . . . me thot i see iesus with the eyes of my soul stand up in heaven a louely g[o]od man with his arms open ready to receive me his face was full of smiles he loockt white and ruddy and was iust such a saviour as my soul wanted.[41]

Men, too, spoke of their feelings toward God in more personal terms after 1740. Benjamin Lyon, a Separatist from Woodstock, Vermont, wrote re-peatedly in his diary of his "Ardent Desire" for Christ. "O to feel Ardent Desire After nearness, After Conformity to my heavenly Father, O to have love Inflamed towards him, O to be made like him & to be near him, to be Swallowed up in Contemplating him, O to be happy in a Delightful Near-ness to him. . . . O to be Encirkled in those Blessed Arms of Everlasting love. O to be kept by his Almighty power, thro' faith unto Salvation. Lord, I would be thine, wholly thine." In the covenant he made on the occasion of his conversion on 5 June 1759, and affirmed every year afterward on that date, Lyon pledged to join with Christ in eternal marriage. "I do here, upon the bended knees of my soul . . . Joyn my Self in Marriage Covenant to him. . . . I do here with all my powers Accept thee, & Do take thee for my head & husband for all times & Conditions, to love, to honour, & to Obey thee before all Others."[42] Such covenantal vows were commonplace in post-Awakening narratives. Abraham Choate of the Chebacco parish declared before the church, "I do avouch the Lord this Day to be my God, and I

---

40. Out of sixteen pre-Awakening accounts, only two contained references to the deity as a personal figure; both spoke of God as king or sovereign. In 106 accounts from the 1740s, 1750s, and 1760s, six references to God as king/sovereign were found; two to God as stern father; six to God as tender father; and eleven to Christ as bridegroom/lover.

41. "The Spiritual Exercises of Hannah heaton," CHS.

42. Ms. Diary of Benjamin Lyon, entries for 26 December 1763 and 23 July 1765, CHS.

avouch and declare myself this Day to be one of his Covenant-Children and People. . . . Henceforth I am thine, entirely thine, and thine forever."[43]

The metaphor of conversion as marriage suggests the sexualized nature of the relationship between man and God in evangelical thought. No other term sums up the evangelical understanding of the conversion experience as well as "ravishment," according to George Rawlyk.[44] The highly sensual descriptions of God's love that Rawlyk finds pervasive in evangelical writings in colonial North America were not new to the revivals of the eighteenth century. In sermons, frequent images of the people of God suckling at the breast of the Church, as well as commonplace references to God as nurturing Mother and to Christ as tender husband or lover, constituted a discursive tradition that first-generation Puritans brought with them to the New World. "Looke what affection is between Husband and Wife," John Cotton demanded in 1655; "hath there been the like affection in your soules toward the Lord Jesus Christ? Have you a strong and hearty desire to meet him in the bed of loves, when ever you come to the Congregation, and desire you to have the seeds of his grace shed abroad in your hearts, and bring forth the fruits of grace to him, and desire that you may be for him, and for none other?" As God shed his "seed" abroad in the hearts of his people, so the experience of conversion "delivers" the fruit of this seed. Conversion in this metaphorical tradition was equated with childbirth, where "deliverance" connoted both physical and spiritual rebirth. One seventeenth-century English woman, Elizabeth White, described being brought "down into" and "up out of" her body and soul by the "begetting" word of God. Mrs. White was, fittingly, delivered from her sins in 1669 at the same time she was delivered of her first child.[45]

However familiar such images of ravishing bridegrooms and divine midwives would have been to John Cotton and other seventeenth-century Puritans, they were dangerously out of place in the 1740s. After the cataclysmic events of 1692, Amanda Porterfield has argued, the trope of erotic female piety lost much of its cultural power in Puritan New England. Horrified by the excesses of the Salem witch trials, Puritan divines turned away from female models altogether in their prescriptive writings. A kind of enlight-

43. Relation of Abraham Choate, 1767, John Cleaveland Papers, PEM (hereafter "Chebacco accounts").

44. George Rawlyk, *Ravished by the Spirit: Religious Revivals, Baptists, and Henry Alline* (Kingston, Ont., 1984).

45. Patricia Caldwell, *The Puritan Conversion Narrative: The Beginnings of American Expression* (New York, 1983). Childbirth, Caldwell has argued, served as an effective "linchpin" for the conversion experience in Puritan discourse.

ened patriarchalism that stressed the benevolent governance of God over his errant children gradually replaced more erotic depictions of spiritual union in the early eighteenth century. As ministers banded together in consociations and sought to tighten the reins of clerical authority over a recalcitrant laity, they turned increasingly to more respectable metaphors to sanction their authority. No longer "Nursing Fathers," the eminent "patriarchs" of eighteenth-century New England resembled more God's emissaries who preached a subdued message of emotional restraint, social benevolence, and paternal duty. Warning that "when the affections wear the breeches, the female rules," Congregational ministers after 1700 decisively altered the gendered connotations of Puritan piety, discarding the more feminine aspects of their faith (such as "raptures, heats," and unrestrained passion) and cloaking their order in the mantle of patriarchal responsibility.[46] To resurrect the discredited language of erotic female piety, as evangelicals did in the mid-eighteenth century, was further proof of their defiant status as religious outsiders.

Although both evangelical men and women chose marriage as the most appropriate simile for their relationship with a gracious God, women's descriptions of this spiritual union were far more physical than men's. As their battles with Satan tended to engage their bodies as well as their souls, women's encounters with Christ in the act of conversion were at the same time corporal and spiritual. The sensation of being "swallowed up" or "melted" by grace, of being subsumed into the body of Christ, was more intense for women, often manifesting itself as physical transportation. Irene Shaw of Freetown "thote my Self in another World, & from this Time I felt ravished with the Love of God."[47] Sarah Osborn, a leader of the evangelical cause in Newport, Rhode Island, also spoke of being "ravished" with the love of God in her memoirs. She invited Christ to "possess every room, every faculty of my soul, and every member of my body, and use me for thyself forever."[48]

---

46. The quotations are from John Corrigan, *The Prism of Piety: Catholick Congregational Clergy at the Beginning of the Enlightenment* (New York, 1991), pp. 12–13. See Amanda Porterfield, *Female Piety in Puritan New England* (New York, 1992), and Ivy Schweitzer, *The Work of Self-Representation: Lyric Poetry in Colonial New England* (Chapel Hill, N.C., 1991), for two recent treatments of the trope of female piety in Puritan writings. On the changing status of the Congregational clergy, see David Hall, *The Faithful Shephard: A History of the New England Ministry in the Seventeenth Century* (Chapel Hill, N.C., 1972); Bonomi, *Under the Cope of Heaven*; and Jon Butler, *Awash in a Sea of Faith: Christianizing the American People* (Cambridge, Mass., 1990).

47. Relation of Irene Shaw, 5 August 1753, in J. M. Bumsted, "Emotion in Colonial America: Some Relations of Conversion Experience in Freetown, Massachusetts, 1749–1770," *New England Quarterly* 49 (1976): 103.

48. Ibid., p. 206.

Susanna Anthony also spoke of her desire to be invaded by the physical presence of God: "O let the Spirit enter the most secret recesses of my soul, and divide between the joints and marrow."[49] The feeling of being subsumed into or swallowed up by Christ in the act of conversion follows from the evangelical demand for complete self-renunciation and alienation. The self was literally dissolved in the moment of conversion and absorbed into the body of God, from whence the regenerate derived their enormous spiritual potency. Caroline Bynum's study of late medieval religious writings finds that "becoming one with God in mystical union was a more frequent aspect of women's devotional life than men's."[50] In the case of eighteenth-century New England, it was not that male evangelicals did not conceive of their relationship with God as one of intimate union, but rather that it was women who seem to have imbued this union with a heightened sensuality that parallels the painful physicality of their encounters with Satan.

Women were also more likely to draw on highly physical metaphors of deliverance in their conversion accounts, perhaps because their lives literally revolved around such embodied events as childbirth. Like Elizabeth White, Jemima Harding of the Sturbridge church was converted in the process of childbirth: "[M]y fears & Concerns about my Sowl did Still Increase Till I Drew near an Hour of Perril & Diffeculty & my fears & concerns about my Self on that account meeting toagether with my other concerns; I was Realy in Destress, but when the Perilous Hour came upon me Even in the midst of my Destress not Long before God was pleasd to Command Salvation & Deliverance for me. . . . He was willing not only to grant me a Safe Deliverance in Child bareing but to Deliver me from my State of Sin & misery."[51] Less directly, Hannah Heaton described the birth of her fourth child in terms strikingly similar to that of her conversion experience.

> i am now fearing the hour that is coming which i cant escape. . . . now there came a turn of extreem fear & terrour upon me about the hour that i can not escape and now it draws near i got into a fit of extream crying i was alone begging for mercy o how fraid i am of the pain. . . . now towards

---

49. *The Life and Character of Miss Susanna Anthony*, p. 150. Only one male account described a similar desire for physical union with God. The Reverend Nicholas Gilman, a New Light preacher from Connecticut, invited Christ to "take Possession of Every Apartment of my Soul." Typescript diary of the Reverend Nicholas Gilman, 7 October 1740, CHS.

50. Bynum, "'And Woman His Humanity,'" p. 260. See Greven's *Protestant Temperament* for a psychological discussion of the evangelical need for complete absorption into the body of Christ; pp. 85–86.

51. Relation of Jemima Harding, 1764, "Sturbridge Experimental Relations," photocopies of manuscript narratives in possession of the Sturbridge Congregational Society, provided by Richard Rabinowitz (hereafter referred to as "Sturbridge accounts").

the last it was so bad some feared how it would be with me but a good god sent salvation Calvin was born and in a moment my soul winged away to glory i felt far away above all these things it seemed as if my soul ioyned with saints & angels round the throne.[52]

After the birth of her child, Hannah experienced the same exultation and physical release that she had felt on the receipt of God's grace. That conversion should be metaphorically likened to the experience of childbirth makes a great deal of sense, for pregnant women—like saints of both sexes, like "women" in general—were believed to be in a liminal condition. Phyllis Mack asserts that early modern medical theories viewed gestation as a process that placed women "outside the pale of strictly human culture."[53]

The underside to the spiritual fulfillment experienced through closeness with a loving God was the ever-present fear of separation which tormented many evangelicals. Susanna Anthony wrote of her anguish at feeling a "Separating wall between god and our own souls." "What! banishment from God! That I cannot bear. I am undone, I am ruined, if separated from God. I cannot. I cannot! What! torn from my centre: rent from my life! O hell of hells, beyond all conception!"[54] Esther Edwards Burr, daughter of the famous revivalist Jonathan Edwards, frequently complained to her friend Sarah Prince of the distance she felt between a once-gracious God and her backsliding soul. "It has pleased him to hide his face and disappoint me in my hopes and expectations when I was ready to think him near," she wrote in August 1756. "I beg to live near him always—nor is it living unless I do— No tis *death*—Worse than *death*."[55] Nathan Cole echoed these sentiments. "Once I had a God but now I have lost him; and it is the loss of God that makes hell."[56] Seasons of backsliding which inevitably accompanied even the most unambiguous of conversions were often described as God's "hiding his face" or withdrawing his love from a wavering convert desperate for reassurance. Benjamin Lyon lamented the "hard Speeches, Unadvised words" that had made "a Separating wall between god and our own Souls."[57] Physical obstacles such as dark clouds and occluded vision intruded between man

52. "The Spiritual Exercises of Hannah heaton," CHS.

53. Phyllis Mack, *Visionary Women: Ecstatic Prophecy in Seventeenth-Century England* (Berkeley, Calif., 1992), p. 35.

54. *The Life and Character of Miss Susanna Anthony*, pp. 148–49.

55. *The Journal of Esther Edwards Burr*, ed. by Carol F. Karlsen and Laurie Crumpacker (New Haven, Conn., 1984), Letters no. 25 and 19 to Sarah Prince, 29 August 1756 and 13 December 1755; pp. 218–19, 176.

56. "The Spiritual Travels of Nathan Cole," p. 99.

57. Ms. Diary of Benjamin Lyon, 14 March 1763, CHS.

and God at these moments, obscuring the channels of affection which bound saint and savior together.

"A holy boldness": The Power of Grace

Because union with God entailed a tremendous transfer of power from God to man, Charles Cohen has aptly described the quest for conversion as "a campaign to tap God's potency."[58] The regenerate state was clearly an empowering one for evangelical saints. Converts recounted the confidence and energy they felt when infused with grace. "I did not fear to ask for anything that was not forbidden by the word of God," exclaimed Susanna Anthony. "O how did these views often fill my soul with a holy boldness, and my mouth with arguments."[59] Sarah Osborn was moved to organize a women's prayer meeting in her native Newport and become one of the leading religious activists within the Congregational community in the town:

> After I was thus revived, my longing to be made useful in the world returned, and I earnestly pleaded with God that he would not sufer me to live any longer an unprofitable servant; but would point out some way, in which I might be useful. . . . And it pleased God so to order it, that I had room to hope my petitions were both heard and in a measure answered. For soon after this a number of young women, who were awakened to a concern for their souls, came to me, and desired my advice and assistance and proposed to join in a society, provided I would take the care of them.[60]

Women in particular described their new-found power as a restoration of sensory facilities that had been deadened under the weight of sin. "The Lord remove[d] the Sk[a]les from mine Eyes. . . . once i was Blind But now i see," wrote Elizabeth Lord to Isaac Backus.[61] The formulaic phrase "I was blind but now I see" can be found in many conversion accounts from the eighteenth century, but women's accounts also speak of a new heart, new ears, or new ability to taste God's love. The importance of sensory input as the channel through which God becomes manifest to the souls of women saints further underscores the physical nature of their spiritual experience.

The empowering experience of being born again is captured by the meta-

---

58. Cohen, *God's Caress*, p. 22. For a more psychological explanation of the source of the potency imbibed during conversion, see Murray Murphey, "Psychodynamics of Conversion," p. 142.

59. *The Life and Character of Miss Susanna Anthony*, pp. 42–43.

60. Samuel Hopkins, ed., *Memoirs of the Life of Mrs Sarah Osborn* (Catskill, N.Y., 1814), p. 49.

61. Conversion of Elizabeth Lord, c. 1770, Backus Papers, Box 6, ANTS.

phor of liberated speech. Twice struck dumb before the power of God's wrath, Nathan Cole struggled to articulate his desire to be saved but could not "stir my tongue or lips." After his rescue by a gracious God, Cole recorded, "[N]ow my heart talked with God." An analysis of contemporary evangelical rhetoric on conversion makes a persuasive case that conversion should be viewed as "a process of acquiring a specific religious language," and indeed, the impotence that inhibits sinners in the unregenerate state is often described as a linguistic failure in eighteenth-century accounts.[62] The inability to speak to God was especially devastating to evangelicals, who had rejected all conduits to God except language.

The progression of the convert from a "listener" to a "speaker" described by Susan Harding in her study of contemporary fundamentalism neatly captures the essence of the transformation effected by the conversion experience. Abraham Choate of Chebacco wrote, "[W]hen I came to lift up my Face to the most high and Heart-searching God, that knew my evil Tho'ts, and worketh as he pleases; He was pleased to stop my Mouth, so that I was not able to speak for some time."[63] The ability to speak was restored only at the moment of grace. Samuel Belcher recorded in his journal, "God was pleased to Show me my one helplessness, and inability to Save my Self, but God was pleased to enable me to Cry mightily unto him in the bitterness of my Soul for mercy. . . . I felt my Load Go of and my mouth was Stopt and I could not utter one word for Some time and I felt as if my heart was Changed and I had that Joy and Comfort come into my Soul beyond Expression and my mouth was opened and I Spake forth the praises of God."[64] Like Belcher, whose "mouth was opened" at the moment of conversion, Sarah Allen of Chebacco recalled, "Afterwards I could not help speaking of what God had done for my soul."[65]

The posture of sinners toward God, on the other hand, was more often that of a passive auditor; many revival converts recalled being awakened by the "voice" of God speaking to them either directly in visions or indirectly through the preached word or the scriptures. Sarah Read of Sturbridge related, "[O]ne Night as I Lay in Bed the Voice of the Son of God Seemed to Sound in my ears Saying Come unto me . . . upon which many temtations Seemed to fall away and my fears Vanished as a Shadow."[66] Anna Bennet of

62. Susan Harding, "Convicted by the Holy Spirit: The Rhetoric of Fundamental Baptist Conversion," *American Ethnologist* 14 (1987): 169–70.

63. Relation of Abraham Choate, 1767, Chebacco accounts.

64. Quoted in Kenneth P. Minkema, "A Great Awakening Conversion: The Relation of Samuel Belcher," *WMQ*, 3d ser., 44 (1987): 125–26.

65. Relation of Sarah Allen, 1764, Chebacco accounts.

66. Relation of Sarah Read, 1762, Sturbridge accounts.

Chebacco recalled Christ "bending his ear" toward her: "I tho't he was speaking in his word to me."[67] Bethiah Foster, also of Chebacco, was particularly struck by a sermon of John Cleaveland in which he urged sinners to open their ears to God's call: "Why says he, you must hearken to the voice of God in the Gospel, for sinners will never be saved in any other way: and I thou't my soul did then really hearken to the voice of God."[68]

Whereas providential occurrences were the most common means of converting sinners before the Awakening, the "Word" in either its spoken or printed form was the most frequently mentioned agent of conversion after 1740.[69] More converts in the Awakening attributed their change of heart to the efficacious intervention of a particularly powerful sermon or timely scriptural text than to any other cause. Although earthquakes and sudden deaths do not disappear from the narratives of revival converts, they are peripheral to the more important process of hearing and responding to the Word of God in its various manifestations. The widow Sarah Davis attributed her conversion to the saving intercession of the word. At first, she confessed, "I thote the more I heard the word the worce I grew and was therefore tempted to leave of Hearing it but God of his Mercy prevented me." After her conversion, she "began to read & hear the Word & pious Discourse with a new Delight."[70] Isaac Backus exclaimed after his conversion, "Never did his Word appear So before as it did now:—it appeared So

67. Relation of Anna Bennet, 1764, Chebacco accounts.
68. Relation of Bethiah Foster, 1766, Chebacco accounts.
69. The following table lists the references to the various means of awakening before and after 1740.

Means	Pre-1740 (n = 16)	Post-1740 (n = 106)
Sudden deaths	6	10
Natural calamities	11	4
Sermon/preaching	0	20
Biblical texts	0	9
Fear of hell/death	3	10
Seeing others under conviction	1	15

The most striking difference is that the "Word," articulated through sermons or in scripture, was not mentioned in a single pre-Awakening conversion account as the means through which the sinner was brought to grace. After 1740, however, sermons and biblical texts became the single largest motivator mentioned.

70. Relation of Sarah Davis, 4 November 1753, in John M. Bumsted, "Emotion in Colonial America: Some Relations of Conversion Experience in Freetown, Massachusetts, 1749–1770," *New England Quarterly* 49 (1976): 105.

glorious and Such Infallible Truth that I could with the greatest Freedom Rest my Eternal Call upon what God hath Spoken."[71]

The centrality of the Word to the experience of conversion after the Great Awakening should not surprise us, given the significance with which evangelicals invested language in their battles with the standing order. As we saw earlier, speech became the terrain on which the meaning of order and disorder was contested in the 1740s and and 1750s. The discourses delivered by the revivalist preachers assumed a heightened importance in the critical task of converting lost souls in the absence of more traditional means of exercising ministerial authority. Lacking the conventional accoutrements of clerical office—state-sponsored licenses, advanced degrees, commanding salaries and other material signs of status—revivalist preachers were forced back upon their ability to reach sinners through the sheer power of words. The novelty of the evangelical style of preaching, with its extemporaneous delivery and extravagant use of vivid imagery, was noted by both contemporary observors and historians of the movement.[72] As Hannah Heaton declared in wonderment on hearing Gilbert Tennant and George Whitefield preach, "it was such preaching as i never heard before."[73]

For some saints, their own conversion prompted a renewed desire for and encouragement of the conversion of others. "I desire perfect holiness," declared Mary Low of the Chebacco parish, "and long for the conversion of every soul."[74] Mary Woodbury "longed for the whole world to come to Christ—and I have found that I could witness to the Gospel."[75] Hannah Heaton recalled how after she was visited with the spirit of God she "went about the room and invited the people to come to him."[76] The concern that new converts felt for the souls of their fellow sinners speaks to their sense of collective responsibility, which transformed them into evangelists for the cause of Christ. Nathan Cole's narrative reveals the extraordinarily strong empathy that bound members of the evangelical community together. Converts "felt all as one, as if they had been made up all into one man, all drinked into one Spirit and oneness," he wrote in 1758. In his vision of a meeting of saints Cole saw "a multitude of people Circled in with great glory all their faces one way *hundreds or* thousands and they sang so gloriously that no

---

71. William McLoughlin, ed., *The Diary of Isaac Backus* (Providence, R.I., 1979), app. 1, p. 1525.

72. For an analysis of the rhetorical innovations of the New Light preachers, see Donald Weber, *Rhetoric and History in Revolutionary New England* (New York, 1988).

73. "The Spiritual Exercises of Hannah heaton," CHS.

74. Relation of Mary Low, 1764, Chebacco accounts.

75. Relation of Mary Woodbury, 1766, Chebacco accounts.

76. "The Spiritual Exercises of Hannah heaton," CHS.

tongue can any way express it to man. . . . I could hear every voice clear and distinct at the same time; and yet hear them all at once and no hindrance at all, every tongue begins the note as one and Ends as one."[77]

This ability to transcend physical and geographical boundaries highlights one aspect of the liminal quality of the conversion experience. For some converts, like Cole, the liminal energy unleashed in conversion served to circumvent community boundaries (those separating town from town) which impeded the formation of a brotherhood of saints. For others, like Susanna Anthony and Sarah Osborn, liminality functioned to dissolve corporal boundaries that barred them from bodily union with God. As these examples suggest, the concept of liminality is important for our understanding of both male and female spirituality, but not in the same way; the nature of the boundaries to be overcome through liminal reversal was perceived very differently by evangelical men and women. Community was the focal point of religious experience for men, such as Nathan Cole, while the individual body was the focus for women.[78] As men sought to reinvigorate the moribund ties of fellow-feeling through the experience of grace, women turned their energies inward in search of perfect physical subsumption into the body of Christ.

Men's accounts reveal a concern for the "perishing" state of others and an emphasis on converting ordinances such as the Lord's Supper as the means through which the community of saints could be sustained. Abraham Choate found his soul "filling with Bowels of Compassion for others" and pleaded with "the whole Race of Mankind to come and cast themselves at the feet of Christ, and to accept of him." His fellow communicant Daniel Low expressed "a longing desire that all the world might be converted I saw there was enough in Christ for all." Such an expansive view of the power of grace to forge bonds of love between saints led men to place special emphasis on sacramental acts in their accounts, both as the means of awakening the sinner to his lost state and as the means of bridging the seemingly impassable gulf that separated him from his fellow sufferers. Jeremiah Kingsman recorded, "[O]n the last Sacrament Day here in the forenoon under the word I had a wonderful Discovery of the suffering and Crucifixion of Christ—which melted my heart within me." Aaron Low similarly found himself

77. "The Spiritual Travels of Nathan Cole," pp. 109–10.

78. This insight counters Epstein's conclusion that "women seem to have valued community ties . . . often more highly than men; women converts rejoiced to find themselves as part of a community and sometimes described heaven as having the same conviviality as a revival." Epstein, *Politics of Domesticity*, pp. 31–32. Her description fits the accounts of such male converts as Nathan Cole more fully than those of women.

brought under conviction at a fast, which gave way to "a sweet peace and calmness in my soul" afterward at meeting. Samuel Belcher "came home" from "the house" of God "full of joy and rejoiceing" and with "strong Desires to Joyn with this Church in full Communion." Like Belcher, Abraham Choate ended his conversion account with the earnest avowal of his "Duty to join a particular Church of Christ in full Communion and to come to that holy Ordinance which he has appointed, even the Lord's Supper."[79]

Women, on the other hand, spoke less of duty to others and more of self-transcendence. Jonathan Edwards' wife, Sarah, recalled, "To my own imagination, my soul seemed to be gone out of me to God and Christ in heaven, and to have very little relation to my body."[80] Hannah Low of Chebacco "longed to leave this World and Join the blessed above to praise God." Some women expressed a willingness to leave family and friends behind, if it would speed their reunion with Christ. "I had rather part with my nearest Friends than that once [one's] soul should be lost," Sarah Butler declared. "I felt love to Christ and tho't I could freely leave all in this world to serve him." Women were not entirely unconcerned with sacramental duties; like many men, Mary Woodbury "intreated" the communicants of the Chebacco church "not to send me away, for where you worship I must worship. . . . I have tho't so much of late that it is my Duty to join to the Chh of Christ and come to his Table, that I can't be easy in the Neglect of it."[81] But their narratives display a greater focus on self than on community, on the subliminal quality of grace rather than on its fraternal nature.

Because men had a sense of connectedness with the larger body of saints, their accounts of religious conversion reveal an important continuity with pre-Awakening accounts. Ties of family and community which bound early-eighteenth-century converts still figure largely in the experience of men under grace after the Great Awakening. The "Land of Light" which male converts sought was the land of the covenant, not so much in its historical manifestation as in its spiritual essence.[82] Seeking a common

79. Relations of Abraham Choate, Daniel Low, Jeremiah Kinsman, and Aaron Low, Chebacco accounts; "The Relation of Samuel Belcher," p. 126.

80. Quoted in Greven, *Protestant Temperament*, p. 85.

81. Relations of Hannah Low, Sarah Butler, Mary Woodbury, Chebacco accounts.

82. The importance of family and community to orthodox Puritans is attested to by the many references to the blessings of godly parents and birth in a "land of light" in the conversion accounts of Old Light or moderate Congregationalists throughout the eighteenth century. The relations recorded in the papers of Ebenezer Parkman provide a good gauge of the popularity of these stock phrases in conventional conversion accounts; over one-half of the 62 relations (23 male, 39 female) that Parkman recorded between 1736 and 1774 pay tribute to the benefits of baptism and a godly

ground on which to anchor the individual spirit, men during the Awakening renewed their sacramental ties to their fellow saints as they revived their piety. The intensely personal religious experience of women saints, on the other hand, represents a sharper break with the past. Female converts more often inhabited a no-man's land of the soul, a state of limbo in which they abandoned themselves to the physical and spiritual ecstasy of divine union. Women's stories of spiritual regeneration thus embodied the most radical features of the Great Awakening model of conversion. Indeed, the figure of the female saint represents the archetype of evangelical religion itself: sensuous, sublime, suspended outside of time and space. In so many ways the evangelical faith was both feminine and feminizing.

The feminine nature of evangelical conversion in the mid-eighteenth century prefigures the emergence of a gender-specific language of authority in the latter half of the century, when women evangelicals would continue to assert the primacy of intimate union with God in the face of a new male enthusiasm for the more abstract, legalistic model of authoritarian relations promoted by revolutionary political discourse. The faint beginnings of a female language of authority which these narratives uncover—a language rooted in physical and emotional attachments rather than in more abstract channels of power—did not, as yet, imply a disjuncture between male and female religious experience in the evangelical community. Not until the late eighteenth century, when the political discourse on government and society engendered by the revolutionary movement gave rise to a new, competing, paradigm of authority (one based on legalistic, rational principles of social contract), did the language used by evangelical men and women to describe their relationship with God diverge significantly. In the mid-eighteenth century, however, the differences in tone and content we can observe in male and female conversion narratives remain largely submerged within the broader evangelical consensus on the personal meaning of religious experience.

---

upbringing in a "land of light." These accounts resemble those of orthodox Puritans in the 1720s far more than those of Awakening converts in the 1740s. See the Papers of Ebenezer Parkman, microfilm of originals in the AAS, "Notes on Church Meetings & Issues," Box 2, Folder 1. I am grateful to Erik Seeman for directing me to this source and providing transcriptions of the relations.

CHAPTER THREE

"TO WATCH OVER EACH OTHER'S CONVERSATION"
Church Discipline

EVANGELICALS FACED A SERIOUS DILEMMA after the Great Awakening: how to balance the communal and individualistic elements of their faith, for those were in constant tension in the eighteenth century. This was a long-standing dilemma within the Reformed Protestant tradition out of which the evangelical wing of American Puritanism grew, yet it assumed a sharper edge in the heated atmosphere of the Great Awakening. For threaded through the classic struggle between the demands of individual conscience and the responsibilities of collective worship was the paradox of gender. The tension between community and individual was, as suggested by the literature of conversion, also a tension between the masculine and feminine, between the male desire for fraternity and the female desire for self-fulfillment. In confronting this dilemma, evangelical churches came face to face with the gendered implications of their own faith.

The struggle to reconcile community and individual (or, in Harry Stout's terms, power and purity), was manifest most vividly in the bitter and unremitting conflicts over the meaning and exercise of internal discipline which rocked the evangelical churches in the years following the Awakening.[1] The evangelical resolution of this century-old tension explicitly privileged purity over power, femininity over masculinity, but at a high cost. Charles Goen's study of Separate congregations in the mid-eighteenth century found an obsessive, almost paranoid concern with discipline which was

---

1. See Harry Stout, *The New England Soul: Preaching and Religious Culture* (New York, 1986), pp. 13–20 and passim, for a discussion of the enduring search for a balance between these two competing principles, which he claims was the most salient feature of American Puritanism.

symptomatic of the unsettling contradictions of evangelical religion.[2] Seemingly trivial disagreements over minute aspects of a church's liturgy or admissions procedures often ignited serious conflagrations which could smolder for decades. "The depth of the feelings seems out of proportion to the incidents," William McLoughlin writes. "Friends and neighbors frequently divided into hostile factions for years after the introduction of a tuning fork or a hymnbook into the service. . . . This widespread discontent hid profound feelings of guilt and anomie as old ways and traditions ceased to match new needs and desires."[3] McLoughlin's use of the term "anomie" is telling, for it rightly directs our attention to the fragility of community in the evangelical ethos.

The potential for contention and strife within the evangelical community was high, given that the church officers (elders and deacons) lacked coercive powers and that church membership was voluntary. Zeal, the Second Baptist Church of Newport warned in 1764, could too easily "degenerate into passion, bitterness, and hatred."[4] Church covenants, subscribed to by all members, provided one measure of control over too-zealous communicants. The terms of the covenant varied somewhat from church to church, but a common set of principles and obligations can be found in each. Some congregations promised simply "to watch over Each others Conversation & not suffer sin upon one another."[5] Others swore more elaborate vows. The Titicut Church of Christ covenanted in 1756 to "watch not only against them that are reckoned more gross Evils, but also against all Foolish talking & jesting which is not convenient; vain disputings about words and things which gender strife; Disregarding promises & not fulfilling of engagements: Tatling & backbiting; Spending time idly at Taverns or elsewhere, and vain and unnecessary worldly conversation on Lords days."[6] Such statements are highly revealing of the conceptual world of the evangelical order in the mid-eighteenth century: the desire to promote social decorum by curtailing worldly behavior in public spaces, the pressing need to defuse sites of conflict within the community by avoiding all "disputings" and "strife," and—above all—the fear of unruly and disruptive speech ("foolish talking," "evil whisperings," "tatling").

2. Charles Goen, *Revivalism and Separatism in New England, 1740–1800: Strict Congregationalists and Separate Baptists in the Great Awakening* (New Haven, Conn., 1962), pp. 164–67.

3. William McLoughlin, *New England Dissent, 1630–1833: The Baptists and the Separation of Church and State* (Cambridge, Mass., 1971), 1:333. Henry Abelove finds a similar tension in early Methodism, as the obsessive "oneness" of the congregation bred periodic discontent. Abelove, *The Evangelist of Desire: John Wesley and the Methodists* (Stanford, Calif., 1990), pp. 47–48.

4. Record Book, Second Baptist Church of Newport, 1764, NHS.

5. Record Book, First Baptist Church of Newport, 4 May 1727, NHS.

6. Covenant of Titicut Church of Christ, 16 January 1756, Backus Papers, Box 6, ANTS.

With little to compel obedience to covenant obligations save an appeal to individual conscience, the churches turned to a system of informal surveillance and policing whereby, as Isaac Backus observed, "the least member might tyrannize over the whole church."[7] The "morbid preoccupation" with the private doings of fellow communicants that Goen observed in the Canterbury Separate Church helped create a climate of constant suspicion and wariness which did little to encourage the cooperation and harmony envisioned by the church covenants. The evangelical disregard for all conventional signs of regenerate status in effect deputized all members of the congregation to search into and pass judgment on the spiritual state of their fellow saints. An overzealous spirit of prosecution was, evangelists well knew, the perhaps inevitable outgrowth of the revival's insistence on purity. As the Reverend James Robe admitted in his narrative of the revival in his congregation, "There were *some Disorders* I could not foresee." When a woman in the throes of conviction admitted to the neighbors assembled to pray for her that she had been guilty of adultery, "there was no preventing the spreading of [the story]; it was reported thro' the Neighbourhood by the Morning Light." To deter such indiscretions in the future, Robe "publickly instructed the whole Congregation, that *they were not bound to confess their secret Sins to any but unto God . . . Discharging* at the same time all to inquire into the secret Sin of their Neighbours, shewing unto them the Evil of it; and most of all their blazing abroad the secret Faults of their Neighbour, when it could tend to no End but the Reproach of their Neighbour, and the Scandal and Offence of others."[8] In this case we can see clearly the damage to personal and communal reputation which the liminal quality of the Awakening portended. Robe was dismayed by the "blazing abroad" of this woman's adulterous behavior, but he was powerless to prevent its spreading.

The result of such unprincipled disregard for conventional boundaries was a community rife with venomous quarrels, schisms, intolerable intrusions into members' private and public lives, and personal feuds that often endured for years. Isaac Backus complained regularly in his diary about the lack of brotherly love which threatened to destroy his fledgling Separate church in Titicut: "[T]here came in such jangling disputes amongst us as seemed as if 'twould have broke us all to pieces. . . . we seemed to be scatered every way."[9] George Gardner withdrew from the Second Baptist Church of Newport in 1759 because of the fractious and quarrelsome nature of the congregation.

7. Isaac Backus, *A History of New England, with Particular Reference to the Denomination of Christians Called Baptists*, 2d ed. (Newton, Mass., 1871), 2:90.
8. Quoted in *The Christian History* (*1743*), 1:49–50.
9. *The Diary of Isaac Backus*, ed. William McLoughlin (Providence, R.I., 1979), 1:137–38.

I know it cannot be consistant with the Christian Religion for Persons to set down at the Lords table and be Reproaching Revileing and speaking all manner of Evil of Each other not only among one another but in all Company Religious and Profane, as to myself. . . . I am villifyed abused and set forth to be a knave a cheat etc. and were it only from the world it would be a small thing if falsely accused, but to be Treated so by some of the members of the church whose Consciences will witness to the truth of what I write . . .[10]

The Preston Separate Church was thrown into disarray by disputes over infant baptism which led its members "into sundry jars and difficulties which occationed Breaches of Charity and intorupted our harmonious sweet Gospill travil." Rather than "Pretend to Govern any Man's Conscience," the Preston church reluctantly agreed to let members decide the issue for themselves: "[W]e leave you to stand or fall to your own master."[11]

The only corrective to the centrifugal tendency of the evangelical church was to harness the energy of the entire laity to the problem of communal definition. The Baptist church faced the challenge handicapped from the start. A religious community without the traditional mechanisms of control over its membership—an educated and powerful ministry, extrachurch structures of ecclesiastical authority such as ministerial consociations, the backing of civil authorities and of establishment symbols and language, the hierarchical ordering of the congregation in the physical layout of the meetinghouse—the Baptists left themselves few resources for preserving the critical boundary between those within and those without which was the overriding concern of the evangelical order.[12] To ensure the purity of the evangelical community, special church meetings for the exercise of discipline were held which resembled religious revivals more than secular trials. As in the courts of the early modern church studied by Martin Ingram, the punishment and rehabilitation of sinners was conducted in a "blaze of publicity."[13] The entire church body, men and women, elders and laity,

---

10. Second Baptist Church of Newport, 28 June 1759, Miscellaneous Unbound Mss., RIHS.

11. *The Parke Scrapbook*, compiled by Ruby Parke Anderson (Baltimore, 1965), 26 January 1757, vol. 1 (n.p.).

12. "Evangelicals constantly sought to ensure that their own immediate households would remain separate from the surrounding world and as free as possible of pernicious influences," Philip Greven has written in another context. "They always knew that corruption and sinful influence could come not only from the outside world, but also from within the household itself." Greven, *The Protestant Temperament: Patterns of Child-Rearing, Religious Experience, and the Self in Early America* (New York, 1977), p. 26.

13. Martin Ingram, *Church Courts, Sex, and Marriage in England, 1570–1640* (New York, 1987), p. 3.

participated in decisions to censure individual members. By drawing the community together in a ritual of expulsion and purification, the churches succeeded in checking the disintegrative tendency of the voluntary principle.

These early efforts to maintain church discipline are reminiscent of the importance that medieval and early modern Christians invested in the principle of charity. Charity in the medieval tradition denoted not discrete acts of benevolence by social elites or state agencies (as it would later in the modern era) but rather the collective responsibility of the community for each member.[14] Deriving from an organic sense of wholeness, of the indivisibility of the body politic, the exercise of charity was designed not to reaffirm social distinctions but to transcend them. Through the act of charity men and women were able to renew their sense of common purpose, of common destiny. Charity can thus be seen as the concrete expression of *communitas*. Where evangelicals parted company from orthodox Puritans was in their attempt to make *communitas* a way of life rather than an episodic occurrence, the very essence of community rather than its occasional representation in acts of revival. And charity—that sense of collective responsibility for the failings and frailties of others—was one answer to the dilemma posed by liminality, that of creating a sense of community among individuals who thought themselves beyond the bounds of conventional social categories.

Charity, of course, never ceased to be of concern in more traditional congregations. But orthodox churches were able to sustain a sense of community by other, less intrusive mechanisms. Rituals such as infant baptism and the ordered presentation of the congregation in the meetinghouse served to reinforce the boundaries of orthodox communities in ways evangelicals found unacceptable. Recalling Rhys Isaac's description of how lesser neighbors filled the church for Sunday worship as the Anglican gentry lingered behind in order to make a united entrance may help us to understand how thoroughly evangelicals (in both the North and the South) rejected the traditional means by which community was enacted.[15] Another way had to be found to sustain the sense of fellow-feeling, of "cohesive brotherhood" (in Isaac's terms), which evangelicals sought in place of the dry and brittle forms of orthodox communion.

The quest for this elusive sense of community led Baptist and Separate churches to confront sin with a determination not seen since the early days of New England Puritanism. An unpleasant spirit of prosecution, which

14. For a lucid discussion of the transformation of the concept of charity in the early modern era, see John Bossy, *Christianity in the West, 1400–1700* (New York, 1985), 143–49.

15. Isaac, *The Transformation of Virginia, 1740–1790* (Chapel Hill, N.C., 1982).

characterized both the vigorous application of church discipline and the "censoriousness" of Awakening converts who presumed to pass judgment on others' souls, was a necessary component in the evangelical scheme to revitalize the faith. Comparisons with Old Light Congregational churches reveal the morbid preoccupation of evangelicals with disorder and corruption. The history of the Old Light Second Congregational Church in North Stonington illustrates the lax orthodox approach to the problem of discipline. In the decade 1740 to 1750, only a handful of communicants were subject to church discipline, for transgressions ranging from fornication to profane speaking to "unchristian practice & behavior." None of the offenders received the ultimate sanction of excommunication, and few cases warranted extensive discussion in the church records. Even such a habitual malefactor as Jehabod Palmer, whose profane swearing and drunkenness were "Notoriously known," was let off with nary a warning when the witnesses against him failed to show up at the church hearing. Over the decade the desultory exercise of discipline by the Second Church presents a sharp contrast to the Canterbury Separate Church, in which, as Charles Goen found, more than one-third of the communicants were suspended or expelled for disorderly conduct in the first three years of the church's existence.[16] Given the rancorous schism that rent the Second Church in the late 1740s, when thirty-six members (15 men and 21 women) were suspended from communion for espousing evangelical beliefs, it may be that behind the revivals and separations of the Great Awakening was a pervasive sense that purity had been sacrificed to the secular ambitions of the Standing Order of New England Congregationalism. Two years after the schism within the Second Church, its members abandoned all pretence to a rigorous exercise of church discipline by creating a standing committee of brethren to handle all disciplinary matters in the future. Citing the "great Expense of Time & Travel" incurred when the entire church met together and the "Perplexity that Some Cases are Involved with," the church reluctantly acknowledged that many in the congregation had simply lost interest in the discipline process. Thereafter discipline hearings were cursory affairs, scarcely warranting a line in the official record; in July 1753 five members were "speedily admonished for their Respective offences" without further elaboration.[17] Only three cases were heard between 1755 and 1762.

16. Goen, *Revivalism and Separatism*, p. 166.

17. Record Book, North Stonington Second Congregational Church, vol. 1: 134, 138, CSL. Jon Butler argues that by the eighteenth century Congregational churches in New England showed little interest in pursuing immorality with vigor. Butler, *Awash in a Sea of Faith: Christianizing the American People* (Cambridge, Mass., 1990), pp. 173–74. My own cursory survey of Congregational

Evangelicals, on the other hand, waged relentless war against sin in the eighteenth century. "When a Saint enjoys the greatest nearness to God," Isaac Backus insisted, "he has then the greatest tenderness of conscience to watch against all sin."[18] But, more important, their understanding of what constituted sin differed markedly from the Old Lights' as well. Whereas the vast majority of the discipline cases considered by the Second Congregational Church of North Stonington in the decade 1740–50 (8 of 11) involved traditional sins of "concupiscence" (lechery, gluttony, sloth), sins of "aversion" (pride, envy, anger) were deemed more deadly in evangelical churches, because they were viewed primarily as an offense against charity, an assault on the affective bonds that held the organic community together. In John Bossy's words, "the sins of aversion destroy community, but without some flirtation with the sins of concupiscence there is unlikely to be a community at all."[19] The relative equanimity displayed by medieval Catholics toward the traditional sins of the flesh was, Bossy argues, a casualty of the wars of the Protestant Reformation, but it persisted to a remarkable degree among those who dissented from dissent. Reaching back to an earlier age in which charity was more important than righteousness, eighteenth-century evangelicals rejected the encroaching moralism evident in such Old Light societies as the North Stonington Second Church.[20] In the discipline records of Baptist and Separate churches there is little sign of the new preoccupation of orthodox societies with personal misconduct; by and large, private lapses in morality were considered incidental to the larger problem of community definition. Instead, evangelical churches marshaled their slender resources against those who broke the bonds of community.[21]

---

church records in the Connecticut State Library reveals that, as in the North Stonington church, discipline was rarely an issue after 1720 or so; there were too few discipline cases heard to count.

18. *The Diary of Isaac Backus*, 1:205. Backus penned numerous accolades to the "cleansing" nature of church discipline in his diary; see the entries for 25 April, 28 May, 22 June 1752, and passim.

19. Bossy, *Christianity in the West*, p. 35.

20. See Joseph Haroutunian, *Piety versus Moralism: The Passing of the New England Theology* (New York, 1932).

21. The sources for this analysis include the church records of twenty Baptist and Separate churches in Rhode Island and Connecticut: First Baptist Church of Lyme, CSL; First and Second Baptist churches of Ashford, CSL; First and Second Baptist churches of Groton, CSL; Hampton Baptist Church, CSL; Waterford Baptist Church, CSL; Fairfield-Stratfield Baptist Church, CSL; First Baptist Church of Providence, RIHS; Warren Baptist Church, JHL; First, Second, and Seventh Day Baptist churches of Newport, NHS; Second Baptist Church of Coventry, RIHS; Westerly Baptist Church, RIHS; Tiverton Baptist Church, RIHS; Canterbury Separate Church, CSH; Preston Separate Church, CSL; North Stonington Separate Church, CSL; Beneficent Congregational church, Providence. Taken together, the records of these twenty religious societies yield over 380 cases in which individual members were brought up on charges of breaking their

We should not, however, make too great a distinction between private lapses and public offenses. In the eighteenth-century evangelical world, the public and private were in large measure indistinguishable. What each member did in his or her private life was also a public testimonial to the power of the Spirit, for evangelicals claimed to have been completely reborn in the act of conversion. The private self was indeed completely absorbed into the public body of Christ through the mystical experience of grace. Yet evangelicals lived in the world, not in the kingdom of God, and the reality of their profane lives often fell far short of the ideal. Evangelical men and women were as prone to sin as believers everywhere; the consequences of their individual lapses, however, were far more severe than those visited upon orthodox societies. To err was human, and that was the rub. To fall from a state of grace into a state of sin was to leave the transcendent community of saints and reenter the conventional world with all its corruptions, to become once again flawed human beings endowed with social characteristics. Androgynous saints became men or women when they sinned. Distinctions of gender were thus reintroduced into the evangelical community when saints became sinners.

"Usurping Authority over the Church": Sins against the Church

In 1760, Lois Adams was censured by the Canterbury Separate Church for "usurp[ing] authority over the Chh in that she Did in a Chh meeting autharitivey teach and admonish the house Church which is contrary to the word of God."[22] In page after page of the records of individual churches, the tenacity of evangelical men and women in asserting what they called their "Christian liberty" is striking. Beholden to no power but that of the Almighty, lay men and women consistently resisted all attempts to enlarge the authority of the church and dilute the individual thrust of the evangelical ethos. In response to such repeated challenges to their authority, Baptist and Separate churches struggled to find a common ground between purity and power, between individual conscience and corporate integrity. Throughout most of the eighteenth century neither principle gained the upper hand, as congregations continued to be rent by the irreconcilable tension between individual and community.

---

covenant vows in the period 1740 to 1780. Because membership data are incomplete for most of these churches, it is not possible to calculate what proportion of church members were disciplined in these forty years.

22. Canterbury Separate Church Papers, 4 July 1760, Larned Collection, CSL.

To evangelicals like Lois Adams, the issue was the right of each individual to improve her gifts. To the Canterbury Separate Church, the issue was pride. Most of the disputes that fall under the heading "Contempt of Church Authority" were, in fact, conflicts rooted in pride—that most deadly of the seven deadly sins. "Remember," Jonathan Edwards admonished a female follower in 1741, "that pride is the worst viper that is in the heart . . . the most hidden, secret, and deceitful of all lusts, and often creeps insensibly into the midst of religion."[23] Rather than creep quietly in, however, pride "roared forth" in evangelical congregations. Mary Ritch, complained the Preston Separate Church, "treated the Church Rufly with Railing accusations." The Preston church had great difficulty in its early years with communicants (especially with women named Mary) who exhibited a similar "Exalted Spirit": Mary Burton was "willfully obstinate" in refusing to commune with the church any longer, Mary Rose "brake out in railing" when questioned by the church for her hasty marriage. When the Swansea Baptist Church cited Patience Miller to explain her absence from worship, the church reported that "she in stid [instead] of giveing Reason writes many Rash and Reproachful sentances against the church, and continues in the same without any Recantation."[24] An unshaken belief in one's spiritual superiority was the inevitable result of the evangelical stress on the new birth and its radically transforming nature. Once reborn into a state of grace, evangelical men and women considered themselves no longer bound by the norms of profane society, including those of civility.

Even such respected evangelical leaders as Isaac Backus were not immune from attacks on their authority by members "puffed up" with pride. Backus himself was upbraided by an irate female parishioner for his superior and condescending attitude. "I look upont that I have a right and may see duty to go into the meeting-house when you preach there to Stand as a witness for god how his word is handled and his Spirit treated by you," Ann Dellis informed her pastor. Backus had admonished Dellis a year earlier for her hot temper and rash spirit, which he claimed had led her into several unseemly disputes with her mother and sister. "I solemnly intreat & charge you not to keep your eyes upon others wrongs or supposed wrongs, so as to guard against seeing your own," he warned. In the face of such disapproval Dellis steadfastly maintained her right to pass judgment on whomever she chose, regardless of rank or family connection.[25] Backus railed repeatedly in

23. Quoted in Greven, *Protestant Temperament*, p. 77.
24. First Baptist Church of Swansea, 4 February 1762, Myles Ms., RIHS.
25. Letter from Ann Dellis to Isaac Backus, 26 April 1772; letter from Backus to Dellis, 26 March 1771; Backus Papers, Box 9, ANTS.

his diary against those who indulged a censorious spirit. In 1751 he noted the case of John Woodward, who had been excluded from the Taunton Baptist Church that year for "Indulging an accusing equi[vo]cating and Bitter spirit. . . . he arose and declared That we wan't acting for God, but Against him and in a Russle and with some bitter and reflecting Language Brok right away out of meeting."[26]

Charges of contempt of the church's authority, which included everything from speaking disrespectfully of the elder to renouncing one's covenant vows, represented more than half of all discipline actions undertaken by Baptist and Separate churches in roughly the period 1740 to 1780 (see Table 1).[27] The wide range of offenses covered by this broad appellation testifies to the depth and breadth of lay activism in the early evangelical churches and to the tenuousness of the churches' hold over their spirited members. A close look at the kinds of transgressions most likely to provoke official censure reveals above all how truly radical was the evangelical scheme of individual and congregational autonomy. After 1740, Baptist and Separate churches faced precisely the same challenges they themselves had directed against the Standing Order during the Awakening: unauthorized preaching by lay exhorters, the setting up of separate meetings for religious worship, attacks on the character and doctrinal purity of ordained elders, women's speaking in public, and so on. Once the power of lay initiative was released in the liminal thrust of the Awakening, the evangelical churches were as hard pressed as their Congregational opponents to contain and channel the enormous energy they had helped unleash.

Caleb Luther was dismissed in 1748 from the Swansea Baptist Church for "invit[ing] strangers to preach in his house without leave from the

26. *The Diary of Isaac Backus*, 1:142.

27. Table 1 separates *sins of aversion* (those that breach the bonds of the community) from *sins of the flesh*. The first is further divided: *contempt of church*, the single largest category, encompassing all direct and indirect challenges to church doctrine, organization, and leadership; *sins against fellow members*, including fighting, quarreling, slander, profanity, cheating one's customers, defaulting on debts, disturbing public order; and *sins against family/household*, including abuse of children or spouse, disobedience toward parents or masters. These designations are not random, but rather reflect the underlying sin at issue in each category. Slander and avarice belong together, for instance, because both weaken the ties that bind neighbors by destroying trust and confidence. Sexual misconduct and drunkenness both represent an inability to restrain one's fleshly appetites. Many offences recorded in the church minutes defy any simple categorization; the figures represented in Table 1 are neither unambiguous nor sufficient in themselves accurately to convey the evangelical construction of disorder in the eighteenth century, but should be taken only as a starting point. We must consider each category in relation to the others, to tease out from the numbers the multi-textured definition of sin which animated the discipline process. To this end, Table 1 includes both the first and second charges listed in the records and tabulates all discrete instances of misconduct.

TABLE I

Discipline of Various Offenses in Baptist and Separate Churches,
by Sex, 1740–80

	Males (%)	Females (%)	Totals
Sins of aversion			
Contempt of church authority	113 (56)	90 (44)	203
Sins against fellow members			
Fighting/quarreling	32 (65)	17 (35)	49
Slander	14 (52)	13 (48)	27
Profanity/unguarded speech	15 (60)	10 (40)	25
Avarice	22 (92)	2 (8)	24
Lying	8 (53)	7 (47)	15
Sins against family/household	2 (22)	7 (78)	9
TOTALS	206	146	352
Sins of the flesh			
Sexual misconduct	1 (6)	14 (94)	15
Drunkenness	8 (80)	2 (20)	10
TOTALS	9	16	25
Unspecified	7	5	12
GRAND TOTALS	222 (61)	167 (39)	389

Church."[28] Twenty years later, the Warren Baptist Church (which had broken off from the Swansea church in 1764 to form a separate congregation) similarly excluded one of its members, Samuel Hicks, for holding unauthorized prayer meetings in his home. In language reminiscent of the orthodox disavowal of unlawful congregational separations during the Great Awakening, the Warren church rejected Hicks's self-appointed status as a preacher and forbade the practice of holding evening meetings "without liberty from the Church or so much as consulting them." In claiming for himself the "right" to preach without license from the church, Hicks in turn was echoing the New Light insistence that an "internal call" alone was sufficient to qualify one for the office of preacher.[29] A few years earlier, members of the Warren church had been so agitated by the unlicensed preaching of one Mr. Blanchard that they took the extraordinary measure of publishing their disapproval in the local paper.[30]

28. First Baptist Church of Swansea, 2 June 1748, Myles Ms., RIHS.

29. Record Book, Warren Baptist Church, 30 March 1769, JHL. I thank the Warren Baptist Church for granting me permission to use these records.

30. "A motion was made with Respect to one Blanchard who under pretence of Preaching by authority is guilty of the most flagicious Crimes by means of which the enemy take occasion to Reproach It was therefore Judged by the Church their duty to let the publick know his Charracter in the Gazette; that he may be prevented for the future." Ibid., 29 August 1765.

The problem of lay preaching was intensified for many eighteenth-century observers by the evangelical precedent of allowing women to speak publicly, either in declarations of faith before the assembled congregation or (less commonly) as exhorters and prayer leaders. Sometimes the practice of female exhorting, so discredited during the Awakening by such orthodox ministers as Charles Chauncy, was criticized by the evangelical churches themselves (witness the attempt by the Canterbury Separate Church to silence Lois Adams). In 1771 the First Baptist Church of Lyme recorded an altercation with two of its members over the church's policy of allowing women to speak in meeting. "The Church called on Sister Lucy to see if she could travil with the Church and she said she had a trial with the Church for Letting the Sisters Improve as they do which is contrary to a divine Rule and I cant walk with the Church." Sister Lucy's husband, Stephen Smith, shared his wife's opposition, and informed the church that "his mind is yet Burdened and said it Grow Rather Bigor than it was Before and still declined to travil with the Church in the Spisial [special] Ordinances: and his Burden was the same as his wifes and Espoused her Cause."[31] Isaac Backus used the issue of women's speaking in church, which he disavowed except in "extraordinary" cases such as prophesying, to validate the principle of lay exhorting generally. Because only women are expressly enjoined in the scriptures to "keep silence in the church," men as *men*—and not as church officers—presumably enjoyed the right to speak publicly: "[I]n that Paul forbids women, he gives liberty to all men, gifted accordingly, opposing women to men, sex to sex, and not women to officers, which were frivolous."[32] As in so many other instances, Backus represents the more conservative wing of the evangelical cause; many churches extended to women the right to speak in "ordinary" as well as extraordinary circumstances, and there are several recorded cases of women's exercising their prophetic powers while in a trancelike state.[33]

As in the Awakening, disputes over the role and qualifications of the

31. Record Book, First Baptist Church of Lyme, 25 January and 16 February 1771, CSL.
32. Backus, *A History of New England*, 2:14.
33. During a church meeting at the Groton Baptist Church, Sister Betty (an Indian member) "fell down on the flower [floor] as tho She was in a trance and afterward got up and said She had Seen her father and he said She must return and be faithful a while." Record Book, First Baptist Church of Groton, April 1764, vol. 1, CSL. Nicholas Gilman, the New Light minister of Durham, N.H., recorded several incidents in his diary of parishioners (mostly women) who claimed to have had visions of the Holy Spirit which empowered them to speak publicly. After one such vision, he wrote, "[Mary Reed] desire[d] me to call the Pple together every wednesday for two Months, for their Time was but Short." Gilman, Ms. Diary, entries for 26 March, 12 April, and 2 May 1742, CHS.

elder constituted one of the most frequent and serious challenges to the authority of the evangelical church. Members were quick to claim the right to pass individual judgment on their elders' qualifications, and they often withdrew from a church when they felt they could no longer in good conscience receive the elements from impure hands. Josiah Cleaveland withdrew from the Canterbury Separate Church because he no longer believed Elder Marshall was "Quallifyed" for the office of pastor. "Therefore I Say that I have free Liberty by the Rules of the Gospell & the Naturall Rights of Mankind to think & Judge for my Self without Being accountable to any But God."[34] In a similar case, the First Baptist Church of Lyme excluded Jonathan Philips in 1772 for "saying that we ware not a spiritual Hous[e]" and asserting that "he was Mistaken in Calling Elder Wightman and seting him apart to the office work of a Watchman and Pasture for he Did not answer the carrector in a perfect manner."[35] The presumption that individual lay men and women were competent, indeed required by their covenant vows, to judge the worthiness and spiritual stature of church officers grew directly out of the evangelical rejection of conventional signs of regeneration. Without the traditional trappings of authority such as superior education, wealth, or social status, Baptist and Separate elders were at the mercy of their congregations' peculiar standards of doctrinal and personal fitness, however idiosyncratic.

If a member's dissatisfaction with a pastor extended to the entire church, an open break with the community was inevitable. The great majority of censures for contempt of church authority were directed at communicants who deliberately withdrew from their congregations and renounced their covenant vows. The Second Baptist Church of Newport excommunicated John Hookey, "formerly a member of this church," in 1761 because he "hath Rent himself from the same breaking through all order as well as his own most Solemn Covenant obligations, in opposition to all our endeavours to Reclaim him."[36] Mary Huntley was suspended by the Lyme Baptist Church in 1754 for withdrawing from the church and "Brething out her unbelievings as to the Chh's being founded [not] on the Gospel but on the divel and that the Spirit by wich the Chh was Governed was of the devil."[37] The Tiverton Baptist Church excluded Mary Wilkins in 1767 for "Reject[ing] the church in going out and openly declaring that [she] was none of us nor ever was."[38]

34. Canterbury Separate Church Papers, vol. 1, 1 April 1767, CHS.
35. Record Book, First Baptist Church of Lyme, 24 December 1772, vol. 1, CSL.
36. Record Book, Second Baptist Church of Newport, 2 April 1761, NHS.
37. Record Book, First Baptist Church of Lyme, 19 April 1754, vol. 1, CSL.
38. Record Book, First Baptist Church of Tiverton, 3 September 1767, RIHS.

Some disgruntled members signaled their disapproval by simply ceasing to attend worship meetings; others publicly declared their disaffection before the assembled congregation. In all cases, the anguish such defections caused was unfeigned, as the illusion of a true community of saints was shattered again and again. Congregations devoted enormous time and energy to "reclaim" these errant members, and they mourned the loss of every soul as a diminishing of *communitas*, the very essence of the church.

More serious than these isolated cases of individual absences from the communion table were the mass defections that periodically confronted Baptist and Separate churches after the Awakening. As New Lights had done in the 1740s, groups of communicants often broke off and formed separate congregations rather than remain in covenant with a society they considered impure. Jemima Rogers, along with six of her fellow sisters in Lyme, was excluded in 1775 for "first usurping the authority over the church and for neglecting the publick worship of God in this place and church meetings and for building up a meeting hild by our admonished members."[39] Two years later two more sisters, Mary Murrow and Jane Clark, were admonished for "joyning with them that cause devisions"; the new congregation was now roughly half the size of the original church.[40] Open schisms occurred in the Baptist churches in Warren, Lyme, and Groton in the 1750s, 1760s, and 1770s, and in the Preston Separate Church in 1757. Separation, it seems, was a dangerous precedent.

"Surely the Tongue is an unruly Member": Disorderly Speech

Although such disputes tell us much about the fractious nature of early New England congregational life, they also confirm the central importance of speech as the primary medium through which community was enacted in the eighteenth century. Godly speech could easily slip into "evil whisperings," "tatlings," and "vain discourse," as the language of the covenants adopted by evangelical congregations attests to. "It is the rash using of the Tongue that greatly enflames our differences," the Second Baptist Church of Newport warned its members. "Surely the Tongue is an unruly Member and full of deadly Poison."[41]

39. Record Book, First Baptist Church of Lyme, 20 January 1775, vol. 1, CSL. The other sisters were Sarah Tubbs, Johannah Miller, Pannel Tubbs, Elisabeth Miller, Martha Beebe, and Dasha Beebe.
40. Ibid., 19 July and 6 July 1777, vol. 1, CSL.
41. Record Book, Second Baptist Church of Newport, 1764, NHS.

Accusations of slander circulated freely in the charged atmosphere of the Great Awakening, as advocates on either side sought to paint their opponents with the tar of subversive speech. One particularly embattled Old Light pastor, the Reverend Nicholas Eyres of the Second Baptist Church of Newport, protested repeatedly against the slanders he charged had been "spread abroad by the Arts and management" of disaffected members of his church to undermine his authority and stain his character. "These men," he fumed in an open letter to the Baptist churches in New England in 1741, "having not been able to contain their ends, nor to compass their designs in our church . . . have drove about from place to place thro the country in their several governments & have kindled the fire of strife and contention, of discord & Divisions in several of our churches abroad as well as ours at home." Ten years later Eyres was still belaboring the point: "Call to your mind therefore sir upon this ocassion," he wrote James Brown, Jr., "the arts pains costs & interests that have been employed against me; the journeys that have been taken to the same view, to different towns churches provinces to places where I have never been & to which I may perhaps never come."[42]

To understand the deeper significance of the charge of slander, we must keep in mind the threat of spatial anarchy which colored the entire debate over the merits of the Awakening. For to slander a member of the church was not only to use speech aggressively but also to breach the moral and, at times, physical boundaries of the community, to air private quarrels in public and thus undermine the exclusive nature of the covenanted community. Slander can thus be seen as a form of communal subversion, a further undermining of those boundaries whose very integrity had been called into question by the revivalists' practices.[43] The connection is particularly vivid in the case of Nicholas Eyres, for whom spatial and verbal anarchy were inextricably linked. The dissidents' campaign to undermine his authority breached both the geographical and speech boundaries of the community and, in the process, utterly destroyed his reputation. "Let one of the Beloved Brethren brake in upon your peace," he warned his fellow clerics, "corrupt your name, wound your Reputation, Reproach your character, smite your

---

42. Letter from Eyres to other churches, 30 September 1741; and letter from Eyres to Brown, 27 November 1751, Papers of Separate Men, RIHS.

43. The problem of "disorderly" speech was irreducibly the problem of community in its most elemental form, for (as Robert St. George and Walter Ong have shown) speech in premodern societies was a powerful force capable of circumventing the physical as well as moral boundaries of a community. St. George, " 'Heated Speech' and Literacy in Seventeenth-Century New England," in *Seventeenth Century New England: A Conference Held by the Colonial Society of Massachusetts*, ed. David Hall and David Grayson Allen (Boston, 1985), pp. 275–322; Ong, *The Presence of the Word: Some Prolegomena for Cultural and Religious History* (New Haven, Conn., 1967).

credit & Estrange your friends . . . let the abused person be a man of publick
character amongst you, and he shall be discasted of his Character, Degraded
from his Office, and thrust out of your Society."[44]

Throughout the eighteenth century the charge of slander retained a special resonance in the evangelical world, as it came to represent the breaching
of the communal ideal at its most pernicious. Ministers, both Old and New
Lights, found themselves caught in a tangle of slanderous rumors which
signified the breakdown of linguistic order initiated by the revival's embrace
of the unstructured word. In one intriguing case, a homosexual Baptist
minister became the target of an extensive slander campaign orchestrated by
dissident members of his congregation who disapproved of their pastor's
unorthodox ministry. The clash between the New London Baptist Society
and its minister Stephen Gorton over the terrain of personal reputation was
at bottom a crisis of communal integrity as both sides resorted to "spreading
evil reports" about the other throughout the Baptist community of New
England.

In 1756, the Baptist church in New London lamented their "broken and
Distressed Condition" to the General Meeting of Baptist Churches, which
they attributed to "ye Awfull and dreadful Reports of [our] Elders unchaist
behaveor with his fellow men," a problem the church had been grappling
with for a decade. These Reports "being spread abroad in the world," the
church conducted an inquiry into the case and found to their dismay that
Elder Gorton "has continued in this unchaste behavior with his fellow man
when in bead with them for many years past." If the sister churches did not
intervene quickly, "ye church will be Entirely broke to peaces and come to
nothing for we can not Receive into the ministry one that has such things
laid to their Charge." In response to this appeal, the General Meeting
suspended Gorton from his pastoral duties until a reformation of character
was evident, despite Gorton's attempts to justify himself. "If you must be
told so," they wrote the elder, "there were & are too many Instances that we
our Selves or some of us do know and are acquainted with who have been
exceedingly grieved & offended at your unchaste Behavior in the Bed. . . .
Therefore which your Paper [appeal] Speaks of must be ineffectual because
the Number of Persons Joining with you is Small and the Rumour offence &
Reproach of your Carriage are Spread abroad into distant Parts & different Churches." After advising Gorton to purge himself "Thoroughly from
every Spark of Inclination or Disposition tending that way," the General
Meeting revoked his ordination.[45]

---

44. Letter from Eyres to other churches, 30 November 1741, Papers of Separate Men, RIHS.
45. Letter from New London Baptist Church to General Meeting of Baptist Churches, 11

Faced with removal as the pastor of the New London Baptist Church, Gorton foreswore his homosexual behavior and promised to refrain from any future scandalous conduct. "Whereas there has been a Rumour gone abroad in the World of my bad Conduct or offencive Carriage towards Men in Bed, as far as I have been Guilty I am heartily Sorry." This confession, he noted, "has Been Read Publickly Sundry times to the Church and the Sabbath day in April to the Church and World."[46] In April 1757 the New London church voted to restore Gorton to the pastorate on condition that he make a full and public retraction. Twenty-seven members (12 men and 25 women) voted to restore him as their minister; 16 (9 men and 7 women) to restore him to church membership but not to the ministry; and 5 (2 men and 3 women) refused to receive him as either brother or minister.[47] It is interesting that many more women than men inclined toward clemency in reinstating Gorton to his full ministerial capacity, perhaps signaling the male brethren's deep ambivalence about Gorton's sexual inclination. The General Meeting was satisfied with Gorton's confession to the extent of restoring his ordained status but recommended: "[Y]ou should of your own Self freely and voluntarily deny your Self so as to abstain from the Communion of the Lords Supper for some convenient time, Several Months at least. . . . We give it as our Sentiments that you do from hence forward Lay aside all Pretensions to a Publick Character in Religion and forbear all Ministerial Services."[48] No further mention of Gorton's sexual behavior can be found in the surviving records, though the New London church (later the Waterford Baptist Church) continued to be rent by quarrels and schisms for the next twenty-five years and finally dissolved around 1772.[49]

As these documents suggest, the sticking point for the New London church and the larger association of Baptist churches was the extent to which Gorton's indecencies had "spread abroad into distant Parts & different Churches." Though no proof was ever offered to the council convened to look into the case other than the persistence of "Rumours" and "Reports" unattributed to any specific source, the Meeting clearly believed that the public nature of the offense alone was serious enough to warrant extreme censure. Interestingly, the churches placed more weight on the public exposure of Gorton's "Unseemly actions" than on the nature of those ac-

November 1746, and Letter from General Meeting to Stephen Gorton, 13 September 1756, Backus Papers, Box 7, ANTS.

46. Confession of Stephen Gorton, 27 October 1746, Backus Papers, Box 7, ANTS.

47. Vote of New London Baptist Church, 8 June 1757, Backus Papers, Box 7, ANTS.

48. Letter from General Meeting to Gorton, 10 September 1757, Backus Papers, Box 7, ANTS.

49. William McLoughlin gives a brief account of the unhappy history of the New London Baptist Church in his *New England Dissent*, 1: 261.

tions. Gorton's homosexuality had, after all, been private knowledge for well over thirty years before the church was spurred to take action; in 1726 the civil authorities of New London had arrested him for having "Lascivously behaved himself towards sundry men Indeavouring to Commit Sodomy with them." The charges were dismissed at this time for lack of proof, and Gorton resumed his preaching duties with no apparent ill effects.[50] Not until knowledge of his sexual preferences had brought public reproach down upon the church did the Baptist community in New London initiate ecclesiastical sanctions against their reprobate elder.

The similarities between this case and the schism in Nicholas Eyres's Second Baptist Church of Newport are striking: both controversies revolved around the damage done to religious communities by "artful" and "scheming" troublemakers "spreading abroad" accusations and innuendos about the character of the church's chief officer. The phrases I have chosen to highlight in the Gorton case suggest the intimate connection between disorderly speech and communal integrity in the mid-eighteenth-century evangelical world. That Gorton's failures as a minister of God took sexual form was incidental to the larger issue at stake in the contest: the inability of the New London congregation to maintain the boundary between itself and the profane world which was so critical to evangelical religion. In "spreading abroad" such "dreadful" lies and rumors, Gorton's persecutors mimicked the actions of itinerant preachers who had themselves circumvented the territorial boundaries of the orthodox parish in their zeal to "spread abroad" the Word of God. Words had, literally, been the means by which a sacred community was created in the 1740s; they could just as easily be the means of destroying that community.

No wonder, then, that the evangelical churches prosecuted disorderly speech with special vigor in the years following the revival. It was no accident that so many of the challenges to church authority described above took the form of verbal attacks—"rash" and "evil" words flung at individual members or the assembled body of saints, unauthorized and undisciplined preaching by lay men and women, "railing" against specific doctrines or unfit elders,

---

50. New London County Court Records, loose files, June Term, 1726, CSL. It is interesting to note in this context Henry Abelove's finding that early Methodists displayed a "quick and unconventional sympathy with same-sex eroticism." See Abelove, *The Evangelist of Desire: John Wesley and the Methodists* (Stanford, Calif., 1990), pp. 66–67. Abelove attributes this tolerance for same-sex affection to the general assault on traditional family arrangements and the intense sense of fellow-feeling within Methodist congregations—characteristics that also apply to the early Baptists. The New London congregation's apparent unconcern for their Elder's homosexual leanings may reflect a similar latitude.

"speaking all maner of Evil of Each Other" during communion sessions.[51] Nor was it coincidental that over half of the sins enumerated in the church covenants concern what I have categorized as crimes of the tongue: "foolish talking and jesting," "vain disputings about words," "evil whisperings" and "backbiting," "unnecessary Discorse about worldly things." Clearly, speech was a potent weapon in the hands of unscrupulous communicants.

In an early case, the Canterbury church excommunicated James and Mary Hides for the sin of defamation, which they condemned as blasphemy against God and his word. "Ye Lord doth hate a Lying tongue," they admonished the pair.[52] A "Lying tongue" was the plaything of the devil, and the means by which evil entered the community of saints. Slander in the evangelical community was understood more in the medieval sense of a breach of Christian charity than in the modern sense of a slur on one's reputation.[53] Evangelicals reserved their sharpest fire for speech that deliberately and maliciously undermined the integrity of the community: slander, spreading false reports, and lying. Lesser offenses, such as profanity and railing, were rarely sufficient to provoke church censure alone, but could aggravate an offenders' guilt in other contexts.[54] Rather than as an act of deliberate aggression, profanity and "unguarded" speech were regarded as temporary lapses of judgment and proper decorum, the unintended consequence of a sudden rush of passion or emotion overcoming the critical faculties. When Nicademus Miller was admonished by the Lyme Baptist Church in 1754 for having "Spoke unadvisedly with his Lips" when in a "grat Pashon," the

51. Second Baptist Church of Newport, 28 June 1759, Misc. Unbound Mss., RIHS.

52. Canterbury Separate Papers, 24 July 1734, vol. 1, CHS.

53. See J. A. Sharpe, *Defamation and Sexual Slander in Early Modern England: The Church Courts at York* (York: Borthwick Papers No. 58, 1980), and Ingram, *Church Courts*, for a discussion of the medieval and early modern concept of slander.

54. The table below breaks down the categories of crimes of the tongue and lists the number of church members censured under each heading from 1740 to 1780. Charges of verbal abuse were often tacked on to other accusations as secondary infractions; cases in which disorderly speech was mentioned secondarily are in parentheses.

Crimes of the tongue	Males	Females	Total
First-order offenses			
Slander	6 (1)	7 (0)	13 (1)
Spreading false reports	7 (0)	6 (0)	13 (0)
Lying	8 (0)	5 (2)	13 (2)
Second-order offenses			
Railing	3 (2)	0 (2)	3 (4)
Profanity	1 (7)	2 (2)	3 (9)
Unguarded speech	1 (6)	2 (4)	3 (10)

church took into consideration the inadvertent nature of the offense in recommending leniency. Miller confessed his fault but insisted that "it was of the spirit of Satan that he thus Spake and Evil Entred the Church." When, however, Anne Smith, another member of the church, was charged with deliberate slander in 1772, the Lyme church did not hesitate to exclude her for "Sundry Defamitory hard ungospel Sayings," including "words not fitting to be mentioned amongst Saints."[55] There is little to distinguish Nicademus Miller's from Anne Smith's verbal barbs save the manner in which they were delivered: both spoke harshly against the church and its elder, but Miller was excused as the passive victim of his own passionate nature, which was stirred, he claimed, by the devil himself, while Smith's assaults were considered to be malicious in intent.

The nervous preoccupation with slanderous speech displayed by the evangelical church is symptomatic of the indeterminate boundary between the church and the world in post-Awakening New England. In a particularly revealing case, the Canterbury Separate Church found itself entangled in a web of rumors about an illicit sexual liaison between two members. In July 1754, Aaron Meach accused John Ormsby and his wife of "telling Lyes about him of what he had said about John [Hibberd] & Elisabeth [Dairy]." Apparently fingered by the Ormsbys as the source of persistent rumors about an adulterous affair between Hibberd and Dairy, Aaron Meach tried to deflect blame for the slanderous report onto his accusers. A "dreadfull Contradiction" then broke out between the Ormsbys and Meach "before many people," prompting Elder Solomon Paine to counsel the three to use "private means" to resolve the dispute, urging them "to discourse before only those who were knowing of it."[56]

The problem with the elder's advice was that the number of people "who were knowing" of the alleged slander proved too large for the dispute to be resolved through private "discorse." In September, the church considered the case at their monthly meeting and invited all members who wished to testify to attend. John Ormsby was the first to speak:

> I do hereby tell you that our Brother Aaron Meach is guilty of . . . spreading an ill Report of his Neighbours (viz.) John Hibberd & Elisa-

55. Record Book, First Baptist Church of Lyme, 11 April 1754 and 18 April 1772, vol. 1, CSL. When Nathan Waldo was charged with talking "in an angry and unchristian maner" to David Kinney, the Canterbury Separate Church found that Waldo did not "premeditatedly & Designedly say that which was not true" and required him to "be Sensable not only that he was wrong in being angray but allso in using words so Rash & Contradictory where no good End could be answered." Waldo duly confessed and was forgiven. Canterbury Separate Papers, 25 February 1783, vol. 2, CHS.

56. Canterbury Separate Church Papers, 25 July 1754, vol. 1, CHS.

beth Dairy trying to make people think they Lived in the Sin of unclean-
ness and that he had seen them in the very act . . . saying he did it because
I and my wife had filled the Neighbourhood with Lyes so that there had
not ben a day for some time but there had ben persons with him to clear
up the Lyes that we had told about what he had said about Hibberd &
Elisabeth Dairy but forasmuch as we never had told anybody what he had
told of Mr. Hibberd and Br. Hide examined what it was that he had told
us aledging that the ill Report is got abroad and must be searched out that
it may be don away.

Sister Ormsby added that she "Reproved [Meach] but never told anybody
of it till after she heard that Elis. Dairy was searching after the maker of sd.
Reports and heard that Meach denied that he ever told anybody etc." The
final witness was Brother Hide, who, acting as the church's agent, testified
that

> he was conferring about Mr. Ormsby till he had made diligent inquiry
> and found that this Report was all about before Ormsby or wife said
> anything etc. and that Meach had tryed to make him believe (when
> talking abt. John Hibd. that he had ben Comon with sd. Elis. Dairy by
> telling him and his wife that he had seen them as plain as he ses that cat
> etc. and he had told her mother and she had gon and said it to her and she
> fell into fits and that he would burn before he wod deny that he had seen
> them etc.[57]

The hidden actor in this convoluted exchange was the larger neighborhood within which the "lyes" and slanders about Hibberd and Dairy circulated. Because an "ill Report" spread by Meach had "got abroad and must be
searched out" accusing the Ormsbys of "filling the Neighbourhood with
Lyes," the church could not wait until private means of reconciliation had
been exhausted. The speed with which rumors of impropriety spread outward into the larger community recalls the orthodox charge of spatial anarchy leveled against the revivalists in the Great Awakening.

The same concern for communal integrity surfaces in other slander cases
during these decades. When Esther Bates "hinted abroad" that "Jonathan
Carver and [Sister Waldo] have ben Lesevius togather," the rumor "fild the
minds of people with Jalosy" and occasioned a major rift in the Canterbury
church. While most of these cases involved sexual reputation, the almost
complete absence (as we shall see) in the disciplinary records of prosecutions
of actual fornication, adultery, and other sexual misbehaviors would suggest

57. Ibid., 11 September 1754, vol. 1.

that sexuality itself was not the issue; the content of the slander was less significant than the means of its dissemination. Like wildfire, untamed words spread confusion and discord outward from their source. When communicants "bite and devour one another," an embattled Isaac Backus wrote to a female parishoner, "ye [will] be consumed one of another."[58]

Like slander, incidents of "unguarded" or impassioned speech were as likely to take place in public settings where church members met socially as in the sanctified space of the meetinghouse. Thankfull Amos was suspended for "treating her Ant Jones uncharitably" and for "not bridling her tongue."[59] In 1731, Jerry Lawton was accused by the Second Baptist Church of Newport of "false Speaking Divers times" and suspended for "his evil conversation with his Neighbours which caused them to Speak much against him."[60] Ten years later his fellow communicant John Moore appeared before the church to answer to charges of "Evil conversation" brought by several of his neighbors: "he being under a bad character of keeping bad company and having a bad conversation and he being talked with about it by some of our Brethren.... They advised him to Refrain such company and Remove his abode to some civil house for where he made his abode was an uncivil house it being a publick house and a very disorderly one and subject to all sorts of bad company."[61] The "Evil" speech of these members was less a premeditated act of malice than a symptom of the disorder evident in their domestic lives, the consequence of keeping "bad company" and residing in an "uncivil" public house. When passion overrode common sense, when private discontents became public quarrels, the evangelical church stepped in to restore goodwill between neighbors and admonish malcontents to "hold their tongues" or face the church's censure. Once again, we see how private acts became construed as sins of aversion when the boundary between the individual and the communal good was transgressed.

"Quarriling all his nabors": The Breakdown of Fraternity

From 1759 to 1775, Peter Brown of the Groton First Baptist Church was in and out of church discipline meetings to answer to a series of charges brought by his neighbors relating to his questionable business practices and uncivil behavior. In July 1759 the church noted "sum dificulty between

---

58. Letter from Isaac Backus to Sister Harvey, 8 May 1775, Backus Papers, Box 10, ANTS.
59. *Parke Scrapbook*, 16 November 1759.
60. Record Book, Second Baptist Church of Newport, 6 February 1731, NHS.
61. Ibid., 8 August 1741 and 4 March 1742.

sd. Brown and some of his nabours." Two weeks later the Widow Hains, John Fox, Caleb Hains, Doctor Fitch, Thomas Williams, and Joseph Elliot gave evidence as to the specific misdeeds charged against Brown, including threats of physical violence, much "bad" and "vain discourse," and general "wicked conduct." This long catalogue of rude and dishonest behavior, culminating with the accusation that Brown was guilty of "quarriling all his nabours that come to mill," bespeaks a neighborhood rife with "hard discourse" and unfriendly dealings.[62] Brown apparently confessed to the satisfaction of his aggrieved neighbors, for the church dropped the case against him at their next meeting. Six years later, however, Brown was again brought up on charges of drinking with "Bad Company," using "Bad Language," and "Medl[ing] with business none of his own."[63] Again, Brown confessed and was forgiven by the church. And nine years later we find Peter Brown indicted along with ten of his fellow communicants (including several of his former antagonists) for "joining in covenant with others in an ungospel manner" in a major schism within the Groton church. Apparently Brown found it easier to retract his defiant withdrawal than face excommunication, for once again he confessed his error and was restored into full church membership. After fifteen years of strained and often rancorous relations with his fellow communicants, Peter Brown finally disappears from the records of the Groton Baptist Church.

A running boil on the body politic, these feuds made a mockery of the evangelical promise to create a godly community of saints out of the tattered remnants of the profane world. When members were estranged from one another, the evangelical churches used every means at their disposal to effect a reconciliation. The First Baptist Church of Middleborough "laboured a great deal" to bring Sister Birchard and Sister Pike together "who have had very great bars against each other." Finally, after months of labor, "they were both of 'em Broken down before God so that they got together next morning and began to confest." Such a display of mutual repentence almost got out of hand, as "they were almost ready to Contend which should Lie the lowest at the others feet."[64] Returning prodigals were as likely to be greeted with "a glorious Shout" as with recrimination.[65] Again and again churches recorded their "labors" to reconcile feuding members, often refusing to admit failure until the entire community had exhausted its reserves of goodwill and charity. In such cases the ultimate sanction of excommunication

---

62. Record Book, First Baptist Church of Groton, 18 July and 2 August 1759, CSL.
63. Ibid., 2 February and 22 February 1765.
64. *The Diary of Isaac Backus*, 1:116.
65. Ibid., 1:176.

was avoided at all costs, because to remove a member permanently from the communion of the church was to admit defeat—to concede that the bonds of fellowship were irrevocably severed. When churches did resort to the extreme measure of excommunication, their decision reflected not the severity of the crime but the unrepentant nature of the offender. Refusing to "make satisfaction" to the church was sufficient grounds for expulsion, however trivial the offense.[66] The reluctance to withdraw the hand of fellowship permanently from an errant sister or brother reflects the central place of charity in the evangelical scheme of discipline.

As the economy of northern New England became more complex in the eighteenth century, with market relations transforming traditional agricultural patterns of economic exchange, the sin of avarice became a growing threat to the harmony of the evangelical community. Disputes over issues of legal and commercial relations punctuate the discipline records of the mid-eighteenth century, and a "covetous" spirit was at the bottom of most of these conflicts. Joseph Morse was charged by the Canterbury Separate Church of "disorderly walk" in "not only Coviting his Neighbours Estate but he is acted upon a Covetus Principals and absolutely taken of his Neighbours Estate and Refuses to Restore it or in any Just way to Reward his Neighbour Justly or Lawfully."[67] John Hayward accused Esther Fobes of "being under the government of a Covetous & dishonest principle" in borrowing things without paying, treating him "hardly" when he remonstrated with her, and "darkening the truth" when confronted with evidence of her thievery.[68] The Preston Separate Church found Brother Tyler's "Cruel Disposition" toward his brother-in-law to derive from "Covetousness" and admonished him to cease harassing him and his father in the hopes of gaining a more favorable inheritance.[69] Disputes over money often proved particularly intractable, as commercial and pecuniary interests drove a wedge between contending neighbors. To "covet" a neighbor's property was more than simply a matter of personal greed; it was a betrayal of the principle of neighborliness itself.

Of all the issues that drove members apart, however, none proved more troublesome than domestic conflicts. As we might expect in a community

66. Emil Oberholzer has found a similar pattern in the disciplinary efforts of Congregational churches; see his *Delinquent Saints: Disciplinary Action in the Early Congregational Churches of Massachusetts* (New York, 1956), p. 38.

67. Canterbury Separate Church Papers, 5 June 1755, vol. 1, CHS.

68. Copy of Middleborough Church Records, 21 June, 8 July, and 12 September 1757, Backus Papers, Box 7, ANTS.

69. *Parke Scrapbook*, 10 May 1754.

that elevated spiritual ties over domestic ones, evangelical households were often torn between the competing demands of faith and family. It was women, however, who felt these conflicts most intensely and who heeded most the evangelical injunction to leave family behind and follow Christ. Sarah Hill accused her husband, Samuel, of "Tiranizing over her by not alowing her Christian Liberty . . . forbid[ing] her going to meeting . . . [and] to Some Christians houses." The First Baptist Church of North Stonington found both parties to be at fault, for each "Did Stand obstainte to Each other."[70] Sister Thankfull Amos of the Preston Separate Church was charged with having "a wicked Quarrel" with her husband and father-in-law in which she talked "Rudely and Railingly." When confronted with the accusations, she too was unrepentant. "She owned she had Quarrel'd with her husband Struck him Pul'd his hair etc. but she denied that she Quarrel'd with her father in Law: which was not Proved. . . . She also owned she had sd she vowed she wood not Lie with such etc. and that she sd she wish'd she might die if she confess'd to her father for she had don him no Rong."[71] In another case, Abigail Standish's disobedience to her husband was explicitly construed as an act of "contempt" against the authority of the church. After quarreling with her sister, Abigail ran away "to Br. Kimbals (although her husband knew not where she was Gon) and there she told of her Quarel and would have staid alnight although she had a young Child at home and the family not knowing what become of her." When she had the further temerity to swear out a warrant with the justice of the peace against her sister Deborah, the church swiftly excommunicated her for "casting Contempt upon the authority Christ has given his Chh."[72] Because the membership records of these churches are incomplete, it is difficult to gauge the extent to which the simple act of joining a church was for some women an act of rebellion against the "Tiranizing" of a husband or father. What is clear from the membership registers is that most women joined not with spouses or other family members but alone.

Churches were as reluctant to enforce other relations of dependency within the household as that which bound wives to their husbands. In one case, a servant who was a member of the Enfield church took advantage of his master's temporary imprisonment to marry without the permission of his master, who had enjoined him "not to marry yet because it would lay him an Impossibility to pay his vows to him and wife." Two outraged brethren

70. Record Book, North Stonington First Baptist Church at Pendleton Hill, 7 July and 17 July 1754, CSL.
71. *Parke Scrapbook*, 17 October 1755.
72. Ibid., 6 March 1756 and 28 December 1757.

from a neighboring congregation charged that Benjamin Simons had deserted "his masters Business to the great greaf and dammage of his master and to the Reproch of the Cause of God." Rather than discipline Simons, the Baptist church at Enfield "neglected to watch over & Restrain sd Simons or to deal with him when he had thus openly in the face of the Church & the world Trespassed against his master." More, the church "have Rather been acsesary to it by Incoraging him to marry while his master was in prison etc. which is a breach of the Solom Charge given to all Esepcially the pastor. . . . Exhort Servants to be obedient to their own masters and to pleas them well in all things." Simons' sin was aggravated, according to Solomon Paine and Thomas Stevens, because he had initially declared his fellowship with his master in his time of trial and had declared "in a great assembly of saints" that "he would be Faithfull in his masters temporal Stuerdship and . . . would work his fingers to the bone."[73] But, however much they may have disapproved in private, members of the Enfield Baptist Church felt honor-bound to uphold the right of their fellow servant of the Lord to order his own domestic affairs. They knew that loyalty to God came before loyalty to man.

"The sin of adultry's breaking out": Sins of the Flesh

In contrast to the severity with which evangelical churches responded to sins of aversion, the discipline records are nearly silent on the subject of sins of the flesh. Only twenty-five men and women were censured between 1730 and 1780 for overindulging their drinking or sexual appetites. The breakdown of the prosecution of these two offenses by sex is exactly what one would expect: almost all drunks were men (8 out of 10), and almost all fornicators were women (14 out of 15). Although the numbers involved are not large, the gender distinctions between these two types of transgressions are significant, for they confirm that community was construed largely as a masculine arena while the self was gendered female in evangelical discourse. Men's drinking was perceived as a public failure, the exposure of the community to worldly ridicule, while women's sexual lapses constituted a violation of the self, of the private world of individual sanctity.

The common theme in cases involving drunkenness is the public nature of the offense and the repercussions of such behavior for the civic reputation

---

73. Testimony of Solomon Paine and Thomas Stevens of the Plainfield Church to the Church of Enfield, 20 December 1752, Canterbury Separate Papers, Vol. 1, CHS.

of the church. Lawrance Clark of the Second Baptist Church of Newport was excommunicated for being "overtaken with drink" in "publick houses": "This [censure] the Ch[urch] were especially moved too because the sin he had been guilty of was publick before the world to the great dishonour of the holy Name of God."[74] The Baptist Church of Lyme admonished John Ingher in 1757 for frolicking, dancing and "adjoining a confideresy with the world."[75] In most cases, corroborating evidence was sought to prove that the offense had indeed taken place in a public setting before witnesses. When Priscilla Lawton was accused by the Second Baptist Church of Newport of drunkenness in 1730, the church solicited testimony from several of her neighbors. One accuser swore that he had "seen her drunk Several times And the Reason he had was because she could not go without Staggering Neither could she Speak plain." Another witness testified that "in her opinion she see Priscilla Lawton was overtaken with Strong Drink at the burial of Edward Smith and Divers People took Notice of the same and talked about it."[76] Caleb Hide was excluded by the Canterbury Separate Church in 1764 only after Jemima Burnam and Elisha Paine testified that they had personally witnessed "many actions which denote a mans being intoxicated with Liquor"; the church concluded that Hide was "in a Publick Mener Left to Behave very unseemly and unbecoming."[77]

In his study of discipline in Congregational churches, Emil Oberholzer argues that the rise in charges of drunkenness after 1800 reflects the new perception of drinking (or "alcoholism," as Oberholzer prefers) as a character flaw rather than a problem of public order. "Recognizing the fact that intemperance is a condition rather than an act, the churches displayed their resourcefulness in placing alcoholics on probation before restoring them."[78] Even if we leave aside the modern bias evident in this analysis, Oberholzer is nonetheless correct in his claim that the eighteenth-century church viewed intoxication as an act carrying public overtones rather than as a personal condition requiring treatment. For this reason, the church did not hesitate to exclude offending members after the briefest of investigations. A mere "report" of Patience Osborne's "Drinking too much Strong Drink" in public was sufficient to compel the Second Baptist Church of Newport to "suspend

74. Record Book, Second Baptist Church of Newport, 22 December 1726, NHS.

75. Record Book, First Baptist Church of Lyme, 6 January 1757, CSL.

76. Record Book, Second Baptist Church of Newport, 6 February and 5 June 1731, NHS. The case was never resolved, because, as the church noted, "Priscilla Lawton was not at our Meeting at that time so we proceeded no further and so she died."

77. Canterbury Separate Church Papers, 25 February and 2 April 1764, vol. 1, CHS.

78. Oberholzer, *Delinquent Saints*, pp. 153–63.

her from our Communion" immediately.[79] The alacrity with which Baptist and Separate churches responded to public reports of intoxicated behavior in the mid-eighteenth century contrasts with the more circumspect approach adopted after 1800, when the sin of drunkenness came to be redefined as an assault on the physiological and moral health of the individual rather than on the corporate church.

Sins of sexual misconduct attracted far less public scrutiny. Isaac Backus fretted about the lack of concern evident among his parishoners over the sexual indiscretions of one Phebe Fobes, who had recently delivered an illegitimate child:

> [At church meeting] I mentioned the case of Phebe Fobes in particular that she fell into the Sin of Fornication. . . . And it Lay with weight upon my Soul that we ought Publickly to proceed with her to have that Iniquity purged out of the Church. . . . But by one means or other we let it alone 'till at Last there was nothing done upon it. . . . twas but 5 or 6 days after, before there came in such jangling disputes amongst us as seemed as if 'twould have broke us all to pieces. Before that there hadn't one member withdrawn from this Church But not Long after we seemed to be scatered every way.[80]

The church's hesitancy to discipline Sister Fobes, which Backus blamed for the fractured state of the congregation, typifies the lethargy with which the early evangelical churches responded to evidence of personal misconduct which did not directly challenge the public reputation of the church. Though Backus was deeply disturbed over the two-year delay in "purging" Fobes's "iniquity" out of the church, he was not particularly successful in instituting a more vigorous discipline process for such personal sins, as his diary from the 1750s and 60s reveals. A lax attitude toward sexual misconduct in particular seemed to Backus to be rife in the fledgling Baptist community in New England: "I think that Since I've Lived in the World I never Heard the like; of the sin of adultry's breaking out; as of late Both before & sience I was at Norwich," he wrote in despair to his brother Elijah in 1756.[81]

Discipline records for the period 1730–80 bear out Backus' concern that sexual promiscuity was undetected and unpunished in the eighteenth century. Only fourteen women and one man, or less than one percent of the total

79. Record Book, Second Baptist Church of Newport, 1 November and 6 December 1729, NHS.

80. *The Diary of Isaac Backus*, 1:137–38.

81. Letter from Isaac Backus to Elijah Backus, 27 May 1756, Backus Papers, Box 7, ANTS.

Baptist membership, were excluded for fornication and adultery during these years, a ratio greatly at variance with the demographic reality of steadily rising premarital pregnancy rates that historians have documented for the century.[82] Church members seem not to have been unduly concerned. The Lyme Baptist Church discovered to its dismay that one of its flock had in fact actively countenanced illicit behavior. "Our said sister," they reported, "had from time to time Knowingly allowed her daughter Ester being a married woman to keep Company with a man who was not her husband."[83] Perhaps the liberalized sexual climate of the Great Awakening was in some measure responsible for the indifferent attitude exhibited by this sister.[84]

Given the organic model of the evangelical church, this inattentiveness to sexual disorder is surprising. For to violate one's own body or the bodies of others in the act of illicit sexual union was in a very real sense to violate the body of the church. When the Seventh Day Baptist Church of Newport excluded Katharine Tabor for the sin of fornication in 1721, they laid out the chain of reasoning which for generations of Christians had justified strict sexual standards. "Know you not," they queried in their letter of excommunication, that "every sin that a man doeth is without the Body Butt he that Commits fornication sineth against his own Body. Know you not that your Bodys and the members of Christ [are one]; shall I then take the members of Christ and make them the members of another[?] Lett God forbid fornication."[85] In mingling the sacred and profane, the elect with

82. The most systematic study of colonial premarital pregnancy is Daniel Scott Smith and Michael Hindus, "Premarital Pregnancy in America, 1640–1975: An Overview and Interpretation," *Journal of Interdisciplinary History* 5 (1974–75): 537–70.

83. Record Book, First Baptist Church of Lyme, 23 January 1773, vol. i, CSL.

84. Other historians have found, in contrast, a heightened concern with sexual promiscuity in post-Awakening church records and have linked such tightened controls to the sexual excesses of the revivals. Charles Francis Adams' study of sexual morality in the colonial period attributes the rise in cases of fornication after the Awakening to the spiritual excitement generated by that movement. After the revival had peaked, those persons aroused by the itinerants sought other outlets for their pent-up emotions; see "Some Phases of Sexual Morality and Church Discipline in Colonial New England," *Proceedings of the Massachusetts Historical Society*, 2d ser., 6 (1918): 497–503. Henry B. Parkes, on the other hand, argues that the Great Awakening did not precipitate an actual rise in sexual violations but rather led to a stricter observance of moral codes; see his "Sexual Morality and the Great Awakening," *New England Quarterly* 3 (1930): 133–35. Oberholzer concludes from his study of church discipline that "it is quite possible that persons influenced by the Awakening were impressed with a sense of guilt of *prior* offences and hence made their confessions. Others may have been converted by the revivals and may have offered confessions, in connection with their admission to church membership, of sins committed years ago." He notes the case of a woman who confessed an act of fornication committed thirty-eight years earlier during her conversion. Oberholzer, *Delinquent Saints*, p. 239.

85. Record Book, Seventh Day Baptist Church of Newport, 28 January 1721, NHS.

the unregenerate, the sin of fornication contributed to the corruption of the body politic. This was powerful incentive for the church to intervene in the intimate lives of believers, but the evangelical community of New England did not follow this path in the mid-eighteenth century.

We can only infer the explanation for this apparent lack of concern. One reason may be that sexual misbehavior, in contrast to drinking or dancing, was a private affair, conducted out of the public eye behind closed doors. When such misconduct came to light, the church was often more disturbed at the dissimulation of the offenders than by the crime of illicit sex. Women who found themselves premaritally pregnant were more apt to be excluded for lying about their condition than for fornication. Robe Thurber was dismissed from the Warren Baptist Church in 1769 when "it appeared [she] had been guilty of Fornication and had agrivated the case by going away in a private manner to conceal her guilt by being delivered of her Child privately."[86] In another case, the Seventh Day Baptist Church of Newport suspended Abigail Barker for "that horrid sin of adultery, having defiled yourself in a shameful manner," adding: "[Y]ou have been guilty of Lying to hide this your wickedness."[87] It was routine for candidates seeking church membership to make a full disclosure of their past sins prior to admission, and premarital sex was the most common sin mentioned in these confessions.[88] These ritualized acknowledgments were sufficient to cleanse the evangelical community of all but the most flagrant carnal sins; only when communicants attempted to evade church censure through concealment did the church step in to bring the offender to justice. It may be that in concealing their sexual misdeeds women lay themselves open to gossip and "whispering campaigns" which—we have seen—were far more threatening to the integrity of the evangelical community. It may even be, to speculate further, that the sexualized nature of evangelical religion itself lent legitimacy to sexual unions that, like the union between the spirit and the flesh, were not natural but of another world. The evangelical "family" was itself an artificial union of men and women who called one another "brother" and "sister" but were unrelated by blood, a marriage of "orphans" not ordained by any earthly authority. The indifference displayed by evangelical congregations to disorderly sexual relations among their members may, in the end, be the unintended consequence of a feminized faith.

86. Record Book, Baptist Church of Warren, 26 October 1769, vol. 1, JHL.
87. Record Book, Seventh Day Baptist Church of Newport, 15 March 1730, NHS.
88. Parkes, "Sexual Morality and the Great Awakening," and Oberholzer, *Delinquent Saints*, p. 239.

Sin was a troublesome concept for evangelicals. Its very existence defied that promise of grace which, evangelicals hoped, had subdued if not defeated their carnal selves. The evangelical scheme provided for the transformation of sinners into saints, but when saints became sinners the illusion of sanctification was shattered. But backsliding was inevitable, and evangelicals were too well versed in Calvinist principles to expect the transfiguration of grace to be complete or eternal. More troublesome was the challenge sin posed to *communitas*. Individuals might slide back into corruption and be rescued by the repeated intercessions of the Holy Spirit, but the community of saints had a fragile existence that threatened to dissolve under the combined weight of individual sins. Special care had to be taken to ensure that the affective bonds holding the community together would not succumb to the extreme individualism of the evangelical ethos.

The exercise of church discipline was thus a highly sensitive and vital component of evangelical Protestantism in the years surrounding the Great Awakening. A close look at the various sins for which evangelical men and women were disciplined in the middle decades of the eighteenth century reveals the primacy of charity in the evangelical understanding of sin and its consequences. Sins of aversion, from contempt of church authority to sins against neighbors, represented by far the largest category in cases of church discipline in the period 1740–80. At bottom, many of these cases represent a reenactment of the bitter debates of the Awakening itself over the meaning of order and disorder in a world increasingly less sure of its institutional and ideological groundings. We have seen how evangelical men and women challenged their churches on precisely the same issues that initially drove Baptist and Separate churches out of the orthodox fold: lay preaching, ministerial qualifications, liberty of conscience in matters of doctrine, the right to secede from impure congregations, and so forth. Such lay challenges were in many ways an inevitable outgrowth of the premium placed on lay activism and individual autonomy within the evangelical order.

An underlying theme in this discussion has been the intimate connection between authority and speech after the Awakening. Words—especially slanderous words—occupied a special place in the evangelical war against disorder, for (as evangelicals learned in the revivals of the Great Awakening) speech had the power to subvert social relations and fracture the bonds of community. Although the number of discipline cases involving disorderly speech are not large, representing only about one-sixth of the total proportion of cases, they were among the most detailed and lengthy records in the church minutes. The case brought by John Ormsby and his wife against

Aaron Meach occupied page after page in the records of the Canterbury Separate Church, and to envision the entire church deliberating for hours, even days, the specifics of the case is to see how slander threatened the entire fabric of a community, not just the personal reputations of the aggrieved.

A striking feature of church discipline in the mid-eighteenth century is the extent to which it was applied equally to men and women. Roughly as many women as men were censured for sins against the community; 44 percent of those accused of "contempt of church authority" were women, while slightly less than 50 percent of all charges of slanderous or false speech were directed against female members (see note 54). When they opposed their covenanted communities over issues of community and institutional authority, evangelical men and women stood together as informed and articulate laity whose religious activism was not yet circumscribed by divisions of gender. Yet there were sharp and distinct associations between other categories of sin and the gender of the offender. Women were far more likely to be disciplined for sexual misconduct and sins against family/household, while men were disciplined in greater numbers for sins of avarice, fighting or quarreling with neighbors, and drunkenness. As neighbors, husbands and wives, servants and masters, producers and consumers, evangelical men and women temporarily abandoned the transcendent realm of sanctification and entered once again into the profane world. Gender was restored to the androgynous evangelical at the moment when he or she forfeited the liminal status conferred by sainthood. The sexual divisions observed in the sins committed by evangelicals in their secular capacities make a good deal of sense, given the different social and economic positions occupied by men and women in eighteenth-century New England. As participants in the market economy and associational life of their towns, men had more opportunities than did women to encounter their fellow communicants in adversarial situations. And as the caretakers of the family and the domestic sphere, women's sexual lives were under greater scrutiny than were men's.

To say that gender entered into the evangelical community when sin was committed is not to say that one gender was subordinated to the other in the discipline process. Although it might be tempting to argue that, as fornicators and disobedient wives, women saints reentered the patriarchal world of female submissiveness to male authority, such a conclusion would be misleading. For "authority" was not construed male in the evangelical church but was exercised jointly by men and women. The discipline process did not pit men against women, church officers against laity, but the androgynous quality of grace against the gendered nature of sin. Where sin was triumphant, grace failed and *communitas* dissolved. When evil was purged and the sinner restored to fellowship, *communitas* could once again emerge. The scenario was replayed over and over in the evangelical church in the middle decades of the eighteenth century, but such constant vigilance took its toll. Imperceptibly, by dribs and drabs, the androgynous essence of evangelical religion was eroded by repeated encounters with the profane world.

The relatively few cases dealing with sins of personal misconduct in the period 1730–80 prefigure the concern with moral character which would become the defining mark of church discipline in the postrevolutionary period. Charges of sexual promiscuity, drunkenness, and "disorderly" or "unchristian" character are important as harbingers of a trend increasingly evident over the course of the eighteenth century: that of investing men and women communicants with disorderly qualities signifying the instability of the individual character rather than the fragility of the larger community. The shift in the focus of church discipline from community to character opened the way for a more fundamentally gendered notion of sin to develop, one that located certain disorderly qualities in the feminine character and others in the male. Once gender was lodged firmly within the individual character, rather than in the contest between grace and sin, the way was clear for evangelicals to reconstruct their community along the conventional poles of masculinity and femininity. The beginnings of such a paradigmatic shift can be seen in the sporadic efforts of the evangelical churches to discipline fornicators, rogues, and drunkards in the decades immediately after the Awakening.

CHAPTER FOUR

"TO GROW UP INTO A STATE OF MANHOOD"

The Sexual Politics of Evangelicalism in Revolutionary America

As THE NEW ENGLAND COLONIES NEARED CRISIS with England in the 1760s and 1770s, the evangelical community stood poised on the cusp between two worlds, one existing above time and space, one grounded in the contingencies of history. The delicate balancing act that the churches had performed successfully for a half century between the competing demands of power and purity was upset, and the evangelical ethos was both politicized and historicized as the British imperial structure of church and state crumbled. Faced with the choice of maintaining their otherworldly stance or joining with their colonial brethren in common cause against Britain, the evangelical leadership chose rebellion. In so doing they compromised the very essence of the evangelical community.

From the vantage point of religious dissent, the American Revolution appears both more and less revolutionary. More, for dissenters not only wished to abolish the monarchy but the entire edifice of church and state which had long sanctioned legal oppression against religious outsiders, particularly Baptists (in both the North and the South). Less, for the decision to rebel was itself an act of renunciation, in which the most radical features of evangelicalism were sacrificed to the political ambitions of the dissenting community. Dissenters had first to make themselves more like New England's orthodox in order to challenge the orthodox on the vexing question of religious liberty. As we shall see, the surest way for dissenters to engage the Standing Order on their own terrain was to reorganize their polity along the model of the patriarchal household. Where renunciation was required, it was evangelical women who paid the price, while evangelical men reaped the civil benefits that came with patriotic service.

The story of how dissenters became patriots is a familiar tale, an almost archetypical reenactment of the Weberian evolution of a marginal religious society with charismatic origins to a rationalist, bureaucratic institution. Beginning in the 1760s with the establishment of the first Baptist college to train prospective ministers and the formation of the first regional association of Baptist churches, the Baptist community entered into a period of sustained institutional maturation. Translating secular political terms like "natural rights" and "liberty of conscience" into religious slogans, the Baptist order fought a well-orchestrated and ultimately successful campaign in the 1760s, 1770s, and 1780s to secure de facto relief from oppressive ministerial taxes and legal harassment, gaining in the process the recognition and respect of New England's orthodox religious establishment. The successful transformation of the dissenting community from a maligned, outsider sect to a respectable, mainstream denomination was, in this reading, a prototypical example of the more general success of the revolutionary effort in transforming the American colonies from a straggly provincial backwater to a national power. Just as the fledgling Baptist church joined the Standing Order as a legitimate ecclesiastical partner, so the United States assumed its rightful place among the community of nations in the early republican period.[1]

In McLoughlin's 1971 rendition, the parallels between the experience of the Baptists and the revolutionary cause are straightforward and direct, grounded institutionally in the denominational associations that sprang up in the late eighteenth century to spearhead the campaign for religious liberty. More recent attempts to link religious dissent with revolutionary protest focus on ideology rather than on formal politics. John Brooke, for example, sees in the religious culture of the Separate Baptists the ideological roots of a world view that, in the hands of the patriots, would become associated with Lockean liberalism. In their embrace of pietistic individualism and rejection of traditional notions of covenant, the Separate Baptists heralded the advent of a new conception of society which privileged the autonomous individual over the moral community. In his words, the "explosion of New Light Separatism engendered by the Awakening, finding stable institutional form in the Separate Baptists, brought the priorities of Lockean voluntary contractualism directly to bear on local society. Breaking away

1. William McLoughlin, *New England Dissent, 1630–1833: The Baptists and the Separation of Church and State* (Cambridge, Mass., 1971); "The Role of Religion in the Revolution: Liberty of Conscience and Cultural Cohesion in the New Nation," in *Essays on the American Revolution*, ed. Stephen G. Kurtz and James H. Hutson (Chapel Hill, N.C., 1973); and the essays collected in *Soul Liberty: The Baptists' Struggle in New England, 1630–1833* (Hanover, N.H., 1991).

from orthodoxy in a swirling series of local rebellions—moral insurgencies—
the Lockean impulses of New Light separatist dissent would reach their
most powerful political expression in the constitutionalist movement of
1776–80."[2] Whether we locate the protorevolutionary potential of religious
dissent in the institutional forms of denominational politics, in the theological premises of the Great Awakening, or in the rhetorical innovations of revivalist preachers, the consensus seems to be that there was a direct and immediate link between religious and political dissent in eighteenth-century
America.[3] So powerful was the confluence of evangelicalism and political
dissent by 1776 that a full-blown "Christian republicanism," as one historian
calls it, came to dominate the political landscape for the remainder of the
eighteenth century.[4]

It is easy to misread the enthusiastic endorsements of the war cause
emanating from the evangelical press as confirmation of the "liberal" pre-
disposition of the dissenting societies, as I believe McLoughlin and Brooke
have. There is, to be sure, abundant evidence that the Baptist leadership, in
particular, did respond to the revolutionary settlement of the 1780s in decidedly Lockean terms. Declaring this to be "an age when mankind are regain-
ing their natural rights, and assuming the privilege of thinking and acting
for themselves," the circular letters of the Warren Association in these times
celebrated the American Revolution in language indistinguishable from

2. John L. Brooke, *The Heart of the Commonwealth: Society and Political Culture in Worcester
County, Massachusetts, 1713–1861* (New York, 1989), p. 67.

3. Harry S. Stout, *The New England Soul: Preaching and Religious Culture in Colonial New
England* (New York, 1986), and "Religion, Communications, and the Ideological Origins of the
American Revolution," *WMQ*, 3d ser., 34 (1977): 519–41; Donald Weber, *Rhetoric and History in
Revolutionary New England* (New York, 1988); Rhys Isaac, *The Transformation of Virginia, 1740–
1790* (Chapel Hill, N.C., 1982). This same link has been made, with reference to orthodox religious
groups, by Patricia Bonomi in her *Under the Cope of Heaven: Religion, Society, and Politics in
Colonial America* (New York, 1986). Jon Butler has raised a dissenting voice to this general consensus; see his "Enthusiasm Described and Decried: The Great Awakening as Interpretive Fiction," *Journal of American History* 69 (1982–83): 305–25.

4. Mark A. Noll, "The American Revolution and Protestant Evangelicalism," *Journal of
Interdisciplinary History* 23 (1993): 615–38. Noll points out that this synthesis altered not only the
way Americans thought about their government but the way they thought about God and *his*
government. The migration of languages and symbols from one sphere to another was reversed
after independence was secured: "Religious language put to the use of politics turned back to alter
religion," p. 630. For particularly successful attempts to address the impact of the Revolution on
religion, see Nathan O. Hatch, *The Democratization of American Christianity* (New Haven, Conn.,
1989); Alan Taylor, *Liberty Men and Great Proprietors: The Revolutionary Settlement on the Maine
Frontier, 1760–1820* (Chapel Hill, N.C., 1990); Randolph Roth, *Democratic Dilemma: Religion,
Reform, and the Social Order in the Connecticut River Valley of Vermont, 1750–1850* (New York, 1987);
and Jon Butler, *Awash in a Sea of Faith: Christianizing the American People* (Cambridge, Mass.,
1990).

that of the most fervent patriots. "The American Revolution," the association proclaimed in 1793, "is wholly built upon this doctrine that all men are born with an equal right to what Providence gave them, and that all righteous government is founded in compact or covenant, which is equally binding upon the officers and members of each community."[5] Yet while orthodox Congregationalists may have made the transition to revolutionary patriots with little or no disruption to their religious ethos or pastoral responsibilities, such political commitments marked a decisive departure from both for the Baptists. For in celebrating the triumph of political unification, the evangelical clergy also celebrated the death of an older ideal, one that found its highest expression in the communalism of the individual covenanted church. The commitment to "integration" or "assimilation" with mainstream religion and society adopted by the evangelical order in the postrevolutionary years stands in stark contrast to the isolationism of the early churches from worldly concerns.[6]

McLoughlin's claim that "not surprisingly, the Baptists came to identify their own search for liberty and power with that of the emerging nation" is, on the contrary, very surprising indeed.[7] Dissenters, no less than many American patriots, were deeply suspicious of the centralization of power at whatever level—the church or the state.[8] The picture drawn by McLoughlin and others of steady and generally uncontested progress on the part of reli-

5. *Minutes of the Warren Association . . . 1793* (Boston: Manning and Loring, 1793), p. 9; ibid., *. . . 1783* (n.p., n.d.), p. 6.

6. William McLoughlin, "Massive Civil Disobedience as a Baptist Tactic in 1773," *American Quarterly* 21 (1969): 710–27. While I agree that these terms are useful in describing dissenters' political position vis à vis the religious establishment, I would reverse McLoughlin's claim that the path followed by the Baptists was from integration to separatism in the eighteenth century. He argues that the Baptists prior to 1750 sought to assimilate with the Standing Order, whereas from 1750 to 1800 they adopted a more pluralistic approach. Our differences derive from our sources; if one looks only at the formal, public political activity of the Baptist clergy, then separation was the goal in the revolutionary era. If, on the other hand, one considers Baptist ecclesiology and polity (how they practiced their faith and organized their churches), then an integrationist stance is observable in the 1770s and 1780s.

7. McLoughlin, *New England Dissent*, 1:438. Noll has argued that the convergence of evangelicalism and republicanism in the revolutionary period was by no means "natural" but rather an entirely unexpected phenomenon that deserves close study, which he has begun to provide in his article "The American Revolution and Protestant Evangelicalism."

8. The conflict between federalists and antifederalists, for example, over the limits of central government was replicated within the Baptist community between those societies who favored joining a federated association of churches and those who refused to surrender the principle of congregational autonomy. The strong and repeated assertions of the "independency" of individual congregations against the interrogatory powers claimed by the various regional Baptist associations in the 1780s (peaking, significantly, in 1788) surely drew on (and fed into) the well-spring of resentment against centralized power of any sort generated by the federal Constitution.

gious dissenters toward mainstream denominationalism obscures the very real opposition such developments engendered.[9] Similarly, Brooke's depiction of the evolution of Separate Baptists from radical dissenters to staunch constitutionalists posits an unbroken continuity in world view which belies the sharp contrast between the corporate culture of the Baptists in the 1740s and that of the 1780s. However committed to the cause of political unification and Lockean liberalism the Baptists may have been in the 1770s and 1780s, such secular entanglements represented a radical break with the evangelical ethos as shaped by the revivals of the First Great Awakening.[10]

Women are conspicuously absent from accounts of institutional development and political awakening—indeed, they are rarely to be found in the byways of Baptist church history after 1770. But, in an ironic twist familiar to feminist scholars, gender is everywhere. As an organizing principle for social perception, gender was deeply implicated as evangelicals became political insiders rather than religious outsiders. Far from being just a story of how the evangelical leadership came to embrace the "sacred cause of liberty" and in so doing transformed themselves from uncompromising separatists into devout patriots, the politicization of religious dissenters in the revolutionary era came about through a fundamental renegotiation of gender relations within the evangelical community. The political capacity of the evangelical clergy, in other words, did not (could not) fully emerge until they had essentially defeminized the evangelical polity and reclaimed for themselves a more masculine identity. Their story has larger resonances for the student

---

9. See, for example, the letter from the Second Baptist Church of Ashford to the Warren Association in 1788 withdrawing its membership on the grounds that "it would interfere with the Independency of Churches" (Record Book, Second Baptist Church of Ashford, 24 August 1788, CSL); or the indignant refusal of the Westerly Baptist Church to allow investigators from the Warren Association to inquire into a dispute between the congregation and its pastor, similarly protesting "Other Churches Intermeddling with their Discipline or Intruding on the Independency of that Church." Record Book, Westerly Baptist Church, 13 April 1788, CSL.

10. In contrast to the Baptists, who at first were reluctant patriots, nationalist sentiments were not at all uncommon among more evangelically minded Congregationalists and Presbyterians in the revolutionary period; as Russell Richy has noted, "We have considerable evidence that many in the evangelical camp . . . worked assiduously during this same period, after the Revolution and particularly after the Constitutional Convention, to reassociate, not dissociate, religion and nation." Richy, *Early American Methodism* (Bloomington, Ind., 1991), p. 34. See also John Berens, *Providence and Patriotism in Early America* (Charlottesville, Va., 1978). While Richey may be right about the nationalist proclivities of mainstream denominations, his claim that the association of evangelicalism with individualism and an otherworldly sense of community is a "misguided" assumption does not ring true for Baptists and Separates. In fact, as R. Laurence Moore points out, American religious groups have always been profoundly ambivalent toward the political, displaying both an aversion and enthusiasm for formal politics which defies easy categorization. See his *Religious Outsiders and the Making of Americans* (New York, 1986).

of revolutionary political culture. Conflating femininity and marginality, the evangelical clergy echoed the implicit message of a revolutionary age in which dependence in all its forms—religious and familial, as well as geopolitical—was denounced as effeminate. Their struggle to rise above the disabilities of a feminized faith suggests the degree to which gender subordination was implicated in political discourse in the "age of democratic revolution."

"Becoming Important in the Eye of the Civil Powers": The Transformation of the Evangelical Church

No longer an *ecclesia* in the original sense of the word (which, as the Danbury Baptist Association reminded its members in 1801, meant to "call out of, separate from, or set apart"),[11] suspended outside of time and history, the evangelical church came fully to embrace the orthodox congregational model it had once rejected. No longer positioned outside (and against) the world, the evangelical church was now fully *of* the world. As the Warren Association of Baptist churches put it in their *Sentiments and Plan* of union for the churches in 1767, the desired goal of the Baptist community was no longer maintaining its isolation from the corruptions of the secular world but rather "becoming important in the eye of the civil powers."[12] "We wish," declared the "very fashionable" Thomas Baldwin, elder of Boston's cosmopolitan Second Baptist Church, "to make our denomination respectable as well as the rest."[13] The grumblings of a few die-hard primitivists such as Elder Young of Smithfield, who complained that "it has got so far already as scarcely to do for a common Illiterate Minister [like himself] to preach," were brushed aside in the general enthusiasm for reform.[14]

"Becoming important" in the eyes of the world meant, first and foremost, adopting the dominant cultural metaphor of the eighteenth-century church

11. *Minutes of the Danbury Association . . . 1801* (n.p., n.d.), p. 7.

12. *The Sentiments and Plan of the Warren Association* (Germantown, Pa.,: Christopher Sower, 1769), p. 3. Interestingly, the association retreated from this rather naked assertion of the evangelical community's need for civil recognition fourteen years later, when it "Resolved, that the paragraph in the plan of this Association—'And becoming important, in the eye of the civil powers' . . . be erased." *Minutes of the Warren Association . . . 1781* (Providence, R.I., 1781), p. 5.

13. As quoted in Hatch, *Democratization of American Christianity*, p. 94. Hatch's account of the encounter between Baldwin and the "rustic" preacher Elias Smith is very revealing; when Smith was called to pastor the Woburn Baptist Church in 1798, Baldwin tried to persuade him to put aside his plain attire and dress "in fashionable black, a large three cornered hat, and black silk gloves." A shocked Smith asked if the Baptists "were going back to the place from whence we came out[?]" Baldwin replied with the plea for respectability quoted above.

14. *The Literary Diary of Ezra Stiles*, ed. Franklin B. Dexter (New York, 1901), 1:49.

and state, that of the patriarchal household. In 1776 the Warren Association
directed its member churches to undertake a census for the first time; significantly, whole families, not individual converts, were to be counted. Each
society was requested to "collect an exact account of the families which
belong thereto, and of the number of souls in each family . . . that it may be
known how many are against the ecclesiastical oppressions which have long
been practiced in this country."[15] New covenants adopted in the late eighteenth century reaffirmed this assertion of the family unit as the cornerstone
of the church; the Second Baptist Church of Ashford, organized in 1774,
reported to the Warren Association that "about Eighteen Heads of families
have entered into Agreement to encourage the Preaching of the Gospel
amongst us by the Baptist Ministry."[16] By elevating the family over the
"souls" of individual members as the foundation on which the church was to
be built, Baptists rejected the earlier evangelical dictum that only those who
had, in the scriptural phrase, "left fathers and mothers, brothers and sisters"
could enter the kingdom of God. Now, members were told, the "chain of
duties" binding parents and children, husbands and wives, masters and
servants, rulers and ruled, had to be preserved for the greater good of the
church. The Danbury Association admonished its members, in effect, to
consecrate these domestic ties:

> That parents may be ready to do the duties which God requires of them
> towards their children; that children may be ready to do their duty to their
> parents; that husbands and wives may be ready to perform their relative
> duties to each other; that ministers and people, servants and masters,
> rulers and ruled may be ready to perform what God has enjoined upon
> them in his Word. . . . Should the chain of duties be broken by any one's
> regarding iniquity in their heart, our churches may be tossed to and frow
> like the Heathen Mariner's ship with a Jonah on board.[17]

Fifty years earlier, the main enemies had been Satan and the corruption of
one's own heart; now disorderly domestic relations threatened the welfare of
the church.

   This new preoccupation with external order and government was accom-

---

15. *Minutes of the Proceedings of the Warren Association, 1776* (Boston: Thomas & John Fleet,
1776), p. 5.

16. Letter from Ashford First Baptist Church to Warren Association, 28 August 1774, Backus
Papers, Box 10, ANTS. For a recent study of how the communal ethos was transformed into a
familial one in another dissenting community, see Beverly Prior Smaby, *The Transformation of
Moravian Bethlehem: From Communal Mission to Family Economy* (Philadelphia, 1988).

17. *Minutes of the Danbury Association . . . 1802* (n.p., n.d.), pp. 5–6; see also ibid. . . . *1793* (n.p.,
n.d.), p. 6.

panied by a new distaste for the emotionalism that had characterized the Great Awakening. "It is to be feared," warned the Warren Association in 1790, "there are too many who place the whole of religion in certain feelings, and have their goodness by fits and starts. . . . It should be the Study of the Christian to be useful in the Church of Christ, to promote the welfare and happiness of society; by which he will glorify God, honour and recommend religion."[18] The act of conversion now became a largely utilitarian gesture, designed to "promote the welfare" of church and society, rather than a sublimely personal religious experience. The concept of the "new birth" was not entirely discarded; the Warren Association affirmed in 1788 that "believers are commanded to put on this new man," but by this they meant "not to put it into them in some mystical sense, but to put it on evidently in sentiment, temper, and conduct."[19] Such unabashedly pragmatic sentiments confirm that character had become more important than soul in the evangelical ethos, as Richard Rabinowitz has recently argued.[20] And a godly character, it was equally clear, was most properly formed within the family circle, under the salutary influence of pious mothers and fathers. "Our pious predecessors," the Warren Association lectured its member churches in 1785, "were justly distinguished for walking with God in their families, and paying strict attention to the education and morals of the youth. Nor is any part of practical religion of greater moment; especially as the character of the *rising generation* will, in great measure, depend on a proper discharge of these obligations."[21]

At times, this renewed interest in the family came dangerously close to embracing the Congregationalist model of baptism and conversion. Since the adoption of the Half-Way Covenant in 1662, New England's Congregational churches had been moving steadily (though not without dissension) toward a vision of grace as a gift to be passed from generation to generation, through the intercessory efforts of the family. Baptists explicitly rejected the notion of the "Abrahamic covenant" in which the elect traced their heritage back to the biblical "father-figure" of Abraham and which was the theological justification for the practice of infant baptism among Congregationalists. Rather, only adult men and women, unfettered by considerations of family, were appropriate candidates for conversion. In the late eighteenth century, however, a new sense of continuity between the generations of converts

18. *Minutes of the Warren Association . . . 1790* (Boston: Samuel Hall, 1790), pp. 7–10.
19. Ibid. . . . *1788* (Boston: John W. Allen, 1788), p. 9.
20. Richard Rabinowitz, *The Spiritual Self in Everyday Life: The Transformation of Personal Religious Experience in Nineteenth-Century New England* (Boston, 1989).
21. *Minutes of the Warren Association . . . 1785* (n.p., n.d.), p. 5.

began to surface in the didactic literature distributed by the Baptist clergy. "Our *families*," exhorted the Warren Association in 1785, "should be so many *nurseries* for the Church of Christ." "The notion of *federal holiness*, and that our offspring, by virtue of any connection with us, have a right to the special privileges of God's house," the association hastened to add, "we reject." Nevertheless, parents held a special responsibility to help their offspring "in acquiring whatever shall tend to render them extensively useful in their day and generation."[22]

Revivals themselves became family affairs in the 1770s and 1780s. A powerful Baptist revival swept through rural New England in the war years, netting over two thousand new converts in the year 1780 alone, according to the enthusiastic Isaac Backus. As church after church succumbed to the fires of revival, a new pattern of conversion became apparent. Rather than individual professions of faith in glorious defiance of family and friends, the family itself now occupied center stage in the drama of regeneration. In Wilbraham, Massachusetts, Backus saw "the hearts of fathers . . . turned to the children, and children to the fathers." In Meredith, New Hampshire, entire families were brought to submission. "The wife, when she saw her husband going forward, began to weep to think she was not worthy to go with him; in like manner the husband the wife, the parent the child, the children the parent." Spiritual conviction flowed through the arteries of the evangelical family, connecting household to household into one vast "family of God." By reinvigorating the evangelical family, the great revival of 1779– 80 also redeemed the new nation. "This revival of religion was undoubtedly a great means of saving this land from foreign invasion, and from ruin by internal corruption," Backus proclaimed.[23]

The fate of the family and of the nation were explicitly linked in the epistolary writings of the evangelical clergy. A spate of circular letters stressing the importance of maintaining "family government" among the faithful issued from the presses of the various denominational associations in the 1770s and 1780s.[24] This heightened sense of the need to maintain strict order

22. Ibid. . . . , pp. 6–7.

23. Isaac Backus, *A History of New England, with Particular Reference to the Denomination of Christians Called Baptists*, 2d ed. (Newtown, Mass., 1871), 2:279–80 and 265.

24. The first missive devoted to the subject of family government was issued by the Warren Association in 1771; thereafter the topic was featured regularly in circular letters prepared by the Warren, Danbury, and Stonington associations; see the *Minutes of the Warren Association . . . 1771* (Boston: John Boyles, 1771), p. 6; *Minutes of the Stonington Association . . . 1772 to 1785* (n.p., n.d.), p. 16; *Minutes of the Proceedings of the Baptist Association of Warren, 1775* (Norwich, Conn.: Robertsons and Trumbull, 1775), p. 7; *Minutes of the Proceedings of the Warren Association . . . 1776*, p. 5; *Minutes of the Warren Association . . . 1782* (Providence, R.I.: Carter, 1782), p. 5; ibid. . . . *1785* (n.p.,

within families was one element in a larger campaign to strengthen the "government" of church and state more generally; and indeed, the two processes were seen to be inextricable. The Danbury Baptist Association stated bluntly in 1797 that "the government of Church and State must depend on family government."[25] In its annual meeting the Warren Association in 1785 heard the case of a controversy in the New-Salem church, where "differences have subsisted for a considerable time respecting family government and the government of the Church." Such "disorders," the association concluded, "have so long and so extensively prevailed, that an entire reformation is not to be expected at once." It then prepared a circular letter deploring the neglect of family government which concluded, "When children and servants are allowed to conduct themselves in a lawless way in *private life*, and they have transgressed the laws of the *family* with impunity, we *can not expect them* to become good citizens, or friendly to *good government in civil society*."[26]

Good government, clearly, depended on the maintenance of proper order within the family. And it was the father as head of the family who was explicitly charged with overseeing the government of both the family and (as we shall see) the church. The powers that devolved on the father were broad indeed. "Every head of a family should exercise the characters of prophet, priest and king in his family," the Stonington Association declared in its *Sentiments and Plan* in 1787. "As a king, and governor in his family, like the father of the faithful, he ought to command his household, and to restrain them from following the superfluous and vain fashions of the children of the world. . . . Every faithful head of a family will endeavour . . . to restrain his family, and all under his care, from associating, keeping company, and spending their precious time in the frolicking chambers, with the giddy, irreligious rabble."[27] The ultimate source of the father's authority lay, of course, in the resemblance between the head of the family and God, the head of the church. "Every head of a family should represent the Great

---

n.d.), pp. 4–7. Renewed concern over family government is also evident in the Baptist periodicals of the early nineteenth century, which printed (and reprinted) articles with such titles as "On Neglecting Parental Restraint," *ABMMI* 3 (1821): 98–100; "On the Influence of Parental Character," *ABMMI* 5 (1825): 335–37; "On Family Worship," *ABMMI* 5 (1825): 334–35; "A Father's Advice to His Children," *BM* 3 (1811): 21–22; "The Importance of Piety in Parents and Guardians of Youth," *MMM* 1 (1803): 160–61.

25. *Minutes of the Danbury Baptist Association . . . 1797* (Hartford, Conn., Elisha Babcock, 1797), p. 7.

26. *Minutes of the Warren Association . . . 1785*, pp. 4–7.

27. *Sentiments and Plan of the Stonington Association* (New London, Conn., 1787), pp. 7–10.

Parent of the universe, who provides for his numerous dependants, and most reasonably expects subjection to his authority."[28] Or as the *Massachusetts Missionary Magazine* put it in 1803: "As every private family is a part of the numerous family of God; and, as pious parents harmonize with the great and good Parent of the Universe in affection, interest, and pursuit, they will like him, seek the permanent felicity of their families."[29] Supreme in his earthly kingdom, the evangelical father thus basked in the reflected glory of God the Father, on whom he patterned himself.

From adopting the language of patriarchy to embracing the cause of political unification was a fairly small step. The transition from family to nation was inherent in the political rhetoric of the revolutionary movement, in which familial metaphors helped prepare Americans for separation from the mother country. But whereas secular patriots exploited the analogy of family and state to justify their adolescent rebellion against both, evangelicals grounded their patriotism in filial piety.[30] The Groton Union Baptist Conference endorsed the principle of confederation in 1799 in both familial and nationalistic terms. "The division among the Baptists, has for a long time been a matter of grief to many," it declared, "and truly, union is a desirable thing. . . . It is grand and pleasing; it makes nations powerful, and families delightful. Union, brethren, is our topic; it is the image of heaven, & the picture of paradise."[31] Strong as a nation, harmonious as a family, the evangelical church would become, in this view, the very "image" of divine government. Similar analogies had earlier filtered down to the rank-and-file through sermons that, in the words of the Baptist elder Job Seamans in 1774, elaborated the common experiences of "Nation Church fammily and Private Persons" in God's providential plan for the "American Israel."[32]

Familial metaphors thus became the chief idiom through which the evangelical community envisioned its role in revolutionary America. A kind

28. *Minutes of the Warren Association . . . 1785*, p. 6.

29. "The Importance of Piety in Parents and Guardians of Youth," *MMM* 1 (1803): 160. The image of God as parent also recurs in the correspondence of churches to the Warren Association in this period; see reference to God as "the great head of the whole Family in & Earth" in the letter of the Warren Baptist Church to the Association, 8 [n.d.] 1788, Backus Papers, Box 13, ANTS.

30. On the Revolution as adolescent rebellion, see Catherine Albanese, *Sons of the Father: The Civil Religion of the American Revolution* (Philadelphia, 1976); Melvin Yazawa, *From Colonies to Commonwealth: Familial Ideology and the Beginnings of the American Republic* (Baltimore, 1985).

31. *Minutes of the Groton Union Conference . . . 1799* (Norwich, Conn.: John Sterry, 1799), p. 7.

32. Diary, Selected Portions (trans. and annotated by William R. Miller), 15 December 1774, Job Seamans Papers, ABHS. The term "American Israel" was a commonplace phrase in sermons delivered during the revolutionary crisis; see Nathan O. Hatch, *The Sacred Cause of Liberty: Republican Thought and the Millennium in Revolutionary New England* (New Haven, Conn., 1977), and *Minutes of the Stonington Association . . . 1772 to 1785*, p. 29.

of masculine self-fashioning can be glimpsed in the epistolary and sermonic literature of the late eighteenth century as the evangelical clergy urged the faithful to take up arms against the British Antichrist. Once "brides of Christ," evangelicals now became "soldiers of Christ" who "would fight manfully 'the good fight of faith'" in a striking reversal of gender identity.[33] Soldiers afield, evangelical men were patriarchs at home, administering family government with one hand and civil government with the other. But, as any New England son knew, there were dangers inherent in the patriarchal system, even for those for whom the system was created. Males who were not yet heads of households faced an uncertain economic and political future; death could interfere in the orderly transmission of power from one generation of males to the next, fathers could lose their land, or sons could be disinherited. For male evangelicals whose patriarchal pretensions did not yet match their legal status, the late eighteenth century was a precarious moment. The path from second son to New England patriarch was not a smooth one, as the fledgling Baptist community in New England learned again and again.

"Turn'd naked into the wide World": The Paradox of Patriarchy

Patriotic service did not immediately translate into civil recognition for New England's dissenting community. In the decades preceding the War for Independence, the Standing Order directed many legal and political harassments against the growing power and size of the Baptist community. Isaac Backus' *History of New England*, commissioned specifically by the Warren Association to chronicle the misfortunes of the Baptist denomination, documents cases of imprisonment for nonpayment of ecclesiastical taxes, seizure of property and goods, public mockery of Baptist rituals, and even physical abuse of Baptist men (and women). The prosecution continued apace throughout the 1770s. Eighteen men were imprisoned in Warwick in 1774 for nonpayment of taxes, and the minister of the Baptist church in Haverhill was subject to physical abuse by enemies in that town: "A stone, large enough to kill him, was cast through a window near his head, where he was in bed. And his enemies went so far as to cut off his horse's mane and tail in the night."[34]

What is most significant about these trials is that they were essentially squabbles between the older son of New England Congregationalism and

33. Letter from the Stonington Association to the Warren Association, 20 October 1784, Backus Papers, Box 12, ANTS.

34. Backus, *A History of New England*, 2:164.

an upstart brother who lay claim to a larger share of ecclesiastical authority. In the revivals of the Great Awakening, as dissenters clashed with orthodox Puritans over the boundaries of religious life, evangelicals had assumed a feminine persona, privileging the sensuous and the sublime over hierarchy and reason. In the late eighteenth century, however, evangelicals fought with their Congregational brethren over their respective positions within the hierarchy, battling to gain a higher rung. At stake were the privileges of patriarchy—civil and legal power, the deference of dependents, and eventual assumption of the mantle of household headship—and the dangers of disinheritance. Nowhere was the battle phrased more starkly than in Ashfield, Massachusetts, where the Baptist community feared it would be driven from town "naked" like an illegitimate brother if it failed to gain a political foothold.

In Ashfield, the Baptists should have been secure. The Baptist church had been the first religious society organized in the town, predating its Congregational competitor by some two years. Yet, according to an account left by a Baptist, in 1763 the Congregationalist minority "over power'd us [the Baptists] in Voting" and succeeded in imposing uniform taxes on all the town's inhabitants for the support of their church.[35] When the Baptists refused to pay the tax, the civil courts confiscated their property. The Elder of the congregation, Ebenezer Smith, complained that the town sold "the best of my Home Lot; and then on to my brethren till they had sold about 400 acres of the baptist Lands for the payment of their minister and for their meeting House." One piece of property, he continued bitterly, that was appraised at 115 pounds was sold at a stupendous loss for less than two pounds sterling, "and so all the Rest at a very small part of the Value."[36] In the spring of 1770 the Baptist community in Ashfield petitioned the General Court of Massachusetts for redress, complaining that their lands "were set up at Publick Vandue, and sold but for a very Small part of their Vallue." "We are not only Deprived of Liberty of Conscience," they protested, but "we Are also in a great measure Disinherited and in a fare way to be turn'd naked into the wide World."[37]

What stands out from the Baptists' account of these trials is the extent to which they pursued their rightful "inheritance" through political and legal channels. Rather than hold themselves aloof from the corruption of secular

35. "A Breaf account of the first rise increase and sufferings of the Baptist Church of Christ at Ashfield," by Chileab Smith, 1769, Backus Papers, Box 8, ANTS.

36. Letter from Ebenezer Smith to Samuel Sennet, 2 June 1772, Backus Papers, Box 9, ANTS.

37. Petition of the Baptists in Ashfield to the General Court, 29 May 1770, Backus Papers, Box 8, ANTS.

politics and assert their spiritual superiority as the Elect, as we might expect a similarly beleaguered Baptist congregation to have done in the 1740s, the Ashfield Baptist Church engaged their religious rivals over the spoils of power: land and votes. After being "over power'd" at the polls, the dissenters faced being "turn'd naked into the world." Such a fate was to be avoided by asserting the political power of the majority, petitioning the higher authorities to intervene on the Baptists' behalf, and contesting the seizure of goods and land in court.

More was involved in the Baptists' cry against "disinheritance" than the threat of physical ruin. Underlying the material crisis represented by the loss of land and goods was a much deeper fear of communal disinheritance—the fear of being cut off from community and place, for these were no longer dissociated in the evangelical mentality. The reassertion of a territorial notion of the church, repudiated by the itinerants of the Great Awakening, can be seen in the efforts of the Ashfield Baptists to define their society as the legitimate representative of the town's faithful. As historians have noted, the cultural ideal of inheritance seemed increasingly vulnerable to ideological and social reformulation in the years preceding the Revolution.[38] For the evangelical community, the problem of disinheritance was perhaps even more acute, for its status as a member of the ecclesiastical family of New England was uncertain.

The established Congregational church in Ashfield was equally determined to deny civil recognition to its religious rival. Town officials looted Baptist homes and shops in an effort to unmask the radical vestiges of evangelicalism, including furtive meetings for worship held behind closed doors, breaking the Sabbath, and convening secret assemblies "in the woods" for ostensibly religious ends. Confirmation of the subversive nature of Baptist worship seemed at hand when a small amount of mercury (a substance used in the manufacture of paper money) was found in the shop of a leading dissenter, Chileab Smith. The charge of counterfeiting was the *pièce de résistance* in the orthodox offensive, revealing the dissenters themselves to be "false specie"—religious imposters. Whether true or not, these charges carried significant symbolic weight as the town's orthodox sought to identify the Baptist order with communal subversion. In manufacturing and distributing false currency, the Baptists were accused of corrupting the medium of exchange between members of the community; in holding "secret" religious services in their shops they transformed the workplace from a public arena

38. See Gordon Wood's "Rhetoric and Reality in the American Revolution," *WMQ*, 3d ser., 23 (1966): 3–32, for a discerning discussion of how fears over the precariousness of inheritance undergirded the revolutionaries' frenzied and seemingly irrational rhetoric.

for the exchange of communal resources into a private sanctuary; in breaking the Sabbath, they undermined the communal organization of time into profane and sacred segments; and in "carrying out into the woods" provisions sufficient for the conduct of "their pretence of Religious worship," they moved the site of worship from sacred to profane space. Such transgressions warranted the harshest punishments available to the community—the alienation of private property and goods.[39]

Though the charges leveled against the Baptists were, on the surface, patently absurd, their opponents accurately perceived the ground on which the battle between dissent and orthodoxy would be joined. Baptist insistence on political recognition was met by a counteroffensive that placed the dissenters outside the pale of the religious establishment altogether. Whether the Baptists really worshiped "in the woods" or not, the woods represent an apt metaphor for the kind of unconsecrated space favored in the evangelical style of worship. "Breaking" the Sabbath, moreover, was precisely the intent of the original evangelists of the Great Awakening who eschewed traditional liturgical forms. To their enemies, the Baptists of Ashfield had never left the disorders of revivalism behind as they pretended; rather, sincere enthusiasts had become hypocritical imposters. Every effort of the dissenting community to move beyond their otherworldly origins was met by orthodox determination to put them back in their place. No wonder the Baptists of Ashfield feared being "turn'd naked into the wide world." More would be required of the evangelical community than pious invocations of the sacred duty of family government for them to be accorded the full privileges of orthodoxy.

"Cutt off from the Church": Women and Church Governance

The language of patriarchy which evangelicals drew on to construct an alternative model of community was reinforced in practice by the adoption, beginning in the 1770s and 1780s, of a bureaucratic edifice within each church which in large measure replicated the hierarchical ordering of society outside the church. The first step in the bureaucratization of the churches was to determine precisely who belonged and who did not; the haphazard record keeping of the early years was replaced by more rigorous accounting procedures.[40] In some cases, the accounting impulse extended back into a church's

39. Narrative of Chileab Smith, 1771, Backus Papers, RIHS.
40. The Fairfield-Stratfield Baptist Church voted in 1784 that "Nehemiah Gruman, John Staples, John Edwards, Sam'll Mallitt, Abel Curtis should serve as a committee to take a list of all

past as its congregation sought to recapture its own history. The Warren Association recommended in 1793 that each member church "appoint one or more of their members, to collect an account of the time and manner of the constitution of each Church, and when their ministers were ordained; with any revivals of religion among them."[41] This renewed sense of history is yet another indication of how far the evangelical community had traveled from its liminal origins, from a community existing outside of time to one with historical purpose.

The most vigorous efforts at improving record keeping occurred in the area of church discipline. Almost without exception, the Baptist churches of New England instituted standing committees in the late eighteenth and early nineteenth centuries to handle discipline matters. Whereas, in the past, ad hoc delegations of men and women had been appointed by the collective membership to investigate rumors of impropriety on a case-by-case basis, now standing committees (of men only) were charged with the responsibility of reporting all breaches of conduct directly to the pastor, who alone was empowered to call a general meeting of the church to decide the issue.[42] In part, this procedure was a response to the tremendous increase in church membership during these years and the difficulty of monitoring the conduct of far-flung parishoners. The Tiverton Baptist Church, "desirous of Knowing that their conversation & conduct be as it becometh the Gospel of Christ," appointed a committee in 1785 to serve as "Constant or continual Messengers of the Ch. unto such of the Brethren and Sisters as Live nearest to them respectively."[43]

One by one, those elements of the evangelical liturgy which celebrated the collective power of the laity succumbed to the bureaucratic impulse. The Providence Baptist Church appointed a committee in 1798 to "prepare some method to be laid before the next Church meeting as to the most reliable mode of reviving our Singing." The committee's response was, not surprisingly, to recommend the establishment of another committee; it urged at the next meeting that "a number of the Members of the Church Qualified to conduct the Musick should convene in the Choiresters seat, in order to take the lead."[44] By 1816 the Second Baptist Church of Newport found it expedi-

the Names of our parishoners for the present year." Record Book, Fairfield-Stratfield Baptist Church, 28 February 1784, CSL.

41. *Minutes of the Warren Association . . . 1793*, p. 7.

42. See, for instance, the records of the Westerly Baptist Church, 8 September 1797, RIHS; and the Warren Baptist Church, April 1805, JHL.

43. Record Book, First Baptist Church of Tiverton, 26 May 1785, RIHS.

44. Record Book, First Baptist Church of Providence, 23 August 1798, RIHS.

ent to regularize their musical practices; they appointed three influential brethren to form a committee to "superintend the concerns of the chh. as it respects conducting the singing of publick worship."[45] Other churches similarly appointed select groups of brethren to serve as "leaders in singing."[46]

This attempt to formalize what had previously been a spontaneous expression of religious feeling on the part of the congregation is indicative of the evangelical community's retreat from the more flexible and individualistic features of its earlier liturgical style. The introduction of such bureaucratic reforms seriously undermined the ability of the laity as a whole to shape the institution in their own image. The delegation of large chunks of church governance to standing committees effectively rechanneled power away from the membership as a body to leading brethren within the congregation, and finally to the pastor as the ultimate head of the evangelical household. Casting aside the more egalitarian title "elder," Baptist ministers began to assume the exalted title of "reverend" as they acquired a college education and a professional demeanor.[47] In this hierarchical restructuring, women became almost entirely disenfranchised from formal participation in church politics. The tradition of sexual equality which grew out of the Great Awakening was the inevitable victim of the transformation of the evangelical church into a "household" in which men ruled over dependent women and children.

This steady, quiet retreat of the evangelical community from its commitment to sexual egalitarianism in the late eighteenth century is a discouraging story. The immediate losers were, obviously enough, women—though (as I will argue) the community itself lost something vital in the process. Women's loss of status within the church is most evident in the political realm, where they experienced a striking curtailment of their institutional capacities. The process by which women were disenfranchised from church polity is difficult to recreate, because it occurred between the lines of official church records. No policy excluding women from voting to elect or dismiss pastors was ever enacted, for instance, but after 1790 ministers were (with few exceptions) chosen by men only. No decision to remove women from disci-

45. Record Book, Second Baptist Church of Newport, 4 January 1816, NHS.

46. See the Record Book of the Second Baptist Church of Groton, 29 May 1830, CSL. The Stonington Association advised its member churches in 1784 to adopt "the modern rule" of singing in the future. *Minutes of the Stonington Association . . . 1772 to 1785*, p. 23.

47. In 1771 the urbane Ezra Stiles noted approvingly in his diary that "formerly the Baptist Ministers were fond of the Appela[tion] *Elder* & the Baptists usually call their pastors Elder in common Discourse. . . . But since the College is erected they begin to assume the Title Rev." Stiles, *The Literary Diary*, ed. Franklin B. Dexter (New York, 1901), 1:123.

pline committees and other committees dealing with liturgical matters was ever recorded, but after 1790 few women appear on such committees. And, perhaps most tellingly, after 1790 women largely disappear from the church records as lay contestants in the battle over doctrine which engaged so much of the churches' attention in the late eighteenth century. Unlike their sisters from an earlier age who actively participated in the theological debates of their day, evangelical women in the late eighteenth century had little to contribute to the vital struggle over doctrine then being waged by their male brethren.

We can see this process with particular clarity in the First Baptist Church of Providence, the oldest and most venerable Baptist society in New England. A series of votes recorded between 1786 and 1808 shows the progressive marginalization of women in church governance. In 1786 the church had met to reconsider its ordinance requiring all new candidates for admission to undergo the imposition of hands. (The scriptural justification for this ordinance was often contested among the Baptist churches of New England, which had long been divided into Six Principle—those who practiced the ritual—and Five Principle churches—those who did not.) "After considerable conversation on the subject, every brother and sister were asked their opinion, and it was the voice of every individual that transient members of sister churches in good standing that were not under hands might have a place with us at our communion seasons."[48] Five years later, the Providence church formally did away with the ordinance for regular church members as well. "The subject of the imposition of hands was introduced. . . . Every member's name was written down and the voice of every member asked, *Bar or not?*" Twenty-seven men and thirty-six women voted to discontinue the practice, with only four men dissenting.[49]

The controversy over the ordinance of imposition of hands is interesting as a measure of the church's distance from the model of an organic community bound together by human touch which had prevailed early in its history. But even more significant, the vote in 1791 to abandon the practice marked the last time that women exercised the vote in matters of church polity in the Providence church. When, in 1808, the church was faced with the decision to dismiss Elder Stephen Gano for his refusal to administer the ordinance, they recorded that "the Question was then taken, and each of the Brethren was called on [by] the Moderator, and answered Thirty seven not to dismiss; one to dismiss, and one declined voting." The sisters of the

48. Record Book, First Baptist Church of Providence, 1 June 1786, RIHS.
49. Ibid., 4 August 1791, RIHS.

church, the clerk added in a note at the bottom of the page, "also manifested their approbation of the vote which had past, by rising when the question was proposed to them."[50] Women were now merely asked to affirm a decision that had already been made. Between 1786 and 1808 women had been effectively disenfranchised from the Providence Baptist Church.

The same process occurred in other Baptist churches throughout New England. In Connecticut, new covenants and articles of faith adopted in the late eighteenth century specifically designated men as the governors of the church. The Waterford Baptist Church, founded in the early eighteenth century as one of the first Baptist societies in the state, rewrote its covenant in 1786. "Now as to Church power of binding and loosing or in other words, the Church power and Authority in Church Discipline in Government, We Say it is the whole Number or Major Part of male members as God witnesses."[51] When the First Baptist Church of Ashford was asked to decide in 1777 "whether or not the Sisters of the Church take hold of the Sword of Discipline or bare in weight in matters of rule and Determination with the male members," they voted "no" unanimously.[52] Thereafter, women are silent in the church records whenever major issues were debated and voted on. Only men voted to call Elder Daniel Wildman to the pastoral office of the Fairfield-Stratfield Baptist Church in 1818, and the council called to ordain Ezra Miner as pastor of the First Baptist Church in Lyme in 1821 consisted of the "Male Members of this Church" only.[53]

Although churches in Connecticut had always been more reluctant than their counterparts in Rhode Island to allow women to participate in church governance, even the more liberal congregations in Rhode Island excluded women from exercising the franchise in the 1790s and early 1800s. In 1816 the minutes of the Second Baptist Church of Newport recorded that only men voted to dismiss Elder Wydown.[54] By the 1820s discipline cases were decided in the Beneficent Congregational church only after "the Sisters retired" from the meeting, presumably in deference to their more delicate sensibilities.[55]

50. Ibid., 2 December 1808, RIHS.
51. Record Book, Waterford Baptist Church, 14 October 1786, CSL.
52. Record Book, First Baptist Church of Ashford, 19 February 1777, CSL.
53. Record Book, Fairfield-Stratfield Baptist Church, 31 March 1818; Record Book, First Baptist Church of Lyme, 6 November 1821, CSL.
54. Record Book, Second Baptist Church of Newport, 1 August and 29 August 1816, NHS.
55. Record Book, Beneficent Congregational church, 19 July 1820, Beneficent Church Vault, Providence. The Beneficent church was an open communion church formed in 1746 by the "Illiterate" New Light, Joseph Snow. Practicing both infant and adult baptism, the church drew disaffected members away from both the Baptist and Congregational churches in Providence. Its membership was predominantly Baptist throughout the eighteenth century despite the fact that

When a dispute arose in the Westerly Baptist Church over the propriety of the deacon's administering the sacrament of baptism, the issue was resolved through negotiations with the "brethren" only; after Deacon Gardiner confessed that the "Brethren Releasing him from His Ortheration to Baptise in the Church" was not a "Sufficient Cause" for him to "stop travel with his Brethren," the "Church as a body" restored Gardiner and "Bid him well-com."[56] The record clearly distinguishes between the responsibilities of the "brethren" (who alone were empowered to authorize the deacon to baptize) and those of the "Church as a body" (who merely ratified the decision)—a distinction entirely absent in the mid-eighteenth century. This trend away from shared governance was apparent as early as 1771, when a few "Aged Sisters" still exercised the vote in the Baptist churches of Newport while "the younger sisters keep their places and say nothing." Reviewing this pattern in 1771, Ezra Stiles concluded that "probably their Voteing is growing into Disuetude—so that this usage may be intirely dropt in another Generation in these old as well as in the new Churches."[57] Stiles proved a prescient observor.

The silencing of women in the internal politics of the evangelical church was accomplished despite the growing presence of women on church membership rolls. Within a generation after the Great Awakening, women outnumbered men two to one in most Baptist congregations, the same sex ratio that Congregational churches had reached by the end of the seventeenth century.[58] The Baptist community in New England was surely aware of the damage to church prestige and political clout that a feminized membership portended, as Congregational ministers struggled throughout the colonial period to maintain their professional standing in the face of steadily declining rates of male membership. Without the support of men, the Congregational church found it increasingly difficult to sustain the moral authority it

---

Snow himself remained a pedobaptist. See Stiles's account of the history of the Beneficent church in his *Literary Diary*, 1:114–15 and 271–76.

56. Record Book, First Baptist Church of Westerly, 28 January and 13 May 1795, RIHS.

57. Stiles, *Literary Diary*, 1:147.

58. Baptist churches were notoriously lax in keeping strict membership records until the institutional reforms of the late eighteenth century. Where figures exist, they suggest that most Baptist churches had twice as many women as men within a generation after the church's founding. The First Baptist Church of Ashford was founded in 1747 by 22 men and 8 women, for instance, but by 1792 the ratio of women to men was 2 : 1 (69 women, 39 men). Mature evangelical churches in Connecticut such as the First Baptist Church of Groton exhibited a feminized membership as early as the 1760s, whereas most Rhode Island Baptist churches were predominantly female by the end of the seventeenth century. The feminization of church membership can thus be dated to the last third of the eighteenth century for those Baptist churches founded after the Great Awakening.

had enjoyed since the founding of New England.[59] A feminized membership was an even greater threat for dissenters as they struggled to transcend
the limitations of a feminized faith.

By 1810 the institutionalization of sexual difference within the church
polity was a fait accompli and occasioned little discussion or dissension.
The bland assertion in a leading denominational publication that Baptist
churches "take for granted, that the duties and privileges of females in a
Gospel Church differ from those of males" was but to state the obvious;
"this, we conceive, scarcely admits of controversy."[60] But the fact that a few
Baptist women did protest their exclusion from church governance indicates
at least an undercurrent of discontent among women at the new sexual
politics. In a striking case (striking because of its explicit assertion of wom-
en's rights, and also for its rarity in the church records), a disgruntled female
member came before the Warren Baptist Church in 1823 with a long list of
grievances. Betsey Luther charged the church with a number of "improprieties," including "sending Male committees with messages to Females,
which marked a departure from past practices. "[S]he observed that Sisters
were formerly capable of executing the business of Committees, and if they
were not now, they had better be cutt off from the church." A long catalogue of personal insults received at the hands of the church's officers then
followed:

> She censured our Pastor for not visiting her, though she thought the
> Brethren were principally to be blamed, as he was a Stranger. Her princi-
> pal difficulty, however, seemed to be with Dea. Davol, who on a certain
> occasion had said "that she was mad," and that "she was brass mounted";
> and at another time, that "he had treated her grievances with him with
> levity." For all which, she intimated, that she could forgive him as a
> natural man, but could not receive the Elements from his hand; she
> hoped he could be converted before he died. . . . She was hurt also, with
> Brethren John Haile and Theo Salisbury for asking her at a certain time,
> in the meeting house, "if she had come as a spy."

The church rather officiously concluded that "Sister Luther did not manifest a becoming Christian spirit while stating her grievances as above enu-

59. On the feminization of church membership among Congregationalists, see Patricia Bonomi, *Under the Cope of Heaven*, pp. 111–15; Mary Maples Dunn, "Saints and Sisters: Congregational and Quaker Women in the Early Colonial Period," *American Quarterly* 30 (1978): 582–601;
Gerald Moran, "'Sisters' in Christ: Women and the Church in Seventeenth-Century New England," in *Women in American Religion*, ed. Janet Wilson James (Philadelphia, 1976), pp. 47–65; and
Richard Shiels, "The Feminization of American Congregationalism 1730–1835," *American Quarterly* (33) 1981: 46–62.

60. "On the Duties and Privileges of Female Members in a Gospel Church," *BM* 2 (1810): 556.

merated" and excommunicated her five months later for her "disorderly conduct."[61]

Luther's grievances were a bold, though futile, protest against the gradual erosion of women's power within the church. Sisters were, she pointed out, "formerly capable of executing the business" of the Church—and, she bitterly concluded, "if they were not now, they had better be cutt off." She, like a handful of other malcontents, complained of being ignored by both the pastor (though he was a "stranger" and so less to blame, itself an interesting indication of the changing relationship of ministers to their congregations) and by leading brethren in the church, of having her accusations summarily dismissed as the outbreaks of a disordered nature; she was variously accused of being insane, or overbearing, or (cruelest of all) of acting the role of a spy. The image of a "spy" listening at the keyholes of the meetinghouse neatly captures the extent to which women were excluded from the realm of legitimate discourse *within* the meetinghouse.

As in the case of Betsey Luther, overt challenges to church authority by disaffected women were deflected through ridicule and condescension. When Joanna Gano, wife of Elder Stephen Gano of the Providence Baptist Church, accused her husband and several other brethren of advocating freemasonry in 1803, the church—after a lengthy hearing—excommunicated her for "disorderly conduct." Several weeks later, fearing that "she might misinterpret the reasons for which she was excluded," the church brethren clarified their position. We "did not exclude Mrs. Gano on account of her opinions against Masonry," they stressed, "but on account of her hard and unchristian language and conduct." In their final communication with the unrepentant Joanna, the church bluntly dismissed her right to intervene in matters of doctrine or policy: her protestations ("my ideas of our Brethren joining the Masonic Society, and the labours I took with them, I thought scriptural, and do still think") met only condescension—"certainly," they responded, "you must know that we excluded you not for your *Ideas* of the Brethren . . . but solely for your *Conduct*." By these words, she was effectively disenfranchised from the realm of ideology. Denied a legitimate outlet for her opinions, she became an outcast within her own community.[62]

61. Record Book, Warren Baptist Church, 2 October 1823 and 5 March 1824, JHL. Interestingly, two other women who held unspecified grievances against the Warren church before the excommunication of Betsey Luther recanted their complaints in the months following her exclusion. See the case of Patty Cole, 31 October 1823 and 3 April 1824; and the case of Nancy Child, 5 December 1823. Both women were accused of "hardness" toward certain key brethren, including Theo Salisbury and John Haile, who also figured in Luther's accusations.

62. Record Book, First Baptist Church of Providence, 3 and 25 August 1803, 1 November 1810, RIHS.

One of the more telling signs of women's diminished status was the resurrection of the old debate in the evangelical press over the propriety of women's speaking publicly in the church. The fact that the problem of women's right to speak had been an intermittent feature of Christian history since Paul wrote his famous epistle to the Corinthians enjoining silence of women in church should not obscure the importance of the debate re-enacted in the early 1800s. It is the reemergence of this ancient concern at a particular historical juncture, not its seemingly universal presence within western Christianity, that is most significant. "Are there not frequent, and almost daily opportunities, when a pious female may, without infringing in the least on the laws of propriety, speak on God's behalf?" queried a reader in the *Massachusetts Baptist Magazine and Missionary Intelligencer* in 1808.[63] The answer, according to a flood of articles published on the subject of women's speaking in the church in the early 1800s, was a resounding "No." One man, who preferred to remain anonymous, argued that the scriptural prohibition on women's speech contained in 1 Corinthians was "*unlimited*":

> I conceive it to be unscriptural for them to speak in the church *at all*, not only by teaching, or by prayer, leading the devotions of the church, but by professing their repentance toward God, and faith in the Lord Jesus Christ, or their future contrition and confidence; by imparting necessary information on any matter; in giving testimony to confirm any fact; in asking or answering any question; or by verbally assenting to or dissenting from, any proposition *there* . . . for while the wisdom and authority of God *for her own sake* shuts one door upon her in public, he opens a more suitable one for her in private.[64]

That women could deliver public relations of faith before congregations was, another man concurred in 1810, "directly opposite to the apostolic command in 1 Cor. xiv, 34, 35, *Let your women learn to keep silence in the churches.*" The reasons for this injunction, he continued, "are those which arise from the relation they [women] bear to men, as being the weaker vessel, the derived, the dependent part. The circumstances, therefore, of their being required to give a verbal relation of their faith for the satisfaction of the public body, is not only in opposition to scripture, but to nature itself."[65] Another correspondent, while conceding that women were entitled to participate on an equal footing with men in the routine aspects of church business, insisted that in the realm of speech "there is a diversity of conduct

63. *MBMMI* 2 (1808): 76.
64. *BM* 7 (1815): 150–51.
65. Ibid., 2 (1810): 467–68.

to be observed by the sexes." Women, following the prohibition expressly set forth in scripture, were not to preach, or teach, or even pray aloud during church meetings.[66] Any woman who was bold enough to challenge the injunction against public speaking was to be banished from the community: "I should request her to change her name and remove to a distance where her connections were not known," declared one Baptist minister.[67] Intrepid women like Mrs. Rebecca Jones who refused to join the First Baptist Church of Providence unless she "might be allowed to speak in publick when it was strongly impressed upon her mind" were forced to look elsewhere for spiritual comfort.[68]

Women were not without their defenders in the evangelical press. "While *we* are discussing and contriving," wrote one man in 1815, "*they* are acting, and without bustle, carrying mercy and love to the abodes of intemperance, wickedness and misery." Women must be allowed to participate in discussing church business for, the author pointed out, "it is very common for churches to have a large proportion of the members women. At many of their meetings, by far the majority are female. In some of their meetings, all the members present may be females." What would happen to church business if, he continued, "women *there* were not to speak in the Church?"[69] Others were more condescending in their defense of women's speech. "The *speaking* in churches, which the apostle prohibited in Corinthian women," one argued, "was the kind of loquacity, or female inquisitiveness, which, in the early days of Christianity was, perhaps, but too common amongst them, of asking questions in the churches respecting the new doctrine." Women in the current day were far less presumptuous in their speech and behavior, and thus the apostolic injunction was not needed.[70] Presumably, were women to recover their original inquisitiveness, this author would concur in silencing them once again.

The remarkable distance traveled by the evangelical community from its earlier history of sexual egalitarianism (hinted at by the last author in his reference to the bold and unbridled women of the primitive church) can be seen, in part, as the simple consequence of institutional maturation. The evolution of a fringe religious community into a denomination through the

---

66. Ibid., 2 (1810): 556–58.

67. Quoted in Nancy F. Cott, *The Bonds of Womanhood: "Woman's Sphere" in New England, 1780–1835* (New Haven, Conn., 1977), p. 158.

68. Record Book, First Baptist Church of Providence, 29 November 1792 and 3 January 1793, RIHS.

69. Quoted in *BM* 7 (1815): 415–18.

70. Ibid., 7 (1815): 236.

politics of exclusion, particularly sexual exclusion, is a familiar narrative. We know from studies of other dissenting religious societies that those groups furthest removed from the ecclesiastical center have historically allowed women the greatest opportunities to serve in official and quasi-official capacities. Quakers and Primitive Methodists are the two examples that come immediately to mind, although Carla Pestana has recently demonstrated that seventeenth-century Massachusetts Baptists, too, accorded women communicants considerable autonomy. The populist religious groups that sprang up in the early republican period likewise offered women opportunities to preach and lead religious services. The egalitarian instincts of fringe religious groups rarely outlast the first generation of believers, however; within a few decades female preaching, for instance, was quickly abandoned in every denomination in which it had been countenanced.[71] The dynamics of the trajectory from sect to church traveled by religious extremists in every epoch would seem to make the defeminization of the evangelical polity a foregone conclusion.[72]

Yet this scenario partially breaks down during the late eighteenth century. The evidence from recent surveys of those populist religious groups that emerged in the early republican period suggests that the Revolution complicated the path from dissent to orthodoxy for American Protestants. For the religious primitivists of the early 1800s display a marked ambivalence toward sexual equality, despite claims that they embodied a truly democratic pulse. On the one hand, women resumed public roles as preachers and lay exhorters, often in the face of considerable opposition from male authorities, and insisted on their right to share in the collective governance of their religious societies. On the other hand, these societies were often deeply misogynistic, embracing an all-male fraternal culture (as in the case of the Methodists) or relegating women to subordinate roles within the home and church (as in the case of the Mormons). In some cases, misogyny

71. Catherine Brekus, " 'Let Your Women Keep Silence in the Church': Female Preaching and Evangelical Religion in America, 1740–1845," Ph.D. diss., Yale University, 1993; Louis Billington, " 'Female Laborers in the Church': Women Preachers in the Northern United States, 1790–1840," *Journal of American Studies* 19 (1985): 369–94; Stephen Marini, *Radical Sects of Revolutionary New England* (Cambridge, Mass., 1982), pp. 117–19; Alan Taylor, *Liberty Men and Great Proprietors*, p. 136; and Nathan Hatch, *The Democratization of American Christianity*, pp. 78–80.

72. Deborah Valenze, *Prophetic Sons and Daughters: Female Preaching and Popular Religion in Industrial England* (Princeton, N.J., 1985); Carla Gardina Pestana, *Quakers and Baptists in Colonial Massachusetts* (New York, 1992); Phyllis Mack, "Women as Prophets during the English Civil War," *Feminist Studies* 8 (1982): 19–45. For a summary of the classic sociological literature on the transformation of religious sects into denominational churches, see Michael Hill, *A Sociology of Religion* (London, 1973).

was overt rather than merely implicit in the organizational structure of the movement. As one of the new brand of populist leaders, the Prophet Matthias, preached in the 1820s, "Everything that has the smell of woman must be destroyed. Woman is the capsheaf of the abomination of desolution—full of all deviltry."[73]

The case of the Methodists offers the best vantage point from which to view the distinctive egalitarianism of prerevolutionary evangelicals. The Methodists and the American Revolution arrived at almost the same time in the colonies, as missionaries began to travel throughout the Upper South in the 1760s and 1770s under the direction of the austere and uncompromising Francis Ashbury. In many respects, Methodists re-created the sense of otherworldly communalism which earlier evangelicals had found so empowering. For Methodists, holy fellowship was rooted neither in notions of providential history nor in sacred space but in the affective bonds that united saints. Gregory Schneider describes how fellowship might have occurred "in English coal fields, in rude Virginia cabins, or out in the wilderness forest under the open sky. Sacred space was anywhere the saints gathered apart from the world to worship and share their experience."[74] As we saw in the revivals of the First Great Awakening, the practice of worshiping in unstructured settings could be enormously liberating for a people who spurned traditional social hierarchies, especially in the South, where the site of social interaction was inseparable from its cultural meaning. Within Methodist congregations (as within Baptist churches) the racial barrier that so deeply divided southern society was, for a time, broken down. "The chapel was full of white and black, and many were without that could not get in," marveled the Methodist missionary Thomas Rankin in 1776. "Look wherever we would, we saw nothing but . . . faces bathed in tears." Distinctions of race dissolved in these "mighty effusions of the Spirit."[75]

Distinctions of gender, however, proved more intractable in this postrevolutionary vision of *communitas*. From the very beginning, Methodist worship was segregated along lines of gender. At the Ashbury Methodist Episcopal Church on the Delmarva Penninsula (the "garden of American Methodism"), for example, William Henry Williams describes men and women entering the church through separate gates, then through separate

73. Quoted in Paul Johnson, "Democracy, Patriarchy, and American Revivals, 1780–1830," *Journal of Social History* 24 (1991): 846. On the fraternal nature of early Methodism, see Butler, *Awash in a Sea of Faith*, p. 237; and Richey, *Early American Methodism*, pp. 5–11.

74. A. Gregory Schneider, *The Way of the Cross Leads Home: The Domestication of American Methodism* (Bloomington, Ind., 1993), p. 19.

75. Quoted in Isaac, *The Transformation of Virginia*, pp. 261–62.

doors, into a sanctuary "divided down the middle by a four-foot-high partition that prevented either sex from viewing the other while seated." Not
until 1832 could the brothers and sisters of the Ashbury Methodist Church
enter the meetinghouse together, and not until 1845 could they worship side
by side. In more rural congregations, sexual segregation continued well
beyond mid-century. The physical isolation of women within the meetinghouse carried over into the realm of church governance, in which Methodist
women were denied the right to vote for church trustees or exercise church
discipline.[76] Although the Methodists traveled much the same road to religious respectability as had the Baptists a half-century earlier, their journey
bypassed the way station of sexual egalitarianism—an omission all the more
glaring because of the radical eclipsing of racial divisions in Methodist
worship.

The populism of these new religious groups is indisputable. Rejecting the
traditional hierarchies of class and education, insisting on the ability of
ordinary men and women to read and interpret the Bible for themselves,
such primitivist preachers as Elias Smith and Lorenzo Dow touched a raw
nerve in American democratic culture. But most remained patriarchs to the
core—and, in fact, populism and patriarchy often went hand in hand. The
democratic populism of Joseph Smith and the Mormons (that "uniquely
American" religion, in Gordon Wood's words) cannot be separated from
their less savory attempts to revive biblical patriarchy and rural familism.
The intense misogyny displayed by many of these Old Testament patriarchs
was not incidental to but rather inextricable from their democratic pretensions, as Paul Johnson has argued.[77] We need to look more closely at the
internal contradictions of American democracy itself in order to understand

76. William Henry Williams, *The Garden of American Methodism: The Delmarva Penninsula,
1769–1820* (Wilmington, Del., 1984), pp. 107–8.

77. Johnson, "Democracy, Patriarchy, and American Revivals"; on the Mormons, see Gordon
Wood, "Evangelical America and Early Mormonism," *New York History* 61 (1980): 359–86. In
contrast to religious populists in postrevolutionary America, evangelicals in Canada in the same
period exhibited a tolerance for sexual disorder which is reminiscent of the First Great Awakening.
It is highly suggestive that George Rawlyk's review of radical evangelicals in British North America
concludes that Canadian evangelicalism was "more radical, more anarchistic, more democratic and
more populist than its American counterpart." The inspired antics of the "New Dispensationalists"
who practiced spiritual wifery and other antinomian excesses in the 1780s and 1790s had no counterpart in the United States, where "enthusiastical" displays of any kind were discouraged. Rawlyk
rightly locates the source of this discrepancy in the secular "baggage of civic humanism, republicanism, and the covenant ideal" carried by American evangelicals, though I would argue that it was not
the *secular* nature of this ideology which was so constraining but rather its internal contradictions.
Rawlyk, *The Canada Fire: Radical Evangelicals in British North America from 1775 to 1812* (Kingston
and Montreal, 1994), intro. and chap. 8.

the turn toward patriarchy exhibited by New England Baptists in the post-revolutionary years, because the answer lies as much in the political transformations of the American Revolution as in the logic of institutional growth.

"To Grow Up into the fullness and statue of Manhood": Patriarchy and the American Revolution

The political choice faced by Americans in 1776 pitted republicanism against monarchy, independence against dependence, liberty against tyranny, virtue against vice—and manliness against effeminacy. For Americans of an evangelical temperament, the choice was fundamentally about "being or becoming effeminate and being or becoming manly."[78] Philip Greven's insight about the gender panic implicit in revolutionary attacks on luxury, vice, and monarchical corruption, especially when voiced by patriots who struggled mightily to reconcile total submission to God with the responsibilities of patriarchy, has been confirmed by scholarship from other quarters, notably from feminist political theory. Often taking their cue from students of the French Revolution, American historians have probed the rhetoric and iconography of revolution for images that cast the struggle against monarchy in gendered terms. What they have found is a consistent set of associations in which the republic itself was figured male—and all that threatened the republic was figured female.

Evangelicals constructed their own version of this rhetoric of gender opposition in the years immediately following the War for Independence. When the Stonington Association declared in 1785 its desire to "grow up into the fullness and statue of manhood" in order to "be sharers in those glorious things" that would providentially flow from national independence, it betrayed the gendered nature of revolutionary political culture.[79] Equating political vigor with the achievement of a state of manhood was to devalue the otherworldly stance of earlier evangelicals as effeminate. Implicit in the celebratory posture of the various associations was the counter-claim that a "feminine" ethos was responsible for the retarded political capacity of the evangelical community in the prerevolutionary era. The reorganization of the evangelical church along the patriarchal model was thus not simply accomplished by removing women from governing capacities but by repudiating an entire religious ethos as "feminine." As we will

---

78. Philip Greven, *The Protestant Temperament: Patterns of Child-Rearing, Religious Experience, and the Self in Early America* (New York, 1977), p. 351.

79. *Minutes of the Stonington Association, . . . 1772 to 1785*, p. 30.

see in the next chapter, the internal discipline records of the evangelical churches in the postrevolutionary years exhibit a new tendency to associate liminality with disorder—specifically, the disorder of women. Whereas in mid-century certain disorderly behaviors (such as visions, trances, unruly speech, and unsanctioned sexual alliances) were tolerated within the evangelical community as signs of divine grace, by the late eighteenth century such transgressions were considered a sign of female deviance and were vigorously prosecuted. Women who breached the moral and spatial boundaries of the evangelical community became a convenient metaphor for disorder in general, as congregations sought to purge the church of the institutional remnants of otherworldly communalism.

In similar fashion, the very language and ideology of the revolutionary movement cast the struggle against monarchy and tyranny in gendered terms. The pioneering work of Joan Landes on the rhetorical and actual exclusion of women from the public sphere during the French Revolution shows how republican discourse was conducted largely in the idiom of gender opposition. Because all subjects, male and female, shared a subordinate posture under the monarchy, the revolutionary moment assumed a stridently masculine tone as patriots denounced not only the corruptions of the crown but their own emasculation. Proudly heralding the transfer of power from the grasp of an "effeminate" aristocracy to the bourgeoisie in all its public offices, French patriots elevated the "public sphere" (with its masculine connotations intact) to the pinnacle of political life. Once liberated from the humiliating (feminine) position of subjects, male revolutionaries wasted little time in rescuing their fragile masculinity from the grasp of militant women who took up arms and called themselves *citoyennes* in the mistaken belief that they, too, had been liberated from the bonds of subjection.[80]

However persuasive Landes may be in explaining the hypermasculinity of French revolutionary rhetoric, there are obvious difficulties in translating

---

80. Joan B. Landes, *Women and the Public Sphere in the Age of the French Revolution* (Ithaca, 1988), quote on p. 21. Joan R. Gundersen has made a similar point about the shared subordination of male and female subjects in colonial America; see her "Independence, Citizenship, and the American Revolution," *Signs* 13 (1987): 59–77. See also Landes' essay "Representing the Body Politic: The Paradox of Gender in the Graphic Politics of the French Revolution," in *Rebel Daughters: Women and the French Revolution*, ed. Sara Melzer and Leslie Rabine (New York, 1992), pp. 15–37. The importance of men's and women's shared status as subjects in promoting less male-centered theories of state and society is underscored by Constance Jordan's study of Renaissance writers, in which she claims that Renaissance feminists (both male and female) were more able to envision an androgynous political subject than were their counterparts in the eighteenth and nineteenth centuries. Jordan, *Renaissance Feminism: Literary Texts and Political Models* (Ithaca, 1990), pp. 19–21.

her account of the gendered nature of royal absolutism to the American context. If the masculine sensibilities of American patriots were not aroused as fully and visibly as they were in the French Revolution, it may be because women in colonial America lacked the access to the public sphere enjoyed by a few aristocratic women in *ancien regime* France. In their salons and drawing rooms, aristocratic French women participated in a highly select but nonetheless influential arena of public discourse, one that embodied the corruptions of monarchical society even while it undermined the hierarchical principles on which the system rested. The frivolous, artful, passionate woman became a focal point around which frustration at the corrupt and luxury-addicted French court coalesced in the 1780s and 1790s. Landes suggests, in fact, that the vision of the Republican Mother which emerged in the postrevolutionary years was largely aimed at domesticating and neutralizing the powerful figure of the *salonnière*. In America, by contrast, the construction of Republican Motherhood represented a continuation rather than a rejection of the colonial image of woman as pious, subordinate, and domestic.[81] Much of the hostility displayed by male French revolutionaries against the participation of women in the street politics of the Revolution can be traced to their experiences with women of real power and influence under the ancien regime.

Yet if less overtly misogynistic, American patriots deployed a remarkably similar strategy of gender opposition to justify their rebellion against the "mother country." Carroll Smith-Rosenberg has shown how gender displacements were central to the restructuring of revolutionary society and politics. In the early republican period, "middle-class men displaced onto middle-class women criticisms the gentry had leveled against them" in the revolutionary crisis. Just as bourgeois men had been accused of venality and extravagance, so they in turn charged bourgeois women with undermining civic virtue by their irresponsible consumption and addiction to luxury.[82] To patriots across the revolutionary spectrum, the "feminine" was defined as that which most threatened the success of the republic. "In that revolution-

---

81. See Linda Kerber, "The Republican Mother: Women and the Enlightenment—An American Perspective," *American Quarterly* 27 (1976): 187–205. Elaine Crane asks the important question, "What could a Republican Mother do that a colonial mother could not?" and finds little difference. Crane, "Dependence in the Era of Independence: The Role of Women in a Republican Society," in *The American Revolution: Its Character and Limits*, ed. Jack Greene and J. R. Pole (New York, 1987), 253–75.

82. Landes, *Women and the Public Sphere*; Carroll Smith-Rosenberg, "Domesticating 'Virtue': Coquettes and Revolutionaries in Young America," in *Literature and the Body: Essays on Populations and Persons*, ed. Elaine Scarry (Baltimore, 1988), p. 166.

ary moment of discursive, social, and political conflict, the feminine came to represent not only the negative but the most controversial and contested points in these male discursive battles."[83]

We must be careful, however, not to assume that "masculine" and "feminine" meant the same things to all participants in these discursive battles. Although various groups may have justified their revolutionary activities in similarly gendered terms, as a "manly" crusade against an "effete" opponent, what they meant by these terms often differed significantly. For the male evangelical, a political parvenue of uncertain civil credentials, manliness was seen to reside in patriarchal privilege. For other patriots, such as a radical artisan struggling to disengage himself from a deferential labor system as well as a corrupt political regime, manliness was defined as the assertion of the autonomous individual over and above the patriarchal pretensions of the merchant elite. For both, the "feminine" was that which was to be challenged and excised from the body politic. But for the evangelical, the "feminine" was the world of egalitarian social relations, of undifferentiated individuals coming together in spiritual communion; while for the artisan, the "feminine" was the world of hierarchical social relations which privileged ancestry over fraternity. The worlds of the "masculine" and the "feminine" may thus have constituted primal poles of opposition for revolutionary actors across the political spectrum, but the meaning of these terms fluctuated considerably. It is the rhetorical structure of gender opposition, rather than the meaning of gender itself, which ties together the political maneuverings of patriots as disparate as New England evangelicals, urban artisans, middle-class professionals, and the French bourgeoisie.

This reading of the gendered nature of political discourse has called into question the antipatriarchal nature of the Revolution itself. The resurgence of patriarchal norms and structures in the evangelical church at the precise moment that the "revolution against patriarchal authority" (to quote Jay Fliegelman) was being enacted on the political level, with the full support of the evangelical community, is less paradoxical than it first appears.[84] "Patriarchalism has two dimensions; the paternal (father/son) and the masculine (husband/wife)," Carole Pateman has observed. The democratic revolutions of the late eighteenth century were primarily a revolt against the first type of patriarchy—a rebellion of the sons against the father-king. The democratic

83. Carroll Smith-Rosenberg, "Beyond Roles, Beyond Spheres: Thinking about Gender in the Early Republic," *WMQ*, 3d ser., 46 (1989): 573.

84. On the antipatriarchal nature of the Revolution, see Jay Fliegelman, *Prodigals and Pilgrims: The American Revolution against Patriarchal Authority* (New York, 1982); Yazawa, *From Colonies to Commonwealth*; Albanese, *Sons of the Fathers*.

state, in which political and paternal power are no longer conjoined in the figure of the monarch but forever separated, is a compact between men. "The contract is made by brothers, or a *fraternity*. It is no accident that fraternity appears historically hand in hand with liberty and equality, nor that it means exactly what it says: brotherhood." In seizing control of the liberal state for themselves, the sons of the democratic revolution left intact the second form of patriarchy, that of men over women. In fact, Pateman argues, women's subordination to men was not only sustained by the triumph of liberal democracy but was more firmly grounded in the "laws of nature" than ever before. Under absolutist theories of government, the power of men over women was political (hence conventional and arbitrary) as well as natural, because state and society were not conceived of as separate entities but as two parts of the same whole. With the decisive sundering of public and private that was the crowning achievement of the liberal state, sexual rule could no longer be subsumed under political rule. Men's dominion over women now flowed from the natural differences between the sexes rather than from the political authority of kings over their subjects. The democratic contract insists that the subordination of women is rooted in nature, not in politics, and this, according to Pateman, is the fateful move that seals women's fate in the liberal state.[85] When we think of the Baptists as the frustrated second son of New England's religious establishment, seeking to liberate themselves from the oppressive rule of their Congregational "fathers" through the act of rebellion, then Pateman's analysis of the patriarchal dilemmas of liberalism provides an answer for the exclusion of women from the evangelical polity. Only by putting their own household in order could Baptists hope to join the revolutionary fraternity.

Once the sons have assumed their place at the head of the liberal state, political authority is secured not through sexual reproduction, as it is in a monarchy, but rather through the rituals of brotherhood. The *asexual* nature of political succession in democratic republics is, paradoxically, underscored by the predominance of female figures in revolutionary iconography. "Liberty was figured as female because women were not imagined as political actors," Landes explains; the abstract nature of allegory renders the feminine a more appropriate symbol of the nation than any male figure.[86] Excluded from actual participation in the life of the nation, women served the

85. Carole Pateman, "The Fraternal Social Contract," in her *The Disorder of Women: Democracy, Feminism, and Political Theory* (Stanford, Calif., 1989), pp. 37, 40.

86. Landes, *Women and the Public Sphere*, p. 83. See also Marina Warner, *Monuments and Maidens: The Allegory of the Female Form* (New York, 1985); and Lynn Hunt, *Politics, Culture, and Class in the French Revolution* (Berkeley, Calif., 1984), pp. 113–19.

republic only as metaphor. The mythic qualities of female icons such as Marianne, the French figure of Liberty, served as constant reminders that the generative powers of real women were no longer needed to secure the future of the republic. Monstrous images of female sexuality, which reached their height in France in the pornographic literature about Marie ˚Antoinette, circulated alongside virginal portraits of the female republic.[87]

Such desexualized visions of revolutionary fraternity also found their way into evangelical circles in postrevolutionary America. The Baptist reassertion of patriarchal authority was not the only response to the revolutionary reconstruction of the political family. Other evangelical groups sought to reconcile the competing demands of piety and patriotism in different ways. Methodists, for instance, institutionalized the ideal of fraternity in the figure of the circuit rider and rejected familial ties altogether by enjoining celibacy on their clergy and segregating men and women in distinct classes. The collective fraternity of the Methodist circuit was characterized by a severe asceticism that manifested itself in sexual abstinence as well as in conspicuous poverty. The famed mobility of the circuit rider—that "mettlesome figure of gaunt visage, plain black clothes, perpetual motion, and restless preaching"—not only enabled Methodism to expand exponentially into the American interior but facilitated an intense spiritual bonding among men who shared a spartan existence. Circuit riders resembled the monastic fraternity of the Catholic priesthood, as Jon Butler has astutely noted; but they also resembled the brotherhood of revolutionary patriots. As the first denomination to organize nationally, as indeed "the most national American church" from the 1780s on, early Methodists collapsed the religious into the political in ways that affirmed the dual meaning of fraternity. The goal of the circuit rider as he traveled with his "yokefellows" was to convert the nation as he converted individual souls. Rather than representing two distinct dialects,

---

87. Lynn Hunt, "The Many Bodies of Marie Antoinette: Political Pornography and the Problem of the Feminine in the French Revolution," in *Eroticism and the Body Politic*, ed. Lynn Hunt (Baltimore, 1991), 108–30; Vivian Cameron, "Political Exposures: Sexuality and Caricature in the French Revolution," in ibid., pp. 90–107. Hanna Pitkin makes a similar point about Machiavelli's vision of republican Florence, in which political authority derives from purely masculine generation—the singular paternity of a mythical forefather. Not only are mothers absent from this vision, but female sexuality itself is ruthlessly suppressed because it corrupts the virility of republican soldier-citizens. Pitkin, *Fortune Is a Woman: Gender and Politics in the Thought of Niccolo Machiavelli* (Berkeley, Calif., 1984), chap. 3. As Diane Owen Hughes argues, the communes of republican Italy associated women with the "forces of blood and patronage" which ruled dynastic societies and contributed to the endemic instability of civil life; as a result, women figured only as icons—never as flesh-and-blood actors—in the historical narratives of these communes. See Hughes, "Invisible Madonnas? The Italian Historiographical Tradition and the Women of Medieval Italy," in *Women in Medieval History and Historiography*, ed. Susan Mosher Stuard (Philadelphia, 1987), pp. 25–57.

as Russell Richey has described them, the fraternal and republican languages of early American Methodism were in fact but flip sides of the same coin.[88]

Baptists and Methodists, in other words, constructed different "family romances" of the American Revolution.[89] One emphasized the patriarchal authority of men within the spiritual household; the other emphasized the brotherhood of saints over and against the corrupting influence of women and family. It may be that, in this regard, Baptists were more in line with broader American trends, for the ideal of fraternity was quickly abandoned by patriot leaders who traded in their status as "Sons of Liberty" for that of "founding fathers" once independence was secured. "By the 1790s, American revolutionaries had transformed themselves collectively from political children into political fathers through the mediation of the figure of Washington," Lynn Hunt notes. In France, by contrast, no living figure was so mythologized, and a radical commitment to fraternity persisted well past the initial stages of revolution.[90] In either case, however, women were sacrificed to the political ambitions of rebellious sons. Whether as republican mothers, iconic figures, or sexual monsters, women were props in a drama played out by men for the spoils of patriarchy.

Despite the recent recovery by feminist historians of the contributions of women to the revolutionary movement, both in America and France, there remains a nagging sense that women may have lost more than they gained in the transition from monarchical to republican forms of government. We know from the work of Linda Kerber, Mary Beth Norton, and Laurel Ulrich that women constituted the backbone of various patriotic activities from economic boycotts to manufacture of homespun to ritualized spinning

88. Hatch, *Democratization of American Religion*, p. 87; Butler, *Awash in a Sea of Faith*, p. 237; Richey, *Early American Methodism*, p. 34. Richey's discussion of the competing idioms that together made up Methodism (pietistic, Wesleyan, episcopal, and republican) is a superb analysis of the way religious communities are constructed partially through language, but he perhaps overdraws the lines separating one idiom from another. For a different reading of the familial metaphors of early Methodism, see A. Gregory Schneider, "Social Religion, the Christian Home, and Republican Spirituality in Antebellum Methodism," *Journal of the Early Republic* 10 (1990): 163–89, and *The Way of the Cross Leads Home*. Schneider sees itinerancy as the "great spring that kept the whole machine going, the vital principle that animated the whole body" of Methodism (p. 65), but he does not address the potential contradiction between the exclusive masculinity of this confraternity and the family-centered ethics of Methodist prescriptive literature.

89. Borrowing from Freud, Lynn Hunt uses the term "family romance" to indicate "the collective, unconscious images of the familial order that underlie revolutionary politics." Hunt, *The Family Romance of the French Revolution* (Berkeley, Calif., 1992), p. xiii.

90. Ibid., pp. 72–73. As Hunt notes, her analysis both draws on and departs from that of Carole Pateman: "I have written this book to show how difficult it was to enforce a patriarchal version of fraternity," p. 5n.

bees. Women can even be glimpsed marching side by side with their menfolk in the public protests of the independence movement and serving a vital if unappreciated role in the military effort itself as nurses, cooks, laundresses, and occasionally soldiers. Yet when the drama of war was past and the victorious rebels returned to their civilian lives as farmers and tradesmen, ministers and merchants, women disappeared from the public eye once again. With the legal apparatus of "coverture" firmly intact, the notion that a woman had no political identity or will apart from her husband continued to constrain the possibilities for republican citizenship which seemingly inhered in the rhetoric of natural rights.[91]

Of what significance was the deliberate decision of the revolutionary governments both in America and abroad to deny women the political and legal prerogatives of citizenship? Women, after all, had never been considered a part of the body politic under the imperial monarchy.[92] What did they lose except the brief glimpse of a brighter public life afforded by the dislocations of the war? It seems true that the Revolution offered women little more than the "illusion of change" rather than any substantive improvement in their political status, at least in the immediate aftermath.[93] Yet feminist political theorists argue that women lost far more than an illusory public role that had never really been theirs in the first place. They lost instead the very possibility of contributing to a public sphere that was essentially, not contingently, defined as masculine. *Both* men and women had occupied the position of subject in the old monarchy, in which the capacity to act politically was reserved to one man alone—the king. But under republicanism

91. For descriptions of women's contributions to the revolutionary war effort, see Linda K. Kerber, *Women of the Republic: Intellect and Ideology in Revolutionary America* (New York, 1980); Mary Beth Norton, *Liberty's Daughters: The Revolutionary Experience of American Women* (Boston, 1980); Laurel Thatcher Ulrich, "'Daughters of Liberty': Religious Women in Revolutionary New England," in *Women in the Age of the American Revolution*, ed. Ronald Hoffman and Peter J. Albert (Charlottesville, Va., 1989), 211–43; and Alfred Young, "Women of Boston," in *Women and Politics in the Age of the Democratic Revolution*, ed. Harriet Applewhite and Darline Levy (Ann Arbor, Mich., 1991), pp. 181–226.

92. Linda Kerber's analysis of the case of *Martin vs. Massachusetts* (1805) shows with particular clarity how American jurists and politicians self-consciously and deliberately shaped early republican jurisprudence to construe citizenship as a male prerogative. It is not anachronistic, she insists, to read back into the political record of the early republic an antifeminist ideology that was consciously articulated in law. Kerber, "The Paradox of Women's Citizenship in the Early Republic: The Case of Martin vs. Massachusetts, 1805," *American Historical Review* 97 (1992): 349–78. I thank Linda Kerber for clarifying this point with me in a personal communication.

93. Joan Hoff Wilson, "The Illusion of Change: Women and the American Revolution," in *The American Revolution: Explorations in the History of American Radicalism*, ed. Alfred Young (DeKalb, Ill., 1976), pp. 383–445; Elaine Crane, "Dependence in the Era of Independence"; and Gundersen, "Independence, Citizenship, and the American Revolution."

men (at least some men) now gained a new political identity as citizens which was explicitly denied to women. Politics itself, in other words, had become a peculiarly masculine affair in the age of democratic revolution. Far from severing the link between sex and power which seems so essential to premodern culture, the revolutionary era firmly cemented it in the form of the male citizen. The democratic revolution was, to paraphrase Landes, constructed against not merely without women.[94]

Although some have argued that women's political rights had to await the coming of a more liberal conception of state and society, one in which the autonomous individual replaced the moral community as the basic unit of political analysis, the experience of Baptist women in the late eighteenth century suggests that even the adoption of a Lockean language of "social compact" and "natural rights" was no guarantee of political citizenship for women. As historians of the transatlantic democratic revolution have noted in other national contexts, the gender politics of the late eighteenth century offered little hope of the promise of sexual egalitarianism once thought to reside in republican or democratic political culture. For women, "revolutionary outcomes were far more complex and confused" than for men. "The collective influence that women had enjoyed for centuries in their neighborhoods and communities [and, we might add, churches] was dissolving under the pressures of economic development and political revolution. These personal and corporate bonds were losing political significance, leaving women marginalized and individually isolated."[95] The Baptist church illustrates this with particular clarity, as women were expelled from the body politic as the cost of revolutionary patrimony.

The costs to the church itself are less obvious, though equally real: the loss of that vital wellspring of religious piety which had sustained the evangelical community throughout the eighteenth century. Sexual egalitarianism was not merely an unintended (and thus unvalued) by-product of the communal ethos promoted by the First Great Awakening, it was integral to the evangelical understanding of faith itself.[96] Once the church allowed

94. Landes, *Women and the Public Sphere*, p. 171.
95. Harriet B. Applewhite and Darline G. Levy, "Introduction," in *Women and Politics in the Age of the Democratic Revolution*, p. 17. On the liberating impact of the transition from republicanism to liberalism, see Linda K. Kerber, " 'History Can Do It No Justice': Women and the Reinterpretation of the American Revolution," in *Women in the Age of the American Revolution*, pp. 3–42; Kerber, "The Republican Ideology of the Revolutionary Generation," *American Quarterly* 37 (1985): 474–95; and Jan Lewis, "The Republican Wife: Virtue and Seduction in the Early Republic," *WMQ*, 3d ser., 44 (1987): 689–721.
96. Richey has made the same point regarding the retreat of early Methodism from its antislavery stance in the early nineteenth century as it "took its place in society." "In surrendering this

secular distinctions such as gender to penetrate into and circumscribe its fellowship, the concept of grace as a transcendental outpouring of the Holy Spirit was itself compromised. The very notion of rebirth, on which the entire evangelical understanding of religious community was erected, was undercut by the new emphasis on the natural family of saints. One consequence of this theological muddle over the nature of conversion was a growing convergence between the Baptists and the Congregationalists on a variety of liturgical issues, most notably the question of open communion. This blurring of denominational distinctions was accelerated by the latitudinarian impulse of the Second Great Awakening, in which Christians of all stripes submerged their theological differences to join together in the battle for America's soul. Ironically, the evangelical church succeeded too well in securing for itself a place in mainstream political and religious culture at the cost of its own spiritual center.

---

egalitarianism, Methodism lost something of itself," he writes. "For Methodists, as for so many religious movements, growth and development may look like progress and success from some angles, but appear retrogressive and ambiguous from others." Richey, *Early American Methodism*, p. xii.

CHAPTER FIVE

"THE DISORDER OF WOMEN"

The Feminization of Sin, 1780–1830

WHEN JOANNA GANO STOOD MUTE before the Providence Baptist Church, unable to speak aloud against her husband or for herself while the male leadership passed judgment on her "disorderly" conduct, she participated (however unwillingly) in a scenario repeated in evangelical congregations throughout New England in the late eighteenth and early nineteenth centuries. To redeem its revolutionary patrimony, the evangelical community had to purge "disorderly" women like Joanna Gano and Betsey Luther from its communion. This was no easy task. The feminization of the Baptist membership meant that to an uncomfortable degree the future viability of the evangelical community depended on women's continued support. If too many sisters were "cutt off" from fellowship, the church would suffer irreparable damage to its spiritual and civic core. The challenge was to defeminize the evangelical polity without alienating those pious New England matrons who increasingly dominated the membership rolls of the church. The problem, and the answer, lay more in the semiotics of sin than in the sociology of conversion. In the discipline records of the Baptist churches after the Revolution, "disorder" came to be defined as an inherently feminine quality whose commission did not necessarily implicate women. Men (especially revival converts) were as capable of committing "disorderly" acts as were women, although when they did so they forfeited the prerogatives of masculinity. In subtle but unmistakable ways, the concept of sin was feminized as the political face of the evangelical church assumed a masculine profile. The two processes were inseparable.

The title is taken from Carole Pateman's collection of essays on feminist political theory, *The Disorder of Women: Democracy, Feminism, and Political Theory* (Stanford, Calif., 1989).

The transition from dissenting sect to mainstream denomination which the Baptist churches accomplished in the second half of the eighteenth century conforms to what Richard Rabinowitz has described as a shift in emphasis from "soul" to "character." "By 1800, New Englanders could believe in either themselves or God," Rabinowitz writes; "the challenge to evangelicals was to find a way to believe in both."[1] The final disassembling of the covenant theology of New England Puritanism in the republican period left many evangelicals scrambling for a new "economy" of religious experience which would allow them to "close" with God without relinquishing the social legitimacy they aspired to. The search for a new "character" to replace the compromised "soul" of evangelicalism forced the church to confront once again the paradoxes of gender. Both the political demands of citizenship in the new republic and the domestic imperatives of a resurgent patriarchy required that this paradox be resolved in favor of the "masculine" principles of order and hierarchy.

To meet these expectations, the evangelical saint had to become a godly father, pious mother, obedient servant, attentive child. To ensure domestic order, the evangelical community scrutinized the moral fiber of its constituency with a critical eye. Although the disciplining of covenant breakers was no more crucial a task after the Revolution than before, the focus of church discipline shifted decisively from community to character. While sins of aversion continued to receive serious attention, sins of "unchristian character" were prosecuted with special vigor after 1780. Like their Congregational rivals a century earlier, Baptist and Separate churches in the postrevolutionary period came to understand sin more as a breach of morality than a lapse in charity. And morality, as the Victorian middle classes would come to understand and articulate so well, was an inherently gendered concept. Nineteenth-century men and women were subject to very different codes of moral behavior, both outside the church and in, and in elevating character over soul evangelicals participated in the gendering of religious culture which was to be the hallmark of antebellum America.

In terms of sheer numbers, the efforts of the churches to discipline backsliding members intensified slightly in the decades after 1770. Discipline records of the evangelical churches I studied reveal a total of 99 members censured for breaches of covenant in the decade 1771–80, rising to a high of 282 in the decade 1811–20. In part this increase parallels the growth of membership within the Baptist churches as congregations swelled under the

---

1. Richard Rabinowitz, *The Spiritual Self in Everyday Life: The Transformation of Personal Religious Experience in Nineteenth-Century New England* (Boston, 1989), pp. xxvii–xxviii.

impact of successive waves of revivalism in the Second Great Awakening. Membership figures, where available, depict a steady rise in the total number of church members from 1780 to 1830. The First Baptist Church of Warren, for instance, tripled its membership from the original 57 to 166 after the revival of 1805, and by 1816 had reached a high point of 221. The First Baptist Church of Providence added 53 new converts in the revival of 1801, 144 converts in the revival of 1805, an additional 99 in the revival of 1812, and 128 new members in 1820.

There is reason to suspect that the official figures often understated the number of church members under discipline. Membership figures (including baptisms, deaths, and exclusions) published in the annual reports of the Warren Association, for instance, indicate only the number of excommunications per year, not the number of admonitions or censures. When the Second Baptist Church of Middleborough submitted its membership figures to the association in 1785, it deliberately omitted the 11 members who were being investigated for breach of covenant from its report. "In the minutes to be printed for 1785," the clerk noted in a postscript, "I have taken no notice of the 11 under discipline, as I don't know whether they are excluded or not."[2] Fully one-fifth of this church's total membership was subject to discipline in the year 1785, but there is no mention of this fact in the association's records.

Moreover, while the prosecution of covenant breakers may not have been proportionately more prominent after the Revolution than before, the sheer volume of the churches' disciplinary actions lent them a visibility that must have been difficult to ignore. Before the Revolution, most congregations could expect to consider a half dozen or so discipline cases a year; by 1800, as many as six or seven backsliding members might be under discussion at every biweekly or monthly meeting. Month after month members debated the merits of various cases under review, interviewed witnesses and interrogated defendants, held lengthy discussions on the appropriate punishment for each offense, expounded sentences, and called sinners to repentance.

By purging their congregations of marginal adherents, the churches hoped to attack at the root the disorder that seemed endemic to their institution. Increasingly, women were targeted as the chief source of this disorder. In those categories of sin which Baptist churches deemed most pernicious, women became the overwhelming majority of transgressors after 1780. As slanderers, fornicators, and "disorderly walkers," women repre-

2. Letter from Second Baptist Church, Middleborough, to Warren Association, 16 September 1785, Backus Papers, ANTS.

sented a subversive element. More important, though, disorderly qualities were seen not only to be manifest in individual women members, but to constitute the very core of the feminine character. While women communicants as individuals were singled out as threats to the community, "feminine" qualities in general were redefined as disorderly even when exhibited by men. Women's supposed proclivity to seduce and lead astray, to dissemble and prevaricate, became reified as seduction and dissimulation were gendered female. What is so striking about this cosmology is the new equation of disorder with liminality; in seducing bodies and souls away from the truth, women sinners reenacted the disorders associated with the revivalists of the Great Awakening.

By conceiving of sin and disorder in sociological rather than strictly cosmological terms, the evangelical community thus signaled its final repudiation of the legacy of spiritual liminality inherited from the Great Awakening. For the gendering of sin involved nothing less than a retreat from liminality into a more conventional understanding of human experience. In the postrevolutionary church, members no longer stood "*with* one another of a multiple of persons" but rather "above and below" one another. Individual members no longer "flowed" one into the other, but rather became "us" and "them." The lines separating the core of the evangelical polity from various "others" were manifold and defy easy categorization. By focusing on divisions of gender within the evangelical community, I do not mean to ignore the importance of other factors that worked to structure the community along hierarchical rather than egalitarian lines after the Revolution. Social and economic divisions were certainly not absent in church life, but they seem to have played only a minor role in communal politics. The absence of more detailed sociological analysis in this discussion of sin and conversion reflects both the difficulties inherent in studying an entire denomination rather than a particular congregation and my own sense of the relative unimportance of class distinctions in shaping the religious landscape of the early republican period. The twenty churches that form the core of this study represent a wide spectrum of New England localities—rural and urban, agricultural and commercial, inland and coastal. The strengths and limitations of such a regional study should be immediately apparent: while it allows a more faithful reconstruction of the religious mentality of the evangelical community as a whole, it keeps the social and economic fault lines within individual congregations largely out of sight. Detailed studies of the social composition of dissenting congregations in eighteenth-century New England are scarce, but what little evidence there is suggests that the socioeconomic profile of evangelical religion remained fairly representative of the population as a whole. Drawing adherents from a wide spectrum of social backgrounds and economic orientations, evangelical religion bore no simple relation to economic deprivation, as some historians have presumed.[3] Within evangelical congregations, there is likewise little sign of the class tensions one might expect to surface in an age of rapid economic change. In most evangelical churches the allocation of pews, for instance, betrayed little class bias until the 1810s and 1820s, according to a recent reconstruction of the social profile of dissenting congregations in antebellum Providence.[4] The conspicuous absence of sins against industrial order in the discipline records of the churches is yet another indicator that economic discontents were not a significant factor in church politics during this era; even the sin of drunkenness, which was prosecuted with great vigor after 1800, was condemned more for its demoralizing effect on domestic relations than for its impact on economic productivity. If divisions of gender went deeper than divisions of class in shaping the religious life of such thriving manufacturing and commercial centers as Providence in the early republic period, we can reasonably assume that less developed regions would present a far less economically stratified religious face.

Through their association with disorder, women became the ultimate "other" in a community of religious believers. The distinction between sinners and saints was, after all, the critical distinction for evangelical Protestants; now this essentially spiritual divide became a gendered one as well. In the process, the evangelical churches in late-eighteenth-century New England seemed to have reached a position that historians have argued was immanent in Puritan (indeed Christian) religion from the beginning. The figure of Eve, after all, represents the aboriginal sinner; from time beyond memory women have been associated in Christian religious literature with the vices of seduction and deceit. Women "scolds" were notorious in the criminal literature of the early modern period, and the figure of the woman gossip a stock character in morality plays of every stripe. In this context, the "feminization" of sin evident in church discipline records in postrevolutionary New England seems but a retelling of an old (and some might say well-worn) story. Yet a feminized conception of sin was *not* constant throughout

---

3. See Mark Schantz, "Piety in Providence: The Class Dimensions of Religious Experience in Providence, RI, 1790–1860," Ph.D. diss., Emory University, 1991; Stephen R. Grossbart, "The Revolutionary Transition: Politics, Religion, and Economy in Eastern Connecticut, 1776–1820," Ph.D. diss., University of Michigan, 1989; Curtis Johnson, *Islands of Holiness: Rural Religion in Upstate New York, 1790–1860* (Ithaca, 1989); and John Brooke, *The Heart of the Commonwealth: Society and Political Culture in Worcester County, Massachusetts, 1713–1861* (New York, 1989).

4. Schantz, "Piety in Providence," chap. 1.

the history of the evangelical churches, but rather was the creation of a
specific historical juncture. In the creative ferment of the Great Awakening
women embodied (as I have argued) the archetypal saint. After the revolutionary crisis and the masculinization of the evangelical polity, they came to
represent the archetypal sinner. How such a transformation came about is a
subject of considerable complexity.

"Joining affinity with the World": Sins of Public Disorder

A close examination of the kinds of offenses prosecuted by the evangelical
churches (see Table 2) reveals the degree to which "character" rather than
community had become the focal point of the churches' discipline efforts.
The efforts at reform which preoccupied the evangelical church during the
second half of the eighteenth century had succeeded to the extent that the
simple survival of the community was no longer at risk. Baptist churches
through their associations, colleges, media, and internal reforms had moved
the denomination from its tenuous civil moorings in the 1740s and 50s to a
secure position within the American ecclesiastical structure by 1800. Now
the question was, not whether the community would succumb to its own
antistructural tendencies, but rather whether the community could consolidate the political initiative it had gained during the revolutionary war. The
"character" of the community and not its very existence, in other words, was
at stake. And to defend its character in the increasingly competitive social
arena, the evangelical church in turn scrutinized the characters of its own
membership to an unprecedented degree.

What the churches found was an alarming rise in certain categories of sin.
In particular, sexual misconduct (adultery, fornication), violations of public
order (drinking, dancing, gambling), and breaches of neighborly relations
(quarreling, suing one's neighbor in a court of law) seem to have been more
prevalent (or at least more visible) after the Revolution than before. Baptist
men and women apparently were less scrupulous in the late eighteenth and
early nineteenth centuries about observing a strict code of behavior in the
public arena, as they took advantage of the expanded opportunities for
sociability offered by the new republic. Mary Gregory "publickly denied her
profession" and became "a Voluntary partaker of the vain amusements Rec-
reations & follies of the non-professing world; in short she had turned her
back upon the cause which she once appeared so Enamored with having her
affection alienated from her Brethren & engaged with the unthinking world

TABLE 2.
Church Discipline of Various Offenses, by Sex, 1771–1830

Sins	Males (%)	Females (%)	Totals
Contempt of church	205 (47)	234 (53)	439
Violations of public order	151 (71)	61 (29)	212
Disorderly character	29 (20)	119 (80)	148
Crimes of the tongue	73 (50)	75 (50)	148
Lying/slander	17 (22)	59 (78)	76
Profanity/unguarded speech	56 (78)	16 (22)	72
Sexual misconduct	15 (11)	116 (89)	131
Breaches of neighborly relations	65 (67)	21 (33)	86
Violations of business ethics	40 (93)	3 (7)	43
Contempt of family/household	21 (72)	8 (28)	29
Unspecified	16 (20)	65 (80)	81
TOTALS	688	777	1465

in pursuing happiness in the path of folly."[5] Samuel Tiler was charged by the Second Baptist Church of Ashford with "having walked Disorderly in joining affinity with the World, in Dancing with them in their Carnal Dances, and giving [him]self Liberty to joke and jest, and talk Unadvisedly, etc."[6] Several churches adopted explicit prohibitions against increasingly popular forms of secular entertainment: "Voted that this Church consider it unbecoming and improper for any of our Members to visit the Theater or the Circus, or Green Cottage (so called) and other Places of amusement as sources of dissipation."[7] The Lyme Baptist Church adopted a policy in 1816 that "we can not freely commune with members who do themselves, or parents who permit their children under age, to attending dancing or balls."[8] The churches evidently found it difficult to persuade their members that such "amusements" were improper and ungodly; when the Warren church excommunicated Jonathan Barton in 1822 for "dancing in a public assembly," he declared that "he considered it no crime & thought that he should do it again when opportunity presented; that he did not think God took notice of his dancing."[9]

Revival converts were particularly prone to engage in public disorderli-

5. Record Book, Fairfield-Stratfield Baptist Church, 2 November 1795, CSL.

6. Record Book, Second Baptist Church of Ashford, 21 August 1783, CSL.

7. Record Book, First Baptist Church of Providence, 29 November 1827, RIHS. The Beneficent Congregational Church in Providence also adopted a resolution prohibiting members from attending "places of Publick resort, or Amusements, & Especially that place known by the name of the Green Cottage." Record Book, 19 September 1821, Beneficent Church Vault, Providence.

8. Record Book, First Baptist Church of Lyme, 21 March 1816, CSL.

9. Record Book, Warren Baptist Church, 8 September 1822, JHL.

ness. Highly susceptible to the lure of economic and recreational opportunities now available in the more commercialized areas of New England,
these converts seemed to have participated in a youth subculture that rejected traditional ties of dependence (whether in the shop or the home.)[10]
Kassander Kingman, whose unstable family situation is reminiscent of those
of the economically vulnerable revival converts described by Mary Ryan and
Whitney Cross, was excluded by the Warren Baptist Church two years after
he joined in the revival of 1805: "Reports prevail and is believed that he has
not used that Industry and Oeconimy that was incumbent on him as a good
Citizen for the support of himself and his Wife but hath shamefully been
Idle, and by means of his Idleness wasted what property his Wife brought
him, and run in debt for a sum of money at the bank, and shamefully
absconded himself."[11]

A disproportionate number of revival converts were disciplined for drinking, dancing, gambling, and even prostitution.[12] Jane Truman, a "Sister of
Color," was excluded from the Providence Baptist Church in 1810 when it
was reported to the church that "some time past, two young men came to the
house in which she lives at a late hour in the night, and insisted on being
admitted into the house, that she let them in; that one of them went away,
but the other tarried, and was seen in her bed in the morning."[13] Anonymous
rumors were circulating in 1810 that Brother Palmer Munro and Sister Roby
Johonet, both of whom joined the Warren church in the great revival of 1805,
kept "disorderly houses and entertain persons of bad Charracter at unsuit-
able times; supplying them with strong liquors."[14] Jane Stout was brought
before the same church to answer to charges that "she had been guilty of very
great improprieties such as Falsehood, carrusing at a late hour of the night

10. The existence of youth "subcultures" for the colonial and antebellum period has been
deduced by historians working primarily with legal documents similar in nature to the church
discipline records surveyed here. See Roger Thompson, "Adolescent Culture in Colonial Massachusetts," *Journal of Family History* 9 (1984): 127–44; N. Ray Hiner, "Adolescence in Eighteenth-
Century America," *History of Childhood Quarterly* 3 (1975): 253–80.

11. Record Book, Warren Baptist Church, February 1807, JHL. For descriptions of youthful
revival converts in western New York, see Mary P. Ryan, *Cradle of the Middle Class: The Family in
Oneida County, New York, 1790–1835* (New York, 1981); and Whitney R. Cross, *The Burned-Over
District: The Social and Intellectual History of Enthusiastic Religion in Western New York* (Ithaca,
1950).

12. Out of all the revival converts disciplined in the Warren Baptist Church, 25 percent (20 of
80) were accused of public disorder, as compared to 14 percent (8 of 55) of nonrevival converts. In the
First Baptist Church of Providence, 40 percent (14 of 35) of the revival converts disciplined were
tried under this heading, compared to 20 percent (11 out of 55) of nonrevival converts.

13. Record Book, Warren Baptist Church, 1 March and 5 March 1810, JHL.

14. Ibid., October 1807.

away from home, indulging freely in the use of ardent spirits, and entertaining, as the Committee had a good reason to believe, improper company at her house in the absence of her husband."[15] That disorderly domestic relations were clearly the source of concern in these cases suggests that those who responded to the emotional appeal of revived religion could not be counted on to maintain a sober home life once the fires of revival had been dampened.

Because their piety was so suspect, revival converts as a group presented special problems for the church. They were more likely to be prosecuted for breach of covenant than were those who converted on other occasions, and they also received harsher sentences. The evidence from two congregations that experienced wave after wave of revivals in the early 1800s, the Warren and Providence Baptist churches, reveals just how shallow was the tie that bound religious societies to their newest members. Although revival converts accounted for 35 percent of the total church membership in the Warren Baptist Church from 1800 to 1830, for instance, they represented nearly 60 percent of the discipline cases during the same period. In the First Baptist Church of Providence, revival converts made up 30 percent of the total membership but 40 percent of discipline cases. Moreover, nonrevival converts who broke their vows were apt to receive mild sentences (verbal admonitions or temporary suspensions), while revival converts often faced excommunication for similar offenses. Eighty-three percent of revival converts who were brought up on charges before the Providence church were excommunicated compared to 33 percent of the nonrevival converts; in Warren, only 19 percent of nonrevival transgressors faced the ultimate punishment of excommunication, compared to 56 percent of offenders who had joined during revival seasons. As a final measure of their greater vulnerability, revival converts tended to be disowned within a much shorter span of their admission than were nonrevival converts. Fifty-four percent of revival converts who were disciplined were dismissed within five years of joining the Warren church (83 percent within ten years); the median length of time between admission and rejection was five years. Among offenders from the more established group, on the other hand, fourteen years elapsed on average between the time they joined and their disownment. Clearly, the church considered revival converts to be less valuable members of the community, peripheral adherents whose loyalty and commitment to the cause of evangelical religion was tenuous at best and subversive at worst. The contrast with the Great Awakening of the 1740s, when each new convert was consid-

15. Ibid., 1 April 1825. Stout had joined in the revival of 1820.

ered a sign of God's grace, a triumph for the community—when, indeed, there was no community without revival—is telling. The existence within the church of a core of established saints, generally more mature, more prosperous, and more dependable, against which newly admitted converts were measured and found wanting is yet another indication that the evangelical church was now a respectable "household" rather than a sanctuary for outcasts and vagrants.

From Intoxication to Intemperance:
The Character of Sin

Not only were displays of personal disorderliness on the rise in this period, but the terms with which the churches chastised their errant communicants reveal a very different understanding of the source of this disorder. The sin of intoxication, for instance, had earlier been called simply the act of drunkenness, which, occurring in the public realm, threatened to bring reproach on the entire church. In the early 1800s, drinking was seen to be indicative of a deeper defect of character, and tipplers were censured for the sin of "intemperance" in discipline records. Lydia Miller was admonished by the Warren Baptist Church in 1809 because "it was well known that Sister Miller had been intemperate in drinking to the dishonour of her profession."[16] Sister Collins was excluded from the Lyme Baptist Church for the "intemperate use of ardent spirits . . . and allso of prevarication of the truth in a number of instances."[17] Similarly, members who were found guilty of premarital sexual activity were often accused of "incontinence" rather than "adultery" or "fornication." The growing use of such terms as "intemperance" and "incontinence" suggests that sin itself had been transformed from an external act of disobedience to an internal failure of character.

This distinction between conduct and character represents a significant step in the evolution of the evangelical understanding of sin away from the context of community. In turning a critical eye toward the personal habits of their members, Baptist churches in the years after 1780 began to distinguish external behaviors from the underlying character of the sinner. Isolated incidents of personal misconduct which could be attributed to a temporary lapse in judgment were treated much more leniently; transgressions that were repeated or revealed a fundamental inconstancy of character, however, were dealt with severely. An occasional indulgence at the neighborhood tavern would, more often than not, draw a mild reprimand from the church

16. Ibid., October 1809, JHL.
17. Record Book, First Baptist Church of Lyme, 19 February 1829, CSL.

discipline committee, but habitual drunkenness usually resulted in excommunication or (at the least) suspension from the communion table until the church body was satisfied that the offender had truly reformed.

Yet the distinction between conduct and character signals more than the shift from an external discipline regime rooted in shame to an internal one rooted in guilt. It was, in addition, key to distinguishing male from female offenses. A cursory glance at Table 2 reveals that certain categories of sin were clearly identified with a particular gender. Sexual misconduct, lying and slander were overwhelmingly female offenses: more than three-quarters of all offenders were women. Likewise labels of "disorderly character" attached more frequently to women members than to males. Men, on the other hand, were much more likely to be accused of contempt of family/household, violations of the public order, dishonest business practices, profanity, and unneighborly behavior.[18]

Simply labeling certain transgressions "male" and others "female," however, does not exhaust the gendered nature of sin in the postrevolutionary period. Within each category, there were important distinctions in the way the evangelical churches described men's and women's offenses. As sexual deviants, spreaders of falsehoods, neighborhood scolds, or tipplers, women offenders were uniformly described in terms that brought their entire characters under suspicion. While men were more likely to be disciplined for a single act of misconduct, women were in contrast charged with repeated acts of deviance which signified a fundamentally disordered nature. Sexual misconduct, for example, was often associated with deceit and lying in cases involving women, whereas the sexual crimes of men were more often linked with other, more male, acts of public transgression. Betsey Marsh of Coventry was accused in 1809 of "an unusual fondness for a married man. . . . She first denying the charge then owning part then owning all and then denying a part again, therefore the Church having lost their confidence in her Think it will be for the glory of God and the health of the Church to withdraw the hand of fellowship from her."[19] Phebe Salisbury of Tiverton was rejected in 1783 for "the shameful sin of Fornication committed for a time with deceit & Lies."[20] Sally Stevens of Newport was excluded in 1813 for being "in habits of intimacy with a person of loose character."[21]

18. There was a slight trend toward greater prosecution of women in the postrevolutionary years. Before 1780 the ratio of men to women disciplined was roughly even, but by the 1830s, 57 percent of the cases concerned women's behavior. This rise is not statistically impressive, for women were still underrepresented in church discipline records relative to their large membership (2 : 1).

19. Record Book, Second Baptist Church of Coventry, 11 January 1809, RIHS.

20. Record Book, First Baptist Church of Tiverton, 27 March 1783, RIHS.

21. Record Book, Second Baptist Church of Newport, 29 September 1813, NHS.

Contrast these records, in which the sinner's underlying weakness of character and the habitual nature of the offense was emphasized, to the case of Nathan Davol, who was excluded from the Warren Baptist Church for "having unlawful carnal intercourse with a certain woman."[22] Or the case of Abraham Durfey, excluded in 1785 for "attempting again to commit the horrible sin of Fornication; associating himself with Riotous company And taking nightly walks for sport mischief, etc.!"[23] Davol and Durfey were excluded for discrete acts of sexual misconduct which were moreover associated with specifically male offenses such as public rioting.

The "habitual" nature of women's offenses can be seen even more clearly in discipline cases dealing with drunkenness and intoxication. Although predominantly a male vice, the sin of intemperance was described very differently when women were the offenders. The key to understanding the threat posed by male drinkers is the public and episodic nature of the offense. Brother John Peckham of Providence reported that he saw William Givens "Intoxicated one evening and helped him to bed in that situation; which evidence was corroborated by others who saw him the same evening."[24] William Coggeshall was reported to have been "Intoxicated in public at Bristol" and admonished by the Warren church. In another case, the Warren church inquired of Brother Cary of the Rehoboth church "who works in the yard with Brother Child" whether he had witnessed Child's intemperance; "Brother Cary expressed an opinion that he has seen him frequently intoxicated. Brother Luther says from his own observation he thinks him guilty."[25] In all these instances, the sin of intoxication was accompanied by public exposure—it was observed and corroborated by others who were firsthand witnesses to the event. Whether in the yard or in the tavern, these cases can be characterized as occurring in the public realm of male sociability. Yet they were also discrete episodes that tended to be viewed by the church with a certain tolerance, as occasional lapses rather than as ingrained patterns of behavior.

Women's drinking, by contrast, was more likely to be described in terms of habitual moral failing. The First Baptist Church of Providence found in 1815 that Sybil Coburn "had been guilty of the sin of drunkenness . . . and that it had become a confirmed habit."[26] Betsey Bowen was suspended in

22. Record Book, Warren Baptist Church, 23 June 1822, JHL.
23. Record Book, Baptist Society of Sturbridge, 29 March 1800, OSVL.
24. Record Book, First Baptist Church of Providence, 1 September 1794, RIHS.
25. Record Book, Warren Baptist Church, 3 January 1811, JHL.
26. Record Book, First Baptist Church of Providence, 29 June 1815, RIHS.

1803 for being "in the habit of being Intoxicated and often repeated."[27] Sister Tuell was excluded from the First Baptist Church in Newport for "repeatedly indulging herself in the immoderate use of spirituous Liquors."[28] Jane Stout and Phebe Salisbury of Warren were both excluded for indulging themselves "freely in the use of ardent spirits" and falsehood.[29] The impropriety of self-indulgence, rather than the public nature of the offense, lay behind these accounts of women's intemperance. Once again, a flawed nature is identified as the underlying root of women's inconstancy—Lydia Wright was admonished along with Betsey Bowen for "not fill[ing] [her] Carrecter agreeable to [her] profession by reason of getting often Intoxicated with spiritous Liquors."[30] Rhoda Basto of Providence was summarily dismissed in 1806 not for any one act of drinking but because "it evidently appeared that Sister Basto was a drunkard."[31]

The clearest indication of the churches' distrust of the feminine "character" is the preponderance of women disciplined as "disorderly walkers," an epithet directed at those members whose entire "conversation" (in the dual sense of both speech and behavior) did not live up to Christian standards.[32] Nearly 20 percent of all women censured were disciplined under this heading, compared to only 5 percent of men. The church found it sufficient to exclude such members without specifying the misdeeds constituting their "disorderly walk." "Sorrowful accts. being received from Prissilla Hart of her Conducts being more ungodly than ever," the First Baptist Church of Tiverton voted in 1814 to "withdraw all fellowship from [Sister Hart] as a very Disorderly Walker & profane [person]."[33] Sarah Potter was cited to attend the monthly meeting of the Coventry Baptist Church in 1827 to "give her an opportunity to clear her character of the reports that is out about her." Several months later she too was excluded for her (unspecified) "disorderly behaviour."[34] Mary Gay was found guilty by the Sturbridge Baptist Church

27. Record Book, Warren Baptist Church, 5 March 1803, JHL.

28. Record Book, First Baptist Church of Newport, 31 May 1817, NHS.

29. Record Book, Warren Baptist Church, 4 March 1825 and 1 April 1825, JHL.

30. Ibid., December 1802, JHL.

31. Record Book, First Baptist Church of Providence, 31 August 1816, RIHS.

32. Barry Levy's discussion of the central concept of "conversation" in the context of Quaker religious life emphasizes the dual meaning of character and speech which attached to the term: "The Quaker's concept of 'conversation' included the idea that it was reflective of a person's inner being, and that it communicated meaning. . . . 'Conversation' thus included not only speech but behavior and non-verbal communication." Levy, " 'Tender Plants': Quaker Farmers and Children in the Delaware Valley, 1681–1735," *Journal of Family History* 3 (1978): 116–35.

33. Record Book, First Baptist Church of Tiverton, 28 July 1814, RIHS.

34. Record Book, Second Baptist Church of Coventry, 31 March and 6 October 1827, RIHS.

of "an irregular or disorderly walk—not only in regard to neglect of all Church obligations, but also in other respects, her conduct has been dishonorary to the Christian profession."[35] These examples are notable for the indeterminate nature of the charges leveled against these women and the speed with which they were excluded by their respective churches. It is highly significant that, as the catch-all label of "disorderly conduct" was used increasingly to signify a sinful character in the late eighteenth century (from a total of nine cases in the years 1740–80 to over 120 cases in the period 1780–1820), four times as many women as men were censured by the churches under this heading. Furthermore, those handful of men who were disciplined for "disorderly conduct" were, almost without exception, recent revival converts whose unstable and unreliable characters represented the "disorder of women" in the eyes of the evangelical church.[36]

"Circulating Evil Reports": Slanderous Women and Profane Men

In both their behaviors and their very natures, women seemed to represent a subversive voice in the evangelical discourse on authority after the American Revolution. When the First Baptist Church of Providence excluded Elizabeth Cross in 1816 for "the crime of using profane language . . . and also [for] her general character as a quarrelsome Woman,"[37] they were making a statement that disorderly speech signified nothing less than a disorderly nature, that the inner qualities of women were manifest in their verbal "outbreaks" (to use a popular evangelical term). The Providence church was furthermore drawing on a long tradition within New England Puritanism which viewed unruly speech as subversive of orderly relations in both the sacred and profane spheres. Late-eighteenth and early-nineteenth-century Baptist churches gave this old Puritan legacy a new twist by attributing disorderly speech to a fundamentally flawed character rather than to a temporary excess of passion. As we saw earlier, the evangelical community had always treated "unguarded" speech more leniently than deliberate forms of verbal transgression such as slander and lying, but in the mid-eighteenth century both men and women were considered equally likely to indulge in malicious verbal aggression. After 1780, only women seemed vulnerable to this new construction of the age-old problem of "heated speech."[38]

35. Record Book, Sturbridge Baptist Church, 1 January 1828, OSVL.
36. Twenty-five of the 29 men disciplined under this category were revival converts.
37. Record Book, First Baptist Church of Providence, 31 August 1816, RIHS.
38. The term "heated speech" is Robert St. George's; see his "'Heated Speech' and Literacy in

The dangerous nature of women's speech becomes clearer when we further break down the category of "crimes of the tongue" into its constituent parts. Combining the frequencies for primary and secondary offenses, we see women associated primarily with two particular sins: lying and bearing false witness or spreading reports (78 percent of all cases). The Second Baptist Church of Coventry recorded in 1796, "Whereas certain reports have gone out into the world against Br. Charles Stone and Br. Nathaniel Price by way of calumny whereby Some of the Church is grieved and after much Labor Sister Eunice Potter was by the best evidence we can get very much out of the way and still persists in it. Therefore this Church withdrew the hand of fellowship from her."[39] Susanna Crossing was rejected in 1792 for "concealing the conduct of [Anne] Jones [who was excluded the same day for fornication] and equivocating against the truth."[40] Lydia Jenks of the Pawtucket Baptist Church confessed in 1823 that she had been responsible for "Circulating Evil Reports about Sister Lydia Swetland" and was dismissed with a strong warning.[41] The First Baptist Church of Newport excluded Betsy Woodman in 1797 for "telling often and Repeated Falsehoods."[42] In a lengthy and acrimonious case in the North Stonington Baptist Church, Levi Walker complained that Mrs. Davis had "for a long time been circulating infamous and false things about me to injur me and my family." In charging her fellow communicant with various seductions, attempted and successful, of neighborhood women, David had accused Walker of acting "out of character" before "all the world."[43]

Men's verbal offenses, on the other hand, were concentrated in two categories of a very different order: profanity or swearing, and unguarded speech (78 percent of all cases). Whereas women's disorderly speech was thus described as devious and potentially subversive, men's outbursts were characterized in a much more benign way, as the product of misdirected passion rather than of deliberate malice. The First Baptist Church of Newport admonished Brother Grinnel in 1808 because "being in a Passion he had spoke unadvisedly with his Tongue."[44] James Pearl was accused by Thomas

Seventeenth-Century New England," in *Seventeenth-Century New England: A Conference Held by the Colonial Society of Massachusetts*, ed. David Hall and David Grayson Allen (Boston, 1984), pp. 275–322.

39. Record Book, Second Baptist Church of Coventry, 7 March 1796, RIHS.
40. Record Book, Second Baptist Church of Newport, 1 March 1792, NHS.
41. Record Book, First Baptist Church of Pawtucket, 4 September 1823.
42. Record Book, First Baptist Church of Newport, 20 January 1797, NHS.
43. Record Book, First Baptist Church of North Stonington, 13 May 1832, pp. 119–20, CSL.
44. Record Book, First Baptist Church of Newport, 3 September 1808, NHS.

Hill of lying in front of the Second Baptist Church of Ashford, but the church rejected this charge in favor of the far less serious one of imprudence: the church found that "sd Pearl Did not Lye but Spake inadvertently in saying there was nothing Saide about Money in his first Discorse with Mr. Hill."[45] As incidents of unguarded passion, men's verbal transgressions tended to involve more face-to-face confrontations with their adversaries, and indeed, most took place in highly public venues. Elisha Peck was excluded by the Lyme Baptist Church in 1783 for "Verry Vile Speaches that are Sinfull Rude and Carnal Behavior Before and with the men of this world."[46] Benjamin Jones of Providence was charged with "treating our Sister Simmons with abusive language" and likewise abusing his father and brother "with bad language." Since these charges were "of such a public nature," the discipline committee reported that "it became necessary to lay it immediately before the Church."[47] Because less public, women's disorderly speech can be seen as more dangerous to the larger community because less easily perceived and of broader consequence. A falsehood "spread abroad" can undermine the tissue of social relations more insidiously than a public quarrel in a tavern.[48]

It remains unclear from this evidence whether women's disorderly speech was discounted as slander because male authorities chose to construe it that way, or whether dispirited women in fact took refuge in slander as the last recourse of the disenfranchised.[49] We can, in other words, never know with any confidence whether the association of women with slander was a sign of changed behavior or changed perception. In the final analysis, the distinction may not matter because the consequences for evangelical women were the same: the loss of voice and thus of authority within the religious community. It was, in fact, the very irrelevancy to which women's opinions had

45. Record Book, Second Baptist Church of Ashford, 3 January 1781, CSL.
46. Record Book, First Baptist Church of Lyme, 12 December 1783, CSL.
47. Record Book, First Baptist Church of Providence, 2 October 1806, RIHS.
48. Other scholars have similarly contrasted men's propensity for open verbal confrontations, "face-to-face" verbal disorder, with women's preference for indirect, "behind-the-back" aggression. See Mary Beth Norton, "Gender and Defamation in Seventeenth-Century Maryland," WMQ, 3d ser., 44 (1987): 3–39; Cornelia Hughes Dayton, "Women before the Bar: Gender, Law, and Society in Connecticut, 1710–1790," Ph.D. diss., Princeton University, 1986.
49. As cultural anthropologists have suggested, verbal disorder usually derives from the anomalous status of the offender in the larger community and his or her opportunities to express discontent in more legitimate, sanctioned ways. Only those who have been denied a legitimate voice must resort to inappropriate and inacceptable modes of expression such as slander and lying. Susan Harding, for example, equates socially illegitimate speech such as gossip with powerlessness within the community of the speaker; see her "Women and Words in a Spanish Village," in Toward an Anthropology of Women, ed. Rayna Reiter (New York, 1975), pp. 283–308.

been reduced within the churches which rendered their continued expression so disconcerting. Denied the outlet of a legitimate and respected public voice in the institutional life of the church, women's efforts to express themselves were forced to take on a veiled, underhanded aspect that came to be described in evangelical writings as "dissimulation." The tendency to dissemble, to substitute appearance for reality, false impressions for true observations, was the logical outgrowth of a cultural system that removed all agency from its women members. In 1811 the First Baptist Church of Providence disowned Sister Sally Relph for her "disorderly" conduct in laying bare the implications of this new paradigm of womanhood; "[Sister Relph] did say," the church complained, "that 'if she [had] been in Mrs. Westcott's place (who was excluded from the church [for adultery]), she would not have been cut off, that she would have been more cunning, for she would have lied the church out of it' (or words to the same import)."[50] Of course, the irony is that by taking refuge in such dissembling, women evangelicals like Sally Relph who sought to circumvent the increasingly inflexible discipline process within the church found themselves paying the ultimate price: excommunication and banishment from their covenanted communities.

To understand the dimensions of the problem of women's slanderous speech, we must bear in mind the fear of internal sabotage which haunted the evangelical churches in the postrevolutionary years. If we train our sights only on the official literature of the Baptist leadership, we might be misled into concluding that the evangelical community had by and large succeeded in securing a place for itself in mainstream American culture by 1780. When we look beyond the official discourse to the internal life of the Baptist church, a very different picture emerges. Rather than the self-congratulatory posture of the regional associations, the internal records of Baptist congregations throughout New England reveal a deep sense of insecurity and ambivalence about the future of the evangelical cause. Unsure of its own institutional character and deeply suspicious of the political ambitions of its ecclesiastical rivals, the Baptist leadership of the late eighteenth century increasingly adopted a defensive posture. As Donald Weber writes, "[Patriot preachers] had once *acted* in history; by 1800, their secret desire was to get out of history, to a place where all 'remains the same.'"[51] Yet such a retreat was no longer possible. The decision to reorganize their polity along the twin models of "family" and "nation" was in effect a decision to engage history, to enter into the current of secular change.

50. Record Book, First Baptist Church of Providence, 21 February 1811, RIHS.
51. Donald Weber, *Rhetoric and History in Revolutionary New England* (New York, 1988), p. 149.

In the waning decades of the eighteenth century, evangelicals evinced an acute fear of being swept away by this current. Their fears revolved around the inability of the churches to maintain those boundaries that the evangelical community had erected to insulate itself from the outside world, to ensure the purity of its membership from a variety of temptations ranging from secular amusements to rival religious philosophies. The many references to the beleaguered status of the churches in their internal records—we should be, the clergy repeatedly warned, as "a Garden inclosed & a City wall'd around"—offer a very different window through which to view the alarming association of women with liminal behaviors such as slander.[52]

There was, first, a rise in concerns over the leaking of sensitive information about the church and its members outside the boundaries of the covenanted community in the late eighteenth and early nineteenth centuries. Often it was the confidentiality of the discipline process which was breached by unscrupulous communicants. "Altho it was stated to be very inconsistent to Good order or Discipline for members to open to the world the Transactions of Church Meetings & to make unfavourable statements one against another," the Tiverton church complained in 1815, such "tatling" was "evident to be much in Practice."[53] The Second Baptist Church of Newport canvased its membership in 1816 to uncover the person responsible for "having divulged the affairs of the Chh proceedings in an improper manner."[54] Baptist clergy throughout New England issued similar pleas in the post-revolutionary years for their members not to divulge sensitive information "abroad." The Warren Baptist Church protested in 1807, "It was represented that some persons who meet with us on Church meeting days reveal the confidential business of the Church to those without; who are not friendly to this Church."[55] Such concerns were echoed frequently by Stephen Gano, the elder of the First Baptist Church of Providence, who gave "a solemn

52. See, for example, the Record Book of the First Baptist Church of Tiverton for 30 December 1815, RIHS.

53. Ibid.

54. Record Book, Second Baptist Church of Newport, 29 August 1816, NHS. In another case, the Pawtucket Baptist Church appointed one of the deacons in 1826 to "enquire and ascertain the Person that has bin guilty of reporting the doings of the Church in the case of Sisters Patience & Olive Jenks out of the church contrary to the Rules of the same." At the next meeting it was reported that "William Jenks was the Person that communicated the Doings of the church to his wife Patience Jenks which information he obtained by Listening in a private place during the Time of Meeting." Record Book, First Baptist Church of Pawtucket, 28 December 1826 and 4 January 1827, RIHS.

55. Record Book, Warren Baptist Church, 4 November 1807, JHL.

and affectionate exhortation" in 1804 "enjoning it on the members to keep locked up within their own breasts the business of the church, and also to be very tender of the character of a brother or sister with regard to believing and reporting any thing to their disadvantage." Gano repeated his injunctions against "tatling and backbiting" sporadically throughout the next few years, obviously with little success. By 1811 the church adopted an explicit declaration that "any member who shall divulge the secret transactions of the Church is highly reprehensible for such conduct."[56]

We can see quite clearly in these statements the defensive posture assumed by the churches in their efforts to stem the hemorrhaging of sensitive information (and thus community reputation) from those within to those without, who, in the words of the Warren church, "are not friendly to this Church." This extreme, one might almost say paranoid, fear of the power of unchecked rumors to undermine religious life can be traced in every aspect of organized church life in the early nineteenth century. There was, for instance, a sizable increase in the number of charges and accusations against individual members brought into church discipline meetings by way of vague and unspecified "reports in circulation" not attributable to any one source. The Second Baptist Church of Newport reported in 1816: "Unfavourable reports in circulation concerning Sister Almy being stated in such a manner as precludes all doubt of her being a prophane person, [we] vote to suspend her."[57] The committee of the Warren Baptist Church appointed to "enquire into certain unsavoury reports respecting certain members" reported that "there existed various rumours to the prejudice of the moral & religious character of Br. Samuel Miller. . . . Also a very disadvantageous report was in circulation as to the moral & religious character of Sister Persis Spellman."[58] Lydia Wright and Betsey Bowen, who joined the Warren Baptist Church in the revival of 1801, found themselves facing church discipline less than a year later because of a "report Injurious to the Carrector" of the two women.[59] The number of cases in which no specific charge was ever levied against the defendant (as in the cases just cited)

56. See the records for 25 October 1804, 24 October, 21 November 1805, 30 January, 27 November 1806, and 31 January 1811, First Baptist Church of Providence, RIHS. See also the records of the New Light Beneficent Congregational church in Providence in which "secresy" was enjoined on the communicants in the aftermath of a bitter falling-out with the elder. Record Book, 10 February 1793, Beneficent Church Vault, Providence, RI.

57. Record Book, Second Baptist Church of Newport, 29 February 1816, NHS.

58. Record Book, Warren Baptist Church, 14 September 1821, JHL.

59. Ibid., December 1802, JHL.

increased sharply over the entire period, from only three in the decade 1771–80 to thirty-nine in 1810–20. The phrase "reports in circulation" is littered throughout church records thereafter.[60]

The unsubstantiated nature of these reports was not at issue; whether there was any truth to these reports or not, in the eyes of the church the damage lay in the mere fact of their existence. The Warren Baptist Church voted in 1822 to suspend Seth Peck "in consequence of certain unfavourable reports respecting his frequently visiting a certain neighbour's house" and requested Peck to "refrain from unnecessary visits, especially in the evening; in order to avoid all appearance of evil. Not that the church criminated him for doing such business," they continued, "or that he had not a good right to do so. But the good of the cause in this state of trial of the Church required the greatest circumspection from all its members."[61] The harm done in the spreading of such "reports" can be understood only in the context of the evangelical community's need to consolidate its cultural authority in the wake of the Revolution. The problem of sealing off the borders of the community was a problem in gender definition, as femininity became a metaphor for liminality. If the character of the evangelical community could not be contained within the bounds of patriarchal propriety, then its hidden feminine nature would once again be exposed.

Another source of trouble was the insinuation of newer, more liberal denominations such as the Methodists and the Unitarians into the hearts and purses of Baptist communicants. In the late eighteenth and early nineteenth centuries we see a notable increase in the number of church members disciplined for leaving the Baptist cause and transferring their allegiance to other denominations, chiefly the accursed Methodists. Benson Bean, for example, was excluded from the Warren Baptist Church in 1822 for having "conspired against the church's peace and welfare" in "drawing off from the church, associating with those who were evidently hostile to the church [i.e.,

---

60. In a statistical representation of the sources of accusations against individual members in the discipline records, the category of unidentified and unsubstantiated "reports" becomes the single largest category after 1810. The table below shows the various sources of charges against a church member from 1770 to 1830:

Source	1771–80	1781–90	1791–1800	1801–10	1811–20	1821–30
Elder	0	0	3	0	1	1
Another member	12	19	29	20	24	13
Unidentified "reports"	1	5	4	9	30	48

61. Record Book, Warren Baptist Church, 4 July 1822, JHL.

the Methodists], frequently indulging in unjust & unfriendly remarks respecting its doctrine & discipline, etc. etc." His fellow communicant Miller Barney was charged in the same year with "encourag[ing] a spirit of division in and alienation from the church" and was likewise found guilty of "conspiring against it's [the church's] welfare and union."[62] Even the staid Episcopalians snared a few apostates from the evangelical cause: Walton Fetch was excluded from the Providence Baptist Church for "using his influence to undervalue the baptist cause and in lieu thereof to build up the cause of the episcopalians by having his children by them sprinkled and prefering their society to that of the baptists."[63]

The language in these records is consistently one of conspiracies and rebellions against the parent church by unprincipled adventurers who have allowed themselves to be seduced away from the path of truth. The Preston Separate Church took up the case of Mary Patting, who in 1783 "had Joyned herself to the People and Purswasion Caled Shaking Quakers." Mary was found guilty of apostasy and "Giving heed to Seduced Spirits and Doctrins of Devils Speaking Lies in hypocricy forbiding to marry etc."[64] Two sisters were excluded from the First Baptist Church in Groton in 1782 for joining the society of the Publick Universal Friend (a sect formed by a charismatic former Quaker, Jemima Wilkinson, in the 1770s). Confronted with the evidence of her heresy, Sarah Niles proudly declared before the church that "the Friend did not come to be Taught she came to Teach." When asked if "she thought the Friend was a Greater Teacher than any of the ministers we have in the Land or Grater than any that has ben sence Christ was personally on Earth, she Answered in the affirmative." In its letter of excommunication to Niles and her fellow apostate Sarah Brown, the church warned others who might be tempted to join the Friend "not to give heed to quick Fabels and Commandments of men that turn from the truth . . . be no more children tosted to & fro and carried about with every wind of Doctrin by the Slight of men and cunning Craftiness whereby they Lie in Wait to Deceive."[65] The Baptist church felt itself beseiged in the late eighteenth century by such unscrupulous religious adventurers as Jemima Wilkinson and Mother Ann Lee, whose cunning was no match for communicants of weak will or insufficient understanding.

62. Ibid., 14 July 1822, JHL.
63. Record Book, First Baptist Church of Providence, 30 June 1825, RIHS.
64. "Records of the Separate Church by Rev. Paul Park, from 1747 to 1800," *Parke Scrapbook*, comp. Ruby Anderson (Baltimore, 1965), n.p.
65. Record Book, First Baptist Church of Groton, vol. 1, 21 February 1782 and 11 November 1783, CSL.

This, then, was the context in which the evangelical church disciplined women who slandered: the "secret" business of the church betrayed to "unfriendly" ears, ominous "reports in circulation" about the backslidings of the faithful, members too easily seduced away from the Baptist cause by rival denominations. While their numbers are not especially large, slanderous women came to represent a special kind of disorder—that which most threatened the integrity of the evangelical community as a whole.

"Tatling & Railing to an uncommon Degree": *Challenging the Church*

The silencing of women's disorderly voices extended to their periodic attempts to intervene in the doctrinal and liturgical disputes that engaged the evangelical community in the late eighteenth and early nineteenth centuries. Although charges of "contempt of church authority" were much more evenly distributed among male and female communicants than were accusations of personal transgression, this overall symmetry conceals a fundamental difference in the way men's and women's challenges were conceived and expressed. Men were more likely to mount direct challenges to church doctrine or organizational structure; women, on the other hand, vented their discontent in highly personal attacks on the characters of the church's official representatives, the elders and deacons.

In 1772, Deacon Samuel Munger of Ashford withdrew from the First Baptist church because "the Church Would not fling them Selves into Individuals and begin anew by Way of teling Experience."[66] Like his brethren in other Baptist churches who contested liturgical practices, Munger was participating in a much larger discussion about the role of the laity in defining the terms of membership in the religious community. The erosion of the individualistic bent of the Baptist denomination in the second half of the eighteenth century was by no means uncontested, and male members led the fight to reclaim the principle of lay supremacy from the tyranny of respectability.

Elder Gardiner Thurston of the Second Baptist Church of Newport complained in 1795 that Brother Parker Hall "often spoke against Priestcraft and Manufactured Preaches, to his great grief and discomfort."[67] Thomas Grow withdrew from the Hampton Baptist Church because "he was so Put out with Elder Balding's Preaching in hampton meeting house that he

---

66. Record Book, First Baptist Church of Ashford, 11 October 1772, CSL.
67. Record Book, Second Baptist Church of Newport, 26 February 1795, NHS.

would not go to hear him nor None of his folks."[68] And Isaac Babcock charged the Westerly Baptist Church in 1793 of promoting a "wild fire Religion" and having "so fallen Bee loo the witness that they was like the Hearth in the Desert that did not know where Good came."[69] These men were not simply voicing personal quarrels with their respective churches, but rather expressing a broader current of discontent with the loss of individual autonomy and lay initiative which sporadically engaged the evangelical order in the years after independence.

Issues such as the propriety of a professional ministry and the efficacy of "manufactured" sermons had been perennial bones of contention in the Baptist community throughout the eighteenth century. Increasingly, however, women dropped out of these debates; their challenges to church authority came to be centered not on issues of doctrine and lay control but rather on the much less potent terrain of personal invective. The Tiverton Baptist Church concluded in 1784, "[T]he Speeches [Sarah Taber] hath made from time to time before several of us at her own House and her shocking disorderly behaviour at Ch Meeting since time past; Amount to tatling & Railing to an uncommon Degree."[70] Hannah Burroughs was excluded from the Second Baptist Church of Newport in 1832 for her "personal abuse of the character of our brother Deacon Sweet," which the church labeled "unparalleled and unjustifiable." "Her observations on the Church being corrupt and under an evil influence," the church continued, "were truly astonishing and that she could never again travail with the Church until Deacon Sweet repented of his wicked conduct and the Sisters made an acknowledgment to her for their ill Treatment and in time she made many observations too virulent and shameful to be repeated."[71]

Unlike their sisters from an earlier age, who had actively participated in the theological debates of their day, these women contributed little to the vital struggle over lay control then being waged by their male counterparts. Rather, they were left to rail at the church hierarchy in terms too intemperate to constitute a serious threat. Hannah Burroughs' grievances with Deacon Sweet were "too virulent and shameful to be repeated," and presumably too rash to be taken seriously. Like Betsey Luther, other women found their discontents attributed to mental derangement or instability. In 1828 the Second Baptist Church of Newport found that "Eliza Nagg having behaved in an unbecoming manner and appearing to be Deranged Voted that she be

68. Record Book, Hampton Baptist Church, 1 September 1804, CSL.
69. Record Book, First Baptist Church of Westerly, 30 October 1793, RIHS.
70. Record Book, First Baptist Church of Tiverton, 24 June 1784, RIHS.
71. Record Book, Second Baptist Church of Newport, 3 April 1832, NHS.

suspended."[72] In an earlier case, the church could not decide whether a sister's unchristian conduct was the product of unstable mental faculties or a disordered nature: "It appeared to some that her conduct was from insanity to others from an evil temper all considered that at present she is unfit for communion."[73] The Providence Baptist Church, "considering the deranged state of Sister Polly Allen's mind," voted that she be prevented from attending the Lord's Supper.[74] When we recall the cavalier dismissal of Joanna Gano's complaints against her husband and the other freemasons in the Providence Baptist Church in 1803 as the result of derangement and satanic delusions, a clear pattern emerges. To speak up was to risk ridicule, the label of insanity, and court censure.

Women's loss of voice in the theological discourse of the evangelical churches was primarily a late-eighteenth-century phenomenon, though a similar development had occurred much earlier in the established churches. We find women staking out a particular theological ground in the early years of New England Congregationalism, which was gradually eroded over the next two generations. Mary Maples Dunn has used evidence from heresy trials in seventeenth-century New England to argue that Puritan women actively engaged their churches in disputes over doctrine, though by the end of the century "women had lost the battle for control over doctrine, which now belonged to men." Thereafter female challenges to the church's authority would be seen as breaches of proper moral and social conduct.[75] It is not surprising that women in the newer evangelical churches experienced this same process of ideological disenfranchisement a century later, as their religious communities reorganized along the established congregational model.

The diminished role of Baptist women in matters of theological importance can be seen in the declining frequency with which women were chastised for questioning doctrine. Richard Rabinowitz has recently argued that doctrine was the essential component of the evangelical religious experience in the federalist era and that (correspondingly) doctrinal heresies constituted "the greatest threat to church order" after 1800.[76] A systematic survey of church records reveals in fact that doctrinal heresies accounted for only a

72. Ibid., 22 August 1828.
73. Ibid., 23 December 1814.
74. Record Book, First Baptist Church of Providence, August 1795, RIHS.
75. Mary Maples Dunn, "Saints and Sisters: Congregational and Quaker Women in the Early Colonial Period," *American Quarterly* 30 (1978): 582–601.
76. Rabinowitz, *The Spiritual Self in Everyday Life*, p. 68. Rabinowitz acknowledges in a footnote that this claim is based on "careful reading, not quantitative analysis" of the records of the Baptist and Congregational churches in Sturbridge, and the Congregational churches in Bristol, Hampton, New Hartford, and Somers (p. 68).

small fraction of the total number of discipline cases between 1790 and 1820, but Rabinowitz is right to emphasize the significance of these doctrinal challenges in the eyes of the evangelical churches, who devoted considerable discussion in their monthly meetings to the spread of universalist and other heretical sentiments. For example, the First Baptist Church of Providence agreed not to hold communion in 1819 "untill the difficulty that now existed in the church is settled (meaning the suspicion that some of the members had embraced Arian principles.)" Five months later, "having for some time been agitated and divided in consequence of the Arian doctrine supposed to be holden by some of our members," it took a vote to deny fellowship to all who "openly and avowedly deny the Deity of our Lord Jesus Christ."[77] What Rabinowitz fails to note is that the challenge to such orthodox evangelical doctrines as particular election came almost exclusively from men. Women's challenges to church authority, on the other hand, assumed far less direct and menacing forms after the revolutionary period because they were labeled mere slander by their opponents. Only a handful of women were known to have embraced universalist or other heretical sentiments in the early 1800s, and most of these did so in the shadow of their husbands. When Brother Helms was disowned by the Westerly Baptist Church in 1791 for accusing the church of "having gone Contrary to the Gospel," his wife belatedly declared that she too "co[u]ld walk no further with the Church, for she Believed the Ch had Delt with them Contrary to the Gospel."[78] Other women faithfully followed their heretical husbands out of the church rather than risk domestic discord. When women's domestic fealty conflicted with a troubled conscience, loyalty to home won out. Rarely would women risk alienating husbands or fathers over the finer points of doctrine as they had earlier in the century. One woman admitted in fact that she had joined the church "only to please her Husband" and found herself disowned for her "Hipocrisy."[79]

"In a Deceitful Manner": The Feminization of Sin

So far, we have reviewed the kinds of offenses for which men and women were censured in the postrevolutionary church, and the gendered distinction between character and conduct which seems to have guided the application

77. Record Book, 4 February and 1 July 1819, First Baptist Church of Providence, RIHS.

78. Record Book, First Baptist Church of Westerly, 21 September 1791, RIHS.

79. Record Book, 16 October 1809, Beneficent Congregational church, Beneficent Church Vault, Providence, R.I.

of discipline. To the extent that women were overrepresented in certain categories of sin (illicit sex, crimes of the tongue, railing against church authority), we can speculate about the evangelical understanding of the female character as naturally disorderly. Every time a sister was excluded for fornication, or lying, or (most damning of all) spreading evil reports about a fellow communicant, the image of woman as seductress (i.e., as Eve) was confirmed in the eyes of the community. But the problem of seduction and deceit went far deeper than the verbal and sexual indecencies of women. For if dissembling women were the archetypal sinners, then men who practiced deceit were metaphorically feminized. Every time a brother was accused of cheating on his wife, or defrauding his creditors, or prevaricating about his business affairs, the specter of female disorderliness menaced again.

Significantly, the quality of "dissimulation" or deceitfulness became increasingly attached to other categories of sin at the very time when lying and slander became particularly female vices. When Polly Harrison was charged by the First Baptist Church of Newport with theft in 1792, the church responded harshly because she had lied when confronted with the evidence: "You have rendered your Selfe not only guilty of unjustly takeing that which was anothers property But also of Lying and thareby you have Doubled your Transgression."[80] The sin of lying always "doubled" the import of any particular transgression because it interfered with the churches' ability to enforce their disciplinary codes. Edward Sarnders not only joined "another people or church we did not recommend him to," the Hampton Baptist Church protested, but did so "in a Deceitful manner."[81] Sarah Woodmancy was "not only guilty of vain Dancing & covering it with a lie," the Tiverton Baptist Church complained in 1781, "but also had told other lies to our Sisters Sarah Griswold & Elisabeth Cook!"[82] The hidden motif in these cases was deception, the deliberate attempt to conceal or "cover" sinful deeds. An article published in the *Baptist Magazine* concluded that deceit was the very essence of sin:

> [Sin] assumes a variety of false names, and delusive appearances; it calls light darkness, and darkness light, evil good and good evil. Covetousness is named prudence, and taking care of the main chance; licentiousness is denominated gallantry; drunkenness is called animated cheerfulness; wanton profusion is styled exalted generosity; profaneness is only a

80. Records of First Baptist Church of Newport, 13 December 1792, B.B. Howland Collection, Box 103, NHS.
81. Record Book, Hampton Baptist Church, 23 June 1789, CSL.
82. Record Book, First Baptist Church of Tiverton, 31 May 1781, RIHS.

trifling habit; Sabbath-breaking taking the air; a luxurious man, a gen-
erous soul; Pride and liftiness, maintaining our rank in life; angry passions
are called hastiness, spirit, valour, manliness; deceit, policy. Thus vice is
ornamented and pronounced good.[83]

As this passage suggests, all kinds of sin were considered but variations
on the central theme of dissimulation. The sin of intemperance, for instance, became the tendency to be "disguised" with drink. Reports were
circulating in Pawtucket in 1805 that Benjamin Barrows "had been disguised
with liquor." Abraham Studley confessed in 1813 to the sin of drunkenness,
"so far as at some times to have been disguised with liquor."[84] Accusations of
"frawd" and dishonesty in business dealings also proliferated after 1790. In
contrast to the mid-eighteenth century, deceit, rather than avarice, was at
issue in these disputes over commercial transactions. Jesse Maynard was
admonished by the Lyme Baptist Church in 1795 for "Deceiving one of the
Men of the World in Swapping horses or Not Letting the man have the true
knolidge of his Beasts age." Samuel Nichols, "having left the town after
conducting in such a manner as to destroy our confidence in him," was
excluded by the Second Baptist Church of Newport. James Hammons'
relations with his creditors, the Beneficent Congregational church concluded in 1804, were "fraught with dissimulation," a phrase that particularly
rankled Hammons when he came before the church six years later to make
"satisfaction"; "it appeared he was willing to submit to the admonition but
only with the exception of the words fraught with dissimulation which
terms he conceived bore to[o] severe an explanation for his case." Hammons
made a full confession only after the church agreed to strike the offending
passage from its censure.[85]

The theme of "counterfeit" money runs through many of the cases dealing with transgressions in the commercial arena. Peter Keech was excluded
by the Providence church in 1808 for the metaphorically apt sin of "aiding

83. "The Deceitfulness of Sin," *BM* 3 (1811): 322.
84. Record Book, First Baptist Church of Pawtucket, 29 September 1805, RIHS; Record
Book, First Baptist Church of Providence, 9 October 1813, RIHS. See also the case of Isaac
Brownell, who was admonished by the Beneficent Congregational Church in 1823 for being "disguised with ardent spirits." Record Book, 17 February 1823, Beneficent Church Vault, Providence.
85. Several men were accused of "frawd" in their business dealings in the Beneficent Congregational church; see the records for 12 May 1813 and 8 October 1817, Beneficent Church Vault,
Providence; Record Book, First Baptist Church of Lyme, 23 June 1795, CSL; Record Book, Second
Baptist Church of Newport, 22 August 1828, NHS; Record Book, First Baptist Church of Providence, 5 August 1808, RIHS. The Hammons case can be found in the records for 17 September 1804
and 3 July 1810, Beneficent Church Vault, Providence.

and assisting in Counterfeiting Bank Bills." Several Baptist men, especially in the maritime centers of Newport and Providence, were disowned for attempting to repay their debts in paper money rather than in silver; the Second Baptist Church of Newport suspended John McWhorter from their communion in 1786 "as they look'd upon it as unjust in McWhorter to think to discharge a hard Money contract with Paper Money."[86] His fellow communicant Benoni Peckham was censured a year later for "rendering a Sum of paper Money in order to discharge a Mortgage of Lydia Sanford when the Discount was Six & Seven for one. The Brethren Unanimously conclude it so being unjust on his part and quite unbecoming the Christian."[87] The economic crisis represented by the circulation of paper money was but one manifestation of a larger social problem in postrevolutionary society, namely the inability to determine rank and status in a society in which old standards had been discarded.[88]

As if to emphasize the problem of "bad" money passing for real, the evangelical press of the early 1800s published a series of articles warning against the admission of "impure" Christians (frequently described as "bad specie") into the churches. Just as "spurious money renders them suspicious of the genuine coin with which it may happen to be collected, so these pretenders cast the shade of their own scandal upon the genuine sons of Zion," cautioned the *American Baptist Magazine and Missionary Intelligencer* in 1822. "These fallacious members of Christ's family, conscious of the counterfeit qualities within them, usually make an infinte parade of their Religion."[89] Repeated warnings against "designing imposters," "doubtful and doubting characters" who "disfigure our religious communities," and "false brethren" who will "cover the church with disgrace and mourning" helped raise the fear of deceit to a fevered pitch in a community eager to avoid the least whiff of scandal.[90]

Finally, a new category of sin first made its appearance in the 1790s—that of attending the theater. The First Baptist Church of Providence, noting that "the Church had never expressed their opinion respecting the propriety

86. Record Book, Second Baptist Church of Newport, 20 September 1786, NHS. McWhorter was back in church to answer to similar charges in September 1789 when he attempted to repay Charles Handy in paper money rather than silver; see the record for 2 September 1789.

87. Ibid., 2 August 1789, NHS.

88. See Gordon Wood, *The Radicalism of the American Revolution* (New York, 1992), pt. 3, for the fullest treatment of this problem in postrevolutionary America.

89. "In Discerning between the Righteous and the Wicked," *ABMMI* 3 (1822): 246–48.

90. "Religious Imposters," *BM* 7 (1815): 55; "A Warning to Professors," *BM* 1 (1809): 102–3; "Thoughts on Discipline," *MBMMI* 3 (1812): 244–47; "Things to be Set in Order in the Churches," *ABMMI* 1 (1812): 443.

of frequenting the theatre," voted in 1795 that it was "the general sense of the Church that the Theatre is Productive of many disadvantages to Civil Society, as well as tends to Create undue Levity."[91] This campaign to discourage members from attending theatrical productions can be seen as symptomatic of a larger concern over deceitful appearances, of the growing need to separate inner reality from outward forms. The costumes actors and actresses wore to disguise their natural selves were metaphorically akin to the false masks worn by sinners to hide their corruption. Nothing disturbed the church leadership more than the thought that sin was going undetected because profane men and women had perfected the "art" of dissimulation, an art that, moreover, carried distinct feminine overtones in eighteenth-century social discourse. Harry Stout notes that in the eighteenth-century Anglo-American world the theater was condemned for its association with sex and the passions. The "effeminacy" of the theater, embodied in the common practices of men's wearing dresses, playing women's roles, and singing with high voices made it especially vulnerable to cultural attack.[92] Along with the unstable passions of women, the theater seemed to embody the fickleness of the new market capitalism as well—a dangerous combination. Whether construed as a fickle woman or a fickle market, the theater came to stand for the "labile, formless, qualityless, characterless" nature of social life in democratic America.[93]

In an important sense, then, this new concern with dissimulation was the ideological representation of the uncertain social and economic order of America in the 1790s and early 1800s. The prevalence of commercial metaphors to describe the problem of misrepresentation is highly suggestive in this light. It is surely no accident that the analogy of using paper money in lieu of "real" currency surfaces again and again in evangelical writings in the postrevolutionary period to describe the difficulty of distinguishing true from false conversions. The rise of a monied economy and the increasing reliance on credit to finance economic expansion in the late eighteenth and early nineteenth centuries was as important as the revolutionary crisis in focusing Americans' attention on the problem of deceit. The fear that bad elements would contaminate the pure currency of the evangelical church was inextricably bound up with the fear of economic insolvency which

91. Record Book, First Baptist Church of Providence, 26 November and 24 December 1795, RIHS.
92. Harry Stout, *The Divine Dramatist: George Whitefield and the Rise of Modern Evangelicalism* (Grand Rapids, Mich., 1991), p. 23.
93. Jean-Christophe Agnew, *Worlds Apart: The Market and the Theater in Anglo-American Thought, 1550–1750* (New York, 1986), p. 9 and passim.

plagued fledgling capitalists in the early republic. One historian describes the early republic as the "golden age" of imposters and counterfeiters.[94] And just as revolutionary patriots constructed a political dialogue that pitted effeminancy against manliness in the service of national independence, the language of commerce relied heavily on gendered oppositions in this period. In the discursive wars surrounding the financial revolution of the early eighteenth century, J. G. A. Pocock and others have observed, credit and investment were figured female. Credit in particular was "equated with fantasy, passion, and dynamic change" and with the "hysterical fluctuations" that a commercialized future portended. By personifying "Lady Credit" as an inconstant female figure, popular writers like Daniel Defoe and Bernard Mandeville constructed an image of a "female monster" who would destroy traditional economic and social patterns through her inordinate lust and insatiable ambition.[95] In an age of rapid economic change, it is no wonder that eighteenth-century evangelicals would conflate commercial and sexual disorder in the figure of the female sinner. Nor is it surprising that, as women were presumably being rendered economically irrelevant by the forces of early industrialism, such a rhetorical tradition would persist and indeed intensify in the early nineteenth century. For, as we have seen in the case of women slanderers, irrelevancy is not synonymous with impotence. The ability to deceive is wielded most effectively by the disenfranchised, by those who bear only the form and no longer the substance of power.

Like patriarchs everywhere, evangelical men felt most threatened when women's sexuality threatened to overstep prescribed bounds.[96] There was in the eighteenth-century world a natural connection between deceit and seduction; as "unruly Members," both tongues and sexual organs were especially prone to disorder. "There is the tongue and another member of the body," Jonathan Edwards wrote cryptically in his private journal, "that have a natural bridle, which is to signify to us the peculiar need we have to bridle

94. Nathan O. Hatch, *The Democratization of American Christianity* (New Haven, Conn., 1989), p. 36.

95. J. G. A. Pocok, *Virtue, Commerce, and History: Essays on Political Thought and History, Chiefly in the Eighteenth Century* (New York, 1985), p. 99. See also Deborah Laycock, "Exchange Alley: The Sexual Politics of South Sea Investment," paper presented at the Western Society of Eighteenth Century Studies conference, San Diego, February 1991, for a discussion of the gendered imagery of credit and speculation.

96. See Kenneth Lockridge's essay on the rage expressed by would-be patriarchs when confronted with their own weaknesses: *On the Sources of Patriarchal Rage: The Commonplace Books of William Byrd and Thomas Jefferson and the Gendering of Power in the Eighteenth Century* (New York, 1992).

and restrain those two members."[97] But whereas Edwards was referring to the need to restrain male sexuality in particular, by the early nineteenth century the source of corrupting carnality was lodged firmly in the female body. "Of all the Sources from whence are derived the most injurious results to individuals and to Society in general . . . we apprehend there will be no difference of opinion among the thinking part of mankind if we assert that *abandonned women* have in every age borne away the palm, in the miseries they have produced," declared the *Baptist Magazine* in 1812. The Christian moralist "will find no difficulty in tracing their contaminating influence from the public streets, the theatres, and the more private haunts of general dissipation, through the inventors of fashion, the toilet, and the ball, to the parlor and the drawing room." The "lurking poison" of women's sexuality "insinuat[ed] itself in the most unsuspecting forms." From the street to the home, seducing women thus embodied the very essence of disorder.[98] At the very time when middle-class Americans were beginning to develop a notion of women as naturally "passionless" rather than inordinately lustful, evangelical Christians were resurrecting the ancient model of woman as seducing Eve.[99] In this context the overwhelming association of women with both slander and sexual misconduct in the discipline records sent a message that could not have been missed by discerning evangelical men and women, that to sin was to reenact the disobedience of Eve.

Such fears of female sexuality and dissimulation had a wide resonance in broader American culture after the Revolution. Perhaps nothing suggests more the degree to which evangelicals were now *of* the world rather than a world apart than the tendency to conflate femaleness with deception.[100] By

97. Quoted in Philip Greven, *The Protestant Temperament: Patterns of Child-Rearing, Religious Experience, and the Self in Early America* (New York, 1977), p. 129.

98. Review of "Considerations on the Causes and the Prevalence of Female Prostitution" by William Hale, *BM* 4 (1812): 254–56. The author dismissed the sentimental notion that fallen women were to be pitied as the victims of cruel circumstance: "[N]o woman ever becomes a harlot, or continues in prostitution a single hour, but *by her own choice.*"

99. See Nancy F. Cott, "Passionlessness: An Interpretation of Victorian Sexual Ideology, 1790–1850," *Signs* 4 (1978): 219–36, for a discussion of this shift in the image of women.

100. For an intriguing discussion of how the problem of deception was feminized in a different context in postrevolutionary America, see Toby Ditz, "Shipwrecked; or, Masculinity Imperiled: Representations of Failure and the Gendered Self in Eighteenth-Century Philadelphia," *Journal of American History* 81 (1994): 51–80. For other discussions of eighteenth-century literature associating women with appearance, vanity, and deception, see Tassie Gwilliam, "*Pamela* and the Duplicitous Body of Femininity," *Representations* 34 (1991): 104–33; Lynn Hunt, "The Many Bodies of Marie Antoinette: Political Pornography and the Problem of the Feminine in the French Revolution," in *Eroticism and the Body Politic*, ed. Lynn Hunt (Baltimore, Md., 1991), pp. 108–30.

the early nineteenth century, dissimulation was not a problem peculiar to revived religion but was in fact an inescapable consequence of the new cultural ideal of sentimental womanhood. Women's "influence," as Ann Douglas has most forcefully argued, became a compensatory mechanism for the loss of status and power which accompanied the loss of economic function occasioned by industrialization.[101] Like their allies, the disestablished clergy, sentimental women insinuated themselves into the hearts and minds of those within their sphere by practicing the art of indirect coercion. The stream of feminine discontent embodied in the figures of such earlier rebels as Ann Hutchinson and Anne Eaton in the first years of settlement and Ann Lee and Jemima Wilkinson in the eighteenth century, had simply gone underground by 1800, not to be exposed to the light of public discourse but rather pursued in the dark regions of intimate associations. That Joanna Gano's anger was directed first and foremost at her husband is important in this light. Clearly the vehemence and bitterness of her attack can be read as symptomatic of thwarted domestic "influence" as much as of intellectual impotence. Mrs. Gano can thus be seen as a transitional figure struggling to find an appropriate language in which to articulate her frustrated vision of the church. Stripped of a legitimate intellectual voice in her community, not yet in possession of an ideology of domestic "influence," it is not surprising that she sounds shrill to our ears.

By 1830, as Karen Halttunen has suggested in a study of middle-class Victorian America, the implications of the sentimental ethos of "influence" (especially feminine influence) had come to be recognized as morally as well as socially disruptive. The preoccupation with hypocrisy in middle-class advice literature derived from fears that such "influence" could, and indeed was, being misapplied to corrupt rather than ennoble those who came within its sphere.[102] As Jay Fliegelman has similarly argued, the popularization of Lockean sensationalist psychology in postrevolutionary literature opened the way for a less optimistic reading of the impact of environmental influences on the human character; not only could character be molded by the inspired intervention of virtuous mothers, but it could as easily be deformed by the devious machinations of less sincere figures.[103] And as historians of republicanism have repeatedly stressed, the critical quality of public and private virtue which underpinned the entire republican edifice was its vul-

101. Ann Douglas, *The Feminization of American Culture* (New York, 1977).

102. Karen Halttunen, *Confidence Men and Painted Women: A Study of Middle-Class Culture in America, 1830–1870* (New Haven, 1982).

103. Jay Fliegelman, *Prodigals and Pilgrims: The American Revolution against Patriarchal Authority, 1750–1800* (New York, 1982).

nerability to distortion in the wrong hands. Republican men and, especially, women carried an enormous social responsibility in the post-1790 period to fulfill the promise of the revolutionary struggle to secure the cause of liberty through the creation of a virtuous citizenry.[104] Thus these three strains of ideology—republicanism, Lockean psychology, and early Victorian sentimentalism—came together by 1830 to create a new social problem: that of "mistaking false appearances for reality, words for things," in Gordon Wood's terms—or, more simply, hypocrisy. The evangelical term for this social problem was dissimulation, and the attack in the Baptist churches on the perceived spread of deceit and disorder came to be centered on women after 1780 as the most vulnerable and marginalized members of their community.

To an impressive degree, the churches in the early nineteenth century succeeded in avoiding the marginality associated with femininity. In fact, once the Second Great Awakening erupted with full force in the 1820s and 1830s, the evangelical community had been so effectively reoriented around a masculine model of authority that the by-now predominantly female membership posed little threat to the patriarchal pretensions of the evangelical leadership. Women knew their place, and it was not in the governing structures of the church or in the arena of public opinion. It is thus surprising to find in the late 1820s some signs of a revival in women's public status which coincided with the revivals of the Second Great Awakening. The Warren Baptist Church, which had excluded Betsey Luther in 1823 for insisting on her right to participate in church "business," recanted its position three years later. "Whereas an erroneous opinion has prevailed upon the subject of church meetings," they declared in August 1826, "Resolved, unanimously, that the male members of this church consider it to be compatible both with the duty & the privilege of Female members of this church to attend the monthly Church Meetings for business therof, so far as their domestic concerns will allow them."[105] While continuing to insist that women's "do-

---

104. Gordon Wood, *The Creation of the American Republic* (Chapel Hill, N.C., 1969). Wood's conception of the unstable nature of republican virtue is elaborated in his "Conspiracy and the Paranoid Style: Causality and Deceit in the Eighteenth Century," *WMQ*, 3d ser., 39 (1982): 401–41, in which he argues that concern over deceit was a logical outgrowth of the Enlightenment insistence on attributing social and political effects to human causes rather than on divine providence. On the role of women in the republican experiment, see Linda Kerber, "The Republican Mother: Women and the Enlightenment—An American Perspective," *American Quarterly* 27 (1976): 187–205; Ruth H. Bloch, "American Feminine Ideals in Transition: The Rise of the Moral Mother, 1785–1815," *Feminist Studies* 4 (1978): 125–26; and Jan Lewis, "The Republican Wife: Virtue and Seduction in the Early Republic," *WMQ*, 3d ser., 44 (1987): 689–721.

105. Record Book, Warren Baptist Church, 4 August 1826, JHL.

mestic concerns" should circumscribe their religious activities, the brethren of the Warren church no longer felt it necessary to exclude women entirely from church "business." Perhaps twenty years of extensive revival activity, which netted the church new prestige as well as members, had mitigated the anxiety over status which lay behind the campaign to remove women from church offices. Perhaps the "feminization" of the church which had seemed so ominous in the late eighteenth century, prompted the adoption of a feminized model of sin, had become an accepted fact of religious life by 1820. Whatever the reason, within two years both men and women were once again participating in the exercise of church discipline in Warren. When the case of Rebecca Drawn came before the church in 1828, the church clerk recorded that "some of the Brethren and sisters were dissatisfied" with her testimony.[106] Rather than observing mutely the business of church discipline, as in Betsey Luther's day, women were now voicing their opinions about the merits of individual cases.

In a similar vein, the Second Baptist Church of Ashford in 1830 restored to women the right to speak publicly in church, a right that had been denied them for fifty years; "Voted to keep the door open for all the brethren & sisters to improve their gives [gifts] that is for edification."[107] The restoration of women's right to speak in 1830—given the attack on women's speech as inherently disorderly in church discipline records over the previous half century—was a critical turning point in the evangelical community's relationship with its women members. The vigorous participation of many women evangelicals in the social reform movements of the antebellum period, which was a direct outgrowth of their religious commitments, is perhaps the best evidence we have that the evangelical clergy had finally accepted the alliance with their women communicants which a "feminized" church seemed to require. The question that remains (and it is one that is largely unanswerable) is whether women's qualified resumption of a more public role in church life after 1830 represents a victory or a defeat. It may be that when women spoke it was with the subdued cadences of the disempowered, voices that no longer threatened because they no longer mattered. What women said with their restored voices may have convinced church authorities that it was all right for them to speak. Had the female tongue been truly domesticated by 1830? Or had women reclaimed for themselves a voice that was still discordant, still capable of eliciting powerful male anxieties about their own precarious status?

106. Ibid., 24 August 1828, JHL.
107. Record Book, Second Baptist Church of Ashford, 22 May 1830, CSL.

We shall see in the next chapter that, even while the evangelical churches were waging a campaign to silence the disorderly women within their congregations, a space for women to "speak" was being metaphorically created by the evangelical press. In the model of religious conversion promoted by the evangelical press in the early 1800s, women turned the image of the dissimulating female on its head: as saints, women were "enabled" (in the language of the conversion literature) once again to express their religious needs and desires in an acceptable idiom. Whereas men continually struggled to find salvation through the pursuit of good works (the antidote to the "misdeeds" they were prone to commit in their profane lives), women seemed to recognize (perhaps because of the devaluation of their characters within the institution of the church) that only a complete reformation of character could lead them to God. Ironically, the model of gender created in the internal workings of the evangelical church was appropriated and transformed in the conversion accounts of the early 1800s into a model of the regenerate which promoted an androgynous vision of the saint.

CHAPTER SIX

"IN A DIFFERENT VOICE"

Postrevolutionary Conversion Narratives

THE PROCESS by which the evangelical community became "defeminized" after the Revolution was neither simple nor straightforward. To equate liminality with femininity, thereby devaluing both, as the evangelical leadership attempted to do in the early republican period was to venture into dangerous territory. However much the clergy may have wished to distance themselves from the marginality associated with a liminal position, the essence of evangelical Protestantism remained for most the experience of conversion. And the essence of conversion, as I have suggested earlier, was its transformative quality—its ability to make "old" things "new," sinners into saints, men and women into genderless beings. This ability to transcend, even eradicate, conventional boundaries remained the sine qua non of conversion, and to enter into a state of grace was to encounter liminality once again. How men and women reconciled the paradox of grace, at once sublime and suffused with moral resonance, reveals just how intractable the problem of femininity was for postrevolutionary evangelicals.[1]

By 1820 or so, a new understanding of the evangelical character was firmly in place in the Baptist churches of New England. Men and women

The title is borrowed from Carol Gilligan's *In a Different Voice: Psychological Theory and Women's Development* (Cambridge, Mass., 1982).

1. The meaning of "grace" was itself subtly transformed in the early nineteenth century from a spiritual notion to a more secular one. For nineteenth-century Americans, grace connoted elegant form and outward propriety, not the mighty effusions of the Holy Spirit which in an earlier age subverted form. Jay Fliegelman, *Prodigals and Pilgrims: The American Revolution against Patriarchal Authority* (New York, 1982), p. 130. See also Ruth Bloch's discussion of the gendering of a similar concept, virtue, in the postrevolutionary period: "The Gendered Meanings of Virtue in Revolutionary America," *Signs* 13 (1987): 98–120.

greeted one another within the meetinghouse not merely as religious partners but as social beings whose identities were shaped as much by their
secular pursuits as by their spiritual aspirations. "Religion does not annihi-
late the secular relations of men," admitted the *American Baptist Magazine
and Missionary Intelligencer* in 1822.[2] Baptist communicants in the early
decades of the nineteenth century parceled out their allegiances among a
variety of sacred and profane callings. As business competitors, heads of
well-regulated households, and participants in an expanding public sphere,
Baptist men were unwilling to allow their religious commitments to penetrate into or circumscribe their social lives. As guardians of the home, re-
positories of civic virtue, and shapers of an emergent bourgeois culture,
Baptist women were far more constrained by their spiritual professions. The
emphasis on character over conduct in the disciplining of women offenders
suggests that, unlike men whose essential characters remained unchallenged
while their misdeeds were reproved, Baptist women found their spiritual
selves subject to new scrutiny and censure.

Ironically, at the very time that women's "character" was being redefined as inherently disorderly and unreliable in the internal politics of the
churches, the model of religious conversion disseminated by the evangelical
press offered an alternative reading of the female self. This chapter explores
the ways in which evangelical women created a new persona for themselves
through religious conversion. Rather than the "dissimulating" and disorderly image of the female sinner found in discipline records, the image of the female saint in conversion narratives celebrated women's agency and strength
of self. Perhaps because their characters were so devalued within the meetinghouse, women conceded more readily than men the self-renunciation
required by the act of conversion. And in renouncing the profane self women
evangelicals experienced a regeneration of their spiritual and moral powers
which (on the level of metaphor, at least) placed them once again on an equal
footing with men.

Narratives of religious conversion dating from the 1740s, as described in
Chapter 2, did not make a psychological distinction between masculine and
feminine paths to salvation. Men and women of the 1740s did experience
religious conversion in slightly different ways, but these differences were
subsumed under a broad agreement on the meaning of personal religious
experience. By 1800 two distinct models of conversion, one male and one
female, existed side by side in evangelical stories of religious transformation.
The gender differences observable in these stories of the self reflect in part

2. "In Discerning between the Righteous and the Wicked," *ABMMI* 3 (1822): 248.

the diverse social circumstances of the sexes in nineteenth-century New England, but even more they reveal the psychological gulf between two groups of people who believed their very beings to be inherently different. Such a gulf was created in a variety of ways in postrevolutionary society: in the economic realm as the countryside of New England was inexorably industrialized, in the domestic realm as husbands and wives assumed ever more distinct "spheres" of responsibility, in the social realm as a gendered popular culture took root in the urbanizing areas of the Northeast, and of course in the political realm as deferential, consensual forms of governance gave way to more individualistic, "democratic" forms of political activity among American males. The gendering of religious behaviors which we saw emerging in the Baptist churches after 1780 was but one part of a larger reconfiguration of gender relations which characterized postrevolutionary America.

So it is no wonder that, as they approached the throne of grace, men and women evangelicals of the early nineteenth century brought with them highly articulated notions of gender identity which had been formed in secular contexts. Nor should it surprise us that they were able to some extent to break out of these subjectivities and create new models of gender more adaptable to their religious needs. The process of religious conversion, as evangelical writers continually stressed, was truly an act of rebirth, in which old identities were discarded and new ones formed. As a classic rite of passage, in the anthropological sense, conversion not only made saints out of sinners but allowed individuals to escape their natural selves altogether (at least for the moment) and enter a transcendental realm where social characteristics, including gender, were irrelevant.

For precisely this reason, we might expect early-nineteenth-century evangelicals to downplay the importance of conversion in their religious scheme, to perhaps substitute the more socially appropriate ritual of family prayer for the iconoclastic act of conversion as the defining rite of evangelical Protestantism. And to some extent, this is what happened. The atavistic retreat of the various Baptist authorities from the emotionalism of the Whitefieldian "New Birth" and the elevation of family government as the supreme duty of godly Christians reflect the distaste for the more sublime elements of the evangelical faith among those who coveted the mantle of orthodoxy. The official publications of the evangelical cause which proliferated in the early republican period, from association minutes to religious periodicals, devoted far more attention to issues of home and hearth than to the workings of the Holy Spirit. Once ablaze with the fires of revival, the New England landscape portrayed by the evangelical press was the very picture of domestic peace in the early 1800s.

Yet the demands of grace, however inconvenient, could not be entirely ignored. Evangelical churches continued to require candidates for admission to make public declarations of faith before the congregation, and periodicals continued to publish accounts of particularly noteworthy or dramatic conversions. Although these antebellum conversion narratives often appear dry and perfunctory to scholars accustomed to the vivid theatrics of Great Awakening conversion stories, their very artificiality constitutes a powerful statement of the deep impasse separating nineteenth- from eighteenth-century evangelicalism. The stylized renditions penned in the 1800s suggest a return to pre-Awakening notions of conversion, in which conventional accolades to godly education and pious lineage overwhelm the personal dynamics of the encounter between sinners and God. We know little about the social circumstances or intellectual orientation of these often pseudonymous figures. Pedagogical concerns clearly played a dominant role in the decision to publish these accounts, and editorial discretion was widely exercised. The point, after all, was to instruct the unregenerate, not simply to annoint the Elect. The artful construction of these nineteenth-century accounts by no means vitiates (and perhaps enhances) their significance as cultural markers, but we must proceed cautiously in assessing their importance in constructing new models of selfhood for evangelical men and women so as not to confuse art with life.

For all the attention given by historians to the phenomenon of a "feminized" religious culture which presumably took root in the early nineteenth century, there has been a remarkable resistance among religious historians to the notion that religious experience itself was profoundly structured by gender. Only Barbara Epstein has argued that men's and women's religious experiences diverged significantly after 1800 in ways that (she claims) contributed to the growing alienation of the sexes. In contrast to earlier studies of conversion narratives, which aimed chiefly at isolating the roots of a uniquely American form of self-expression, Epstein uses the conversion narrative to chart the influence of evangelical culture on the emergence of more sharply defined notions of gender and gender relations in nineteenth-century America. Arguing that a popular awareness of distinctiveness from and antagonism to men developed among nineteenth-century American women through their involvement in religious activities, Epstein suggests that men's and women's accounts of religious conversion reflect a different sensibility with regard to issues of authority and guilt.[3]

While Epstein is right to emphasize the gender-specific nature of the

3. Barbara Epstein, *Politics of Domesticity: Women, Evangelicalism, and Temperance in Nineteenth Century America* (Middletown, Conn., 1981), pp. 45–65.

conversion experience in early-nineteenth-century America, her conclusion that sexual differentiation and antagonism were thereby exacerbated in both the religious and secular spheres misses the subtle yet unmistakable leveling of gender distinctions at work in this discourse. To be more specific, close scrutiny of the psychological dynamics of the conversion experience reveals an androgynous model of regeneration which ultimately echoes the biblical affirmation that in Christ there is neither Jew nor Greek, slave nor free, male nor female. Though evangelical men and women reached the pinnacle of grace through very different paths, the final destination was the same for both sexes: a mature union with God which can best be described as the recovery of moral agency and spiritual potency. Ironically, the very existence of sexual distinctiveness in the natural state—which is the thrust of Epstein's argument—is the precondition for the sexual leveling achieved in the regenerate state.

This chapter is drawn from over two hundred (135 male, 90 female) detailed accounts of religious conversion published in six evangelical magazines between 1800 and 1830.[4] Though aimed at slightly different audiences, these six periodicals exhibit significant overlap in content as well as form— exigetical pieces by prominent clergy as well as particularly noteworthy conversion accounts, for instance, were often reprinted verbatim in Baptist and Congregational magazines.[5] The message disseminated by the religious press was consistent across denominational lines, allowing us to speak of a generic "evangelical" model of the conversion experience. Such a theological convergence, moreover, makes a great deal of sense, given the institutional parallels between the Baptist and Congregational orders increasingly apparent after the Revolution. As the evangelical "family" closed ranks against apostates and infidels and put its household in order, men and women articulated their most intimate religious experiences in the language appropriate to their familial positions. For men, the heads of the evangelical household, God appeared as a sovereign king and lord whose power as the ultimate patriarch of the universe was a galling reminder of their own reduced status as sons. For women, as submissive wives and dutiful daughters, the image of God was that of a loving and tender husband or father whose patriarchal authority was softened by the bonds of affection.

4. These magazines are: the *Connecticut Evangelical Magazine* (1800–1807), *Connecticut Evangelical Magazine and Religious Intelligencer* (1807–15), *Religious Intelligencer* (1816–30), *American Baptist Magazine and Missionary Intelligencer* (1817–27), *Massachusetts Baptist Missionary Magazine and Intelligencer* (1803–1816), and the *Massachusetts Missionary Magazine* (1803–8).

5. The account of the Reverend Andrew Fuller's conversion originally appeared in the Congregational magazine *RI* 4 (1820): 636–37, and was reprinted in the Baptist periodical *ABMMI* 3 (1821): 8–10.

"Father" or "King"?
A Patriarchal God

The image of God portrayed in female narratives of the early nineteenth century is most often that of a family member or personal friend. As in the 1740s, many women spoke of their relationship with God as a marriage: "O most gracious God, since thou hast appointed the Lord Jesus Christ as the only way of coming to thee, I do here, upon the bended knees of my soul, renewedly accept of him for my covenant friend, and do hereby solemnly join myself to thee. . . . I call heaven and earth to record this day that I do here solemnly engage myself to thee."[6] The metaphor of God as bridegroom, however, was noticeably lacking in sexual overtones in these nineteenth-century accounts. "My passions are subdued," Mrs. Bishop confided in her account.[7] Women frequently wrote of souls that "panted" after the love of God, but rarely was sexual desire actually realized in the act of spiritual union.[8] Bodily imagery was not entirely absent—one women spoke of "being so nearly allied to our blessed Saviour, as to be a member of his body"[9]—but most accounts emphasized the emotional side of union rather than its erotic dimension. The language of erotic female piety which was so striking in women's conversion narratives from the 1740s had been largely sanitized by 1800. Rather than the ravishing bridegroom of the early colonial period, Christ appeared in nineteenth-century devotional literature as, in Barbara Welter's words, "a very cosy Person" into whom the sinner is urged to "nestle."[10]

Although images of Christ as bridegroom occasionally resurfaced in women's accounts, shorn of their erotic content, for most women God appeared more simply in the guise of a concerned parent whose offer of love was uncomplicated by sexual undercurrents. Several young women referred to God as their father and friend, an appellation at once paternalistic and platonic.[11] Lois Chamberlain recalled that, on receiving God's grace, she heard the words: "I will be your God and you shall be my Daughter."[12] A young woman described the sense of peace and security she found in God: "I felt myself completely safe in the arms of the Almighty Saviour. Christ

---

6. *CEM* 6 (1805): 185–87.

7. Ibid.

8. See, for example, the account of Eliza Jenkins, *MBMMI* 3 (1811): 25.

9. *MMM* 5 (1807): 279.

10. Barbara Welter, "The Feminization of American Religion, 1800–1860," in her *Dimity Convictions: The American Woman in the Nineteenth Century* (Athens, Ohio, 1976), pp. 89–90.

11. *MMM* 4 (1806): 300; *RI* 1 (1816): 348.

12. *ABMMI* 3 (1820): 277.

seemed indeed a rest to a wearied soul; a sweet, refreshing hiding place."[13] Similarly, Mrs. Abbe Ward "found myself encircled in a Saviour's arms. A sweet calm ensued, and something like a small still voice speaking peace to my soul."[14] In fact, for some women the fulfillment of the requirements of grace entailed a desexing of their nature so as to enable them to receive God in pureness of body. Patty Long was so filled with joy at her salvation that "she could not compare herself to anything but the eunuch who went on his way rejoicing. . . . She was willing to leave father and mother, brothers and sisters, to go to Christ."[15] Given the reformulation of women as evil seductresses in the discourse of church discipline, it is perhaps not surprising that female sexuality was effaced from accounts of conversion in the early 1800s which aimed to show fallen women the way to salvation.

As the only way to God for women was through personal relationships, the state of sin was understood as a consequence of failed or flawed attachments. The process of conversion for women was one of removing obstacles to union and establishing lapsed covenants. The language of attachment colors the women's accounts of their efforts to find God. One woman, lamenting that "my sins have made a separating wall between God and my own soul," found, with the renewal of grace, "The partition [is] broken down and I could enter in by the door into the sheepfold." Like the prodigal son, she was once again "admitted into the family" of God.[16] "The first sin of which I was convinced," wrote Mrs. Charlotte Carey, "was the alienation of my heart from God. . . . My most ardent wish is to cleave to him and to walk in his ways; and my continued wandering from him, and his commands, fills me with grief and shame."[17] The fear of becoming distant from God was highlighted in the account of this young woman: "I had sought and strove, but found not, knocked but it had not been opened; nothing, however, but thick darkness spread over my mind, and I had endeavoured to draw near unto him in his appointed means, but still found myself no nearer, but farther off, and had endeavoured to love and serve him with all my heart, and agreeable to the divine requirement, but still he appeared not to regard me."[18]

The desire to "draw near" and to be "regarded" by God seemed to have been felt more keenly by women, for whom the exercise of authority was

---

13. *RI* 2 (1817): 111.
14. *MMM* 5 (1807): 277.
15. *MBMMI* 1 (1805): 158.
16. *CEM* 6 (1805): 186–87.
17. *ABMMI* 3 (1822): 363.
18. *CEMRI* 6 (1813): 463–64.

rooted in personal bonds. Their narratives usually described God in personal rather than functional terms—as "angry," "gracious," "merciful," "strong," "kind," and "compassionate" rather than as "sovereign," "all-sufficient," or "omnipotent." The transformation of God into an "other" endowed with human qualities and capable of expressing human affection and sympathy lent a tenacious strength to the bond between God and women. For to rebel against God was, in a very real sense, to rebel against a loved and revered father whose source of authority lay deeply buried in the emotional bedrock of the personality. That God should assume such patriarchal proportions for women in the postrevolutionary years is not surprising; what is perhaps surprising is that women rejected the more authoritarian aspects of patriarchal power in favor of a gentle paternalism. A particular model of family relations is recognizable in their descriptions of the ideal relationship between God and man, that of the sentimental, affectionate family.

Jay Fliegelman's recent study of eighteenth-century Anglo-American popular literature concludes that, by the time of the American Revolution, "family relations had been fundamentally reconsidered in both England and America. An older patriarchal family authority was giving way to a new parental ideal characterized by a more affectionate and egalitarian relationship with children."[19] Drawing on the research of social historians into the changing balance of power between parents and children, Fliegelman explores the political and social ramifications of the new understanding of paternity which emerged in the middle of the eighteenth century. As Daniel Scott Smith and James Henretta have shown, children increasingly took on a more autonomous role in making crucial decisions such as when and whom to marry, where to reside, and what occupation to pursue.[20] Their quest for autonomy was aided by the realization, popularized through the pedagogical writings of John Locke, that noncoercive authority was more effective than the authoritarian and nonnegotiable control exercised by traditional patriarchs. In the Lockean scheme, the figure of the tyrannical parent who too rigorously or irrationally insisted on total obedience became an object of contempt.

As Fliegelman demonstrates, the new ideal of paternity expressed in the

19. Fliegelman, *Prodigals and Pilgrims*, p. 1.

20. Daniel Scott Smith, "Parental Power and Marriage Patterns: An Analysis of Historical Trends in Hingham, Massachusetts," *Journal of Marriage and the Family* 2 (1963); James Henretta, *The Evolution of American Society, 1700–1815* (Lexington, Mass., 1973). For a review of the literature on changing relations between adolescents and parents in the nineteenth century, see Susan M. Juster and Maris A. Vinovskis, "Adolescence in Nineteenth-Century America," in the *Encyclopedia of Adolescence*, ed. Richard M. Lerner, Anne C. Petersen, and J. Brooks-Gunn (New York, 1991), 2:698–707.

political rhetoric of the Revolution could easily be transferred to the religious realm. "By the rationalist lights of Lockean ideology, it was not only George III who might be convicted of parental tyranny, but Jehovah. For did not the God of the Old Testament send stillborn infants to hell and keep his living children bound in the enslaving determinism of original sin, perversely demanding of them, nonetheless, a 'blind and perfect obedience'?"[21] This concern with abuses of patriarchal authority was articulated with a feminine voice in the conversion narratives of nineteenth-century evangelicals. When we consider that evangelical women faced a resurgent patriarchy in their own religious community, that however benevolent, the rule of men in the church was still premised on the suppression of women's voices, the efforts of women to construct an alternative model of familial authority appear revolutionary indeed. Notions of a more sentimentalized paternalism may have been floating in the air in the early 1800s, but they resonated with particular meaning for women who chafed under the strictures of an older patriarchalism within the evangelical "household."

The influence of new ideas about paternal authority can be seen in the reasons unregenerate women gave for having rebelled against God. Rather than being preoccupied with doctrinal issues, as men tended to be, women focused their anger on the image of God as an unjust father, especially for showing partiality by bestowing grace on some of his children while abandoning others to damnation. The sin of partiality, as Fliegelman has argued, was one of the most frequent violations of the new paternal ideal condemned in the popular literature of the time.[22] The parable of the prodigal son, a common reference in women's narratives, turns on the consequences to a younger son of the father's excessive regard for the eldest. In returning to his family, the prodigal son comes to realize that his father's love is not, in fact, unevenly divided among his children but encompasses all. In like fashion, the woman convert, in affirming her faith in God, recognized the universality of his love.

Narratives of evangelical women show the nature of the cry against partiality: "I hated the bible because it contained my condemnation. I felt that God was partial in shewing mercy to others and not to me. The enmity of my heart rose against him; and indeed I wished there was no God."[23] Mrs. Caroline Woodward complained that "she could not see why God did not save all mankind as well as a part; and that it made God appear partial and

21. Fliegelman, *Prodigals and Pilgrims*, p. 155.
22. Ibid., p. 52.
23. *CEM* 3 (1802): 107.

unjust." When reproached by her minister for such blasphemous thoughts, "She replied that she could not love such a God."[24]

Love, and its betrayal, is the key to understanding the source of the unregenerate women's enmity toward God. The language of these narratives is very different in feeling and tone from that in the men's accounts. The struggle with God's authority was very personal for women, a clash of two personalities—not a reasoned and impersonal debate over abstract principles. These women felt "threatened" and "condemned" by the judgments of a partial father, and felt the injustice in their hearts, not their heads. The plaint of one woman, that "he was not so kind to me as to some others," restates the issue in simple human terms.[25] When scorned by God, as they interpreted their alienated state of sin, women often reacted with anger and hate. "When I found that my sister C—had become hopefully pious," one woman said, "I felt spiteful towards her. I looked upon her with real contempt."[26] "Whenever I heard of any person's having obtained a hope," added another, "it was like adding fuel to the fire. My heart rose against it, and accused God of exercising partiality with his creatures, not considering that he had a right to do what he would with his own."[27] Women responded to God's partiality with all the emotional intensity of hurt, betrayed children, as the response of this young woman to the news of her friend's conversion testifies: "My anguish and distress was so great that I could not shed a tear. I walked the room, but felt as if I should die; several times I took up the bible, and thought I would read, but threw it down again. I thought I would pray; but as God had given that woman relief, and left me in this distress, I would not pray to him."[28]

Male narratives proceed along a very different path, with different emotional inflections. Legalistic terminology pervades male accounts; God is presented as "king," "mediator," "tribune," or, above all, "sovereign." The role of lawgiver rather than that of father or friend predominates, and the metaphor of government displaces that of the family. The Reverend Lynde Huntington, describing his vision of the divine, wrote in his memoirs: "I thought I could see the law, both in its requirements and penalties, to be a most fit, harmonious, and beautiful thing, even should I myself be brought to suffer its curse. . . . I think my soul can say, let GOD be KING, and rule

24. *RI* 7 (1822): 139.
25. *CEM* 7 (1822): 139.
26. *RI* 1 (1816): 59.
27. *CEM* 6 (1806): 430–31.
28. *CEMRI* 3 (1810): 146.

and reign just as he pleases. Let me willingly *submit* to and feel my *dependence* on him."[29] Another man, with grace, "felt reconciled to the divine government and willing that God should sway the sceptre of the universe."[30] A young man, in a letter to his father, expressed the satisfaction he felt in his converted state: "Everything appeared perfectly right in the divine government; I felt submissive, and rejoiced that God was on the throne, and I felt fully resigned to his holy law, as being just and good."[31] While the desire of women under grace was to revive the sense of closeness and affection between themselves and a personal God, a young man stated, "The desire of my soul was that god might be glorified, and his kingdom built up."[32] The rapture women felt for the person of God was reserved by men for the contemplation of his divinely inspired "Code of Laws" (to use Lyman Beecher's phrase), the Bible: reading the scriptures for the first time, Francis Junius "became instantly struck with the divinity of the argument, and the majesty and authority of the composition, as infinitely surpassing the highest flights of human eloquence. My body shuddered; my mind was all in amazement; and I was so agitated, the whole day, that I scarce knew who I was."[33]

The relationship of God to man expressed in the male narratives resembles more a contract between consenting individuals than the familial bond of father to son or husband to wife. The distinction between contract and covenant is useful here. A contractual relationship is based on the assumption that both parties share a rough equality of status which enables them to fulfill their mutual obligations. The purpose of a contract is primarily functional, an agreement undertaken to satisfy certain needs that cannot be met individually. A covenant, on the other hand, is an unconditional pact among two parties of unequal status. Covenantal bonds are rooted not in the balancing of accounts but in the personal convictions of the covenanted partners.

The male view of relationships, as expressed by the Reverend Andrew Fuller, is largely a contractual one: "I was not aware that *any* poor sinner had a warrant to believe in Jesus Christ for the salvation of his soul; but supposed there must be some kind of qualification to entitle him to it; yet I was aware I had no qualifications." This man's mistaken belief in the necessity of

29. *CEM* 6 (1806): 297.

30. *ABMMI* 3 (1821): 8–10.

31. *CEM* 3 (1802): 236. Similar statements can be found in the *MMM* 1 (1804): 353; *MBMMI* 2 (1809): 235; *MMM* 1 (1803): 310.

32. *CEM* 2 (1801): 74.

33. *RI* 9 (1824): 63. Beecher's phrase is quoted in James Turner, *Without God, without Creed: The Origins of Unbelief in America* (Baltimore, 1985), p. 84; a similar analogy is drawn in the account of a lawyer in *RI* 3 (1803), who spoke of the Bible as "the best law book, the eternal rule of right between man and man" (p. 187).

meeting certain conditions before entering into a relationship with God was the primary stumbling block to his conversion: "[I] should have found [rest] sooner, if I had not entertained the notion of my having no warrant to come to Christ, without some previous qualification. The notion was a bar that kept me back for a time, though through divine drawings, I was enabled to overleap it."[34] The essence of God's relationship to man in Calvinist theology is found in the notion of irresistible grace, the call to redemption which must be heeded. Likewise, man can do nothing to warrant God's affection; it is bestowed arbitrarily on grounds not comprehensible to the human mind. Men found this concept very difficult to accept. The mistaken belief of one man that "God was *obliged* to change [my heart] by his promise, if I did the best I could" signals the contractual nature of men's understanding of relationships.[35]

God and his divine plan often appeared "painful and odious" to the unregenerate sinner who was searching for a way out from under the burden of conviction.[36] Different arguments were used by men and women, however, to justify their resistance to divine authority. Where women rejected a patriarchal God for his failure to fulfill his familial responsibilities, men used a legalistic framework of authority, accusing God's rule of being unreasonable and unjust. A tyrannical, unloving father was the anti-God of the women's spiritual dramas; an irrational system of government was the object of men's hostility.

When men in the rebellious stage made efforts to come to terms with God and his government their discussions revolved around the merits of specific Calvinist doctrines, most notably the doctrines of divine election and justification by faith. As in their relations with the official representative of God's authority (the church), evangelical men centered their challenges to divine authority on the ideological ground of doctrine.[37] Men scrutinized the Calvinist creed for evidence of doctrinal truth; a minister, in his account of a general revival, described a man who

> was a violent opposer of religion and the doctrine of grace. He would not admit the truth of revelation. Some part of it, he said, was true. But those passages, which did not comport with his carnal reasoning, he conceived

34. *RI* 4 (1820): 636–37.

35. *MMM* 2 (1804): 34. Emphasis mine.

36. *CEM* 1 (1801): 424.

37. Stephen Grossbart's statistical analysis of conversion and church membership in Connecticut supports the claim that most women were not concerned with doctrine; only men seemed to have been influenced in the decision to join a particular church by the doctrinal stance of that church. See his "Seeking the Divine Favor: Conversion and Church Admission in Eastern Connecticut, 1711–1832," *WMQ*, 3d ser., 46 (1989): 696–740.

to be priestcraft, or the work of some cunning deceiver. He said that there
were typographical mistakes, especially where the doctrine of decrees and
election were mentioned. . . . He said that the divinity of Christ was
contrary to reson. The doctrine of the Trinity had no place in his creed.
This was also an absurdity, imposed on men by cunning priestcraft.[38]

In this passage, the ultimate test of truth is reason; those doctrines which do
not "comport with carnal reasoning" were rejected as mere sophistry (a
favorite expression of male evangelicals) or as deliberate attempts to deceive
and lead astray. In the words of another "infidel," the Bible was but "a
fabrication of man's invention, designed to hold the world in awe."[39] One
man, in his search for a field of knowledge in which "the intellect might
expatiate without control," flitted from one system to another—from the
"Pythagorean delusion of the transmigration of souls" to the "Epicurean
Errors of materialism." After sixteen years of living in "this maze of error
and delusions," he finally began to read the Bible systematically from cover
to cover. "The light of evidence," he recorded, "burst in upon my understanding with rays too splendid to be resisted. . . . no comfort could be found
in the illusions of sophistry, my former companions."[40] Disputing every
inch of ground, male unbelievers were slowly brought to see the truth and
justice of those doctrines which so troubled them in their false search for a
rational basis for revealed religion.[41]

Doctrinal disputes were not absent from the women's accounts. They, too,
felt discomfited by the arbitrariness and injustice of the decrees of election
and justification. Yet the grounds on which they challenged specific doctrines reveal an important, though subtle, difference of perception. This
account of a forty-year-old woman illustrates my point: like many of her
male counterparts, she wanted to believe in the efficacy of good deeds: "[I]
thought that if I lived a moral life, God would not be so unjust as to make me
forever miserable. Thus I continued until I repeatedly heard the doctrine of
election and divine decrees. I found that my heart was dreadfully opposed to
such doctrines. I could not bear to think that I was in the hands of a sovereign
God. It was too mortifying to my proud heart to grant that he is the potter,
and I the clay." After she read the Bible, her minister explained, "she immediately saw that the doctrines, with which she had been quarreling, were
clearly contained in the holy scriptures, and that in opposing them she had

38. *CEM* 7 (1807): 56–57.
39. *MBMMI* 2 (1809): 236.
40. *RI* 2 (1818): 631–32.
41. See the accounts of male converts in *MMM* 1 (1803): 351, and 1 (1804): 356; *RI* 3 (1818): 94,
and 6 (1822): 685.

opposed God. This filled her with extreme distress."[42] This passage differs in two key respects from the male narratives. First, the heart rather than the mind was the faculty of religious understanding for women. God's doctrines appeared unacceptable because "my heart was dreadfully opposed," not because they violated the dictates of reason. Second, only when she realized that her rejection of God's doctrines entailed a rejection of God himself did she abandon her opposition. Once again, the primacy of personal relationships over abstract principles is asserted.

Underlying the male unbeliever's distrust of revealed religion was the conviction that justice properly consisted in balancing deeds with the appropriate consequences. The concern with fitting the proper reward or punishment to particular actions was an overriding one in male narratives. One man initially rejected the notion of hell because "man had never committed a crime deserving of eternal punishment. . . . He said, the law of God was but a finite law given to a finite creature, and a transgression was deserving of but a finite punishment."[43] An "infidel" renounced deism because he could not "recollect ever hearing but one Deist profess really to believe in a future state of rewards and punishments."[44] The desire for a legal system that will rationally determine guilt or innocence and pass appropriate sentence seems to have been at the heart of the male struggle with authority.

To understand the fears associated with arbitrary and unjust authority, on the one hand, and with licentious and unrestrained liberty, on the other, we must bear in mind the historical context that frames these conversion narratives. The early 1800s were a time for working out the implications of republican government and resolving the tensions immanent in a voluntaristic, democratic society. The obsession with tyranny from above and below can perhaps be traced to the persistence of the revolutionary anxiety over the fragility of the republican balance between authority and liberty. In this sense, it could be argued, the conflict over authority articulated in the male narratives was a spiritual reenactment of the revolutionary struggle for natural rights and liberties. Yet I would suggest that beneath this fear of arbitrary authority lay the deeper male fear of disinheritance, that just as an all-powerful father could arbitrarily deny an unfavored son his rightful patrimony, so too an all-powerful God might exercise his patriarchal right to disown his sons on earth.

The concern with legal delimitations of rights and obligations, the appeal

---

42. *CEM* 7 (1807): 394–95.
43. Ibid., 7 (1806): 57.
44. Ibid., 4 (1803): 235.

to abstract concepts of justice and equality, the Enlightenment preoccupation with harmony and balance in natural and social relations, the search for a rationally legitimated system of authority—all these ideas found expression in the rebellion of male converts against the seemingly unjust and arbitrary nature of God's rule. A frequent complaint heard in the male accounts is that God is a "hard master," who requires "slavish" obeisance and unconditional submission.[45] In its extreme form, male resistance to divine authority was couched in explicitly revolutionary terminology: "Not willing the Lord should rule, fain would I have dethroned him, and have taken the reins of government in my own hands; saying, 'I will not have this man to reign over me!'"[46] We would expect such challenges to come from men more than women, as male evangelicals constituted the vanguard of lay resistance to the encroachments of clerical authority within the institution of the church.

For several men, the connection between the political rhetoric of the Revolution and their resistance to God's government was explicit. "At a time of life when the mind is most likely to receive and retain impressions," wrote one veteran,

> I entered into the American army, where I imbibed very pernicious principles, and advanced from bad to worse by almost imperceptible degrees, till I met with Paine's Age of Reason.—This book being exactly suited to my taste, speaking the language of my heart, and satisfying all my desires, I mounted at once upon its authority, superior to every restraint and distinguished myself as one of the most open, daring, and blasphemous infidels of the age.[47]

The Reverend Andrew Fuller attributed his deistical leanings to the "contagious and contaminating influence of a [military] camp" while he was a soldier during the revolutionary war.[48] The practical exposure to such "pernicious" and "contaminating" ideas through participation in the war itself and the ongoing political activity surrounding the implementation of independence obviously affected men more than women. As political and revolutionary actors in an age of intense public and private discourses on the nature of men and their governments, American males more deeply absorbed the spirit if not the letter of the Enlightenment challenge to the Calvinist world view.

45. *MMM* 1 (1804): 354; *MMM* 2 (1804): 281–82; *MMM* 2 (1805): 295; *MMM* 4 (1806): 64–65.
46. Ibid., 2 (1804): 281–82.
47. *CEM* 2 (1801): 315.
48. *ABMMI* 3 (1821): 8.

It is important to recognize the deeper resonance within American political and religious culture of the evangelical fear of deism and infidelity. While Perry Miller, among others, has argued that the actual number of declared deists in the early republic was too small to constitute the chief threat to the evangelical religion, despite the prevalence and virulence of attacks on deism in the evangelical press, he has taken the terms of the debate too literally and misread the significance of the deistical challenge.[49] Deism as the practice of a specific form of religion (or irreligion) was but a small part of a wider impulse to ground religious sentiment in the principles of rationality and the contractual model of human relations. The attempt to find a rational basis for Christian belief was not, after all, limited to confirmed Deists. Evangelical theologians themselves often joined in such a task.[50]

The Enlightenment metaphor of man as machine was also a recurring theme in the male accounts of spiritual rebellion. This excerpt from the narrative of a twenty-year-old man is illustrative:

> For a time I strove hard to disbelieve the doctrines of the gospel. I searched diligently to find arguments against them—particularly the doctrine of the endless future punishment of the wicked. . . . [I] attempted to persuade myself that there was no such thing as free moral agency, or accountability—nor any distinction between virtue and vice—but that mankind were mere machines, actuated by a blind and fatal necessity. But I was unable to reason myself into a belief of this.[51]

Another man wrote, "I supposed myself one item in the grand machine, not accountable, because I acted through necessity."[52] Left to their own devices, men are ruled by a "blind and fatal necessity" that is capricious and arbitrary. The exercise of real human agency requires the presence of some restraining power, some legitimate authority that sets the bounds of permissible action. Male evangelicals seemed to have recognized that power in postrevolutionary America was no longer a matter of personal will but of larger impersonal forces that necessitated new forms of control. Just as republicanism as a political ideology transferred authority from, in Melvin Yazawa's words, "the grasp of the personal to the realm of the impersonal," the religious paradigm of authority found in male conversion accounts relies more on

49. Perry Miller, *Life of the Mind in America from the Revolution to the Civil War* (New York, 1965), pp. 4–9.

50. Turner, in *Without God, without Creed*, credits the evangelical community itself with contributing to the emergence of agnosticism as a legitimate cultural idea through its efforts to invent a rational basis for Christianity.

51. *CEM* 1 (1801): 424–25.

52. *CEMRI* 6 (1813): 254.

the operation of eternal principles than on human agencies.[53] "T.H. Esq." found that "in taking up the cross and following the Lord Jesus" he had "not merely to contend with flesh and blood, but with principalities and powers, with spiritual wickedness in high places."[54] Reconciling abstract power with the rights of human subjects required a restrained version of the balance between authority and liberty.[55]

The masculine conception of authority as an abstract system of rules led male converts to seek grace through conformity with "the law."[56] While the failure of Arminian schemes to achieve grace through good works is well argued in the literature on evangelical conversion, many more men than women seemed to have fallen into the moralistic trap. Women apparently understood the Calvinist tenet that a rule-governed approach to salvation cannot succeed, that conversion was possible only through the personal intercession of God in the hearts and minds of his people. This proved a difficult lesson for men to learn. After they overcame their initial resistance to God's government, most male sinners attempted to effect their own salvation by reforming their external behavior—by becoming moral. A Yale student "began, as I supposed, to reform my conduct and live a better life. I attended the outward means of religion, and was more strict on the Sabbath." He soon found, however, that "[M]y own words did me no good, but rather seemed to make me worse."[57] Another young man thought, "I must try to mend my ways by breaking off from all my evil conduct. I endeavoured to build up a righteousness of my own; but was finally convinced that I could not recommend myself to the favor of God."[58]

In their belief in the power of good works to save souls, male evangelicals exemplified what one historian has termed the shift from "piety to moralism," albeit in perverted form, which distinguished the theological evolution of American Puritanism from Jonathan Edwards forward.[59] For men in the

---

53. Melvin Yazawa, *From Colonies to Commonwealth: Familial Ideology and the Beginnings of the American Republic* (Baltimore, 1985), p. 112.

54. *MBMMI* 2 (1808): 144.

55. Joyce Appleby argues that this balance between liberty and authority shifted in postrevolutionary society as an older conception of liberty as the freedom to participate in self-government gradually gave way to the modern, negative notion of liberty as the right to pursue private interests. In the terms of this discourse, the conception of liberty expressed in the male narratives seems to draw more on the classical republican heritage than on its modern successor. See her *Capitalism and a New Social Order: The Republican Vision of the 1790s* (New York, 1984).

56. A fifty-five-year-old man was "determined to be saved by the law," but to no avail. *CEM* 3 (1802): 104–5.

57. *CEM* 7 (1807): 395.

58. Ibid., 2 (1801): 73.

59. Haroutunian, *Piety versus Moralism*; see also Turner, *Without God, without Creed*.

unregenerate state, the moral dimension of religion was the sole ground of belief. "I was convinced," wrote one, "that the system of moral conduct contained in the bible was by far better calculated to promote public good and private happiness than any other system which had ever been formed."[60] In a more cynical vein, Colonel Robert Barnwall considered the Christian religion "merely a good political engine, and as such highly serviceable to the State in keeping the common people in awe."[61] Such reductionist views of the role of religion in promoting public and private morality were the natural outgrowth of the legalistic conception of authority exhibited by male evangelicals.

Richard Rabinowitz sees the acceptance of the image of God as lawmaker as the essence of religious experience for all evangelicals. In the 1790s conversion accounts begin to reveal that God had become "a distant ordering principle in the universe" rather than a living presence. The law as codified in the Bible "caught the entirety of God's breath for man."[62] Conversion itself became an act of translation, as evangelicals "learned how to substitute a scriptural, authoritative, universal, and conclusive vocabulary for a personal, private, sensual, and confused one."[63] Rabinowitz's description captures perfectly the legalistic orientation that colored men's accounts of conversion, but he mistakenly attributes the male model of conversion to women as well. As we saw above, women resorted to a language of the divine which was personal, private, and sensual—not distant and formal. While male evangelicals adopted with enthusiasm the new rationalist language of the Enlightenment, women retained an older vocabulary of personal attachment which had emerged with such vigor in the revivals of the First Great Awakening.

"My Spirit Looks to God Alone": The Female Experience of Grace

However soft and tender the bonds of God's love for women, to be redeemed was an act of renunciation rather than of espousal. Grace could be found only in the solitude of one's heart, not in the web of dependencies which bound evangelical women to family and friends. This was a strange

60. *MMM* 1 (1804): 355.

61. *RI* 5 (1820): 509; recall also the words of the man who considered the Bible "a fabrication of man's invention, designed to hold the world in awe." *MBMMI* 2 (1809): 236.

62. Richard Rabinowitz, *The Spiritual Self in Everyday Life: The Transformation of Personal Religious Experience in Nineteenth-Century New England* (Boston, 1989), p. 24.

63. Ibid., pp. 63, 25.

concept indeed for nineteenth-century women who had been raised to rely on those stronger and wiser than themselves.

Modern psychological theory suggests that men and women differ in the degrees to which they depend on others to help them resolve moral problems. The terms "communion" and "agency" have been proposed to describe the way women and men in modern society approach moral dilemmas. Because the female principle of *communion* promotes "contact, openness, and union," the chief moral problem for women is that of individuation.[64] Because the male principle of *agency* engenders "isolation, alienation, and aloneness," the chief moral problem for men, conversely, becomes one of forming attachments. In terms of the demands of faith, women were compelled to disengage themselves from overdependence on friends and family in order fully to establish an adult relationship with God. Men, on the other hand, found that they had to overcome their alienating self-sufficiency through interaction with others if they hoped to reach God. Women undertook the quest for salvation alone; men, with the aid of others.

Women were often "awakened" to their sinful state by the loss of a loved one. Sarah Dimmuck first became aware of her need for repentance when her mother died:

> After my mother was taken from me, I began to feel more sensibly the necessity of having a friend in God, and obtaining pardon and sanctification. . . . At times, when the loss of my pious and tender mother was fresh in my mind, my concern for my salvation was so great that I tho't I could be willing to submit to the loss, even of so dear a mother, and to experience a similar loss every day, were it possible, if it might be sanctioned to bring me to the choice of God for the guide of my youth and my eternal portion.[65]

The loss of her mother, although first prompting her to seek a substitute source of nurturance in God, enabled her eventually to realize that separa-

---

64. As described by David Bakan, "Agency manifests itself in self-protection, self-assertion, and self-expansion; communion manifests itself in the sense of being at one with other organisms. Agency manifests itself in the formation of separations; communion in the lack of separations. Agency manifests itself in isolation, alienation, and aloneness; communion in contact, openness, and union. Agency manifests itself in the urge to master; communion in noncontractual cooperation." Quoted in Nancy Chodorow, "Family Structure and Feminine Personality," in *Woman, Culture, and Society*, ed. Michelle Zimbalist Rosaldo and Louise Lamphere (Stanford, Calif., 1974), p. 56. As these oppositions suggest, the self is the motivating principle of all moral action for men; for women, the wider community of which they are a part forms their motive force.

65. *CEM* 4 (1804): 433.

tion from her family might perhaps be necessary to "bring [her] to the choice of God" for her saviour. Another young woman was brought under conviction by the death of her father: "In the midst of their sorrows," the minister reported, "the child was comforted by a pious friend sitting at her side, with the consideration that God would be her Father, if she would put her trust in him."[66] The desire to replace a severed relationship with another, more fulfilling one, drove women to convert.

Once under conviction of their depraved state, women faced the battle with their souls alone. Nancy Bishop, whom we have encountered before, spoke of her desire to renew her baptismal vows for herself: "My thoughts were troubled that I never had owned the Lord Christ, by my own voluntary profession, nor renewed for myself what my parents had done for me."[67] Isabella Leeds's mother used similar terms in reminding her daughter, "Your baptismal vows are upon you, still unfulfilled—We have given you to God; but you have not given yourself."[68] No longer content to have others take responsibility for their spiritual state, these women welcomed the opportunity to recover moral agency for themselves. Moreover, they needed not only to retreat from the protection of their parents but to abandon the support of friends and companions as well. To Nancy Bishop's query, "[Why] there is not one with whom I can, with prudence, converse," the answer came with reluctance: "I think because my heavenly father has called me to the privilege, so he has enabled me . . . to look directly to him alone, when I have no earthly prop, or any one, to whom I might apply, and by whose friendly, Christian conversation I might derive comfort, in my darkest hours; I say to himself alone, the foundation of all good."[69] No "earthly prop" can assist her in her journey to God, which must be undertaken alone. Mrs. Willard, who similarly "had no earthly friend to whom [she] could have access," found comfort in the text "When thy father and mother forsake thee, the Lord will take thee up."[70] "Angelina," a young convert, also expressed the loneliness of her search for God: "I seemed to be alone in my distress. . . . I wanted some friend, to whom I might disclose these feelings of my heart; but I knew of none, in whom I had sufficient confidence to mention so interesting a subject."[71] Claudia Prentice felt that she must choose

66. *RI* 1 (1816): 34.
67. *CEM* 1 (1800): 148.
68. *Christian Cabinet* 1 (1802): 47.
69. *CEM* 1 (1800): 186–87.
70. *ABMMI* 5 (1825): 63.
71. *CEM* 2 (1801): 106.

between "the friendship of the world, which has hitherto been dearer . . . than life," and the loss of her soul.[72] Clearly, the choice was not easy. Thrown back on themselves, many women experienced an acute sense of loneliness, despair, and emptiness. Yet the road to salvation, it was equally clear, lay in this direction.

Loneliness gave way to exultation with the experience of grace. No longer frightened and anxious at leaving their friends and family behind, women converts actively sought out and gloried in being alone. One thirty-year-old woman described her delight in God after conversion: "For a few minutes a sweet calm, and a resignation to God's will followed, till my mind was filled with inexpressible joy and rejoicing in God. I longed to be by myself, away from everybody."[73] Joanna Obear, who had been warned by a dream of the folly of "indulging too much attachment to the world and its objects," awoke one night to the words "My spirit looks to God alone, My rock and refuge is his throne" and heeded God's call to "Come out from among them and be ye separate."[74] Echoed another young woman, "This was the happiest day of my life. . . . I was happy to be alone. I felt humble and unworthy; but I saw a sufficiency in Christ, and felt that all glory belonged to God."[75] Stripped of their worldly attachments, their sense of self reaffirmed, women under grace entered into a new covenant with God.

The experience of grace thus implicitly strengthened women's sense of personal autonomy and moral agency. Mrs. Prudence Stille recounted how, "At times (yea, almost constantly) her soul drank such large draughts of holy delight, that she was filled with such raptures, that she scarcely knew whether she was in the body or out of the body. When engaged in the publick exercises of religion, her spirit was on the wing."[76] Angelina, another convert, "seemed to rise above the world and all its vanities, and all the energies of my soul were unitedly drawn out in fervent supplication to God. . . . I felt the all-subduing power of his grace, melting all the powers of my soul, at his feet, into a rapture of holy love." Like their sisters who converted during the First Great Awakening, these women experienced a fusion of divine and human qualities which strengthened and empowered them. "It seemed to me," continued Angelina, "that, if it had been my proper province, I could have gone out, and convinced all the infidels

72. Ibid., 6 (1805): 186.
73. Ibid., 1 (1801): 306–7.
74. *ABMMI* 3 (1821): 116–17.
75. *CEM* 1 (1801): 306.
76. *ABMMI* 2 (1820): 415.

and scoffers at religion in the world, of their folly and madness, and of the reality of experimental religion. Everything was real, invisible things were no longer hidden."[77] Infused with God's grace, Angelina has been enabled (a potent term in the literature of evangelical conversion) to resume her place as a social actor, with the important qualification that, as a woman, her province of activity was necessarily restricted. Hannah Boardman found with grace that "Her natural reservedness and timidity seemed to be overcome, and she could now, with the utmost freedom, introduce the subject of religion to Christians of any denomination."[78]

The restoration of agency is the key to our understanding of women's experience of grace. As the passages above suggest, grace brought both moral and spiritual ability in its wake. The material and spiritual reality of the world was now accessible—"invisible things were no longer hidden"—and with this new knowledge came the ability to act. I would suggest that these women were empowered by recovering their sense of self through the assertion of independence from others. Though perhaps few would have understood the process in these terms, one woman observed: "I have been enabled, in some measure, to love myself with the same love I bear to beings in general."[79]

Perhaps the clearest evidence of the empowering influence of religious conversion on women evangelicals lies in the restoration of their facility for self-expression. At the core of women's experience of grace was the process of recovering a distinctive voice. "Her liberated tongue now broke out in unknown strains," wrote one minister of a female convert. The metaphor of a loosed tongue recurs throughout the female accounts of conversion: "her tongue [was] loosed to utter the praises of redeeming grace," "her tongue broke out in astonishing strains," "her tongue broke out in unknown strains."[80] If language is, as Smith-Rosenberg claims, the "symbolic medium" through which power relations are shaped, then the experience of conversion offered antebellum women an important entry into the male world of evangelical politics.[81] The ability to speak needs and desires is, after all, the precondition of their fulfillment. The freeing of women's tongues to articulate their experience of grace is an apt metaphor for the recovery of

---

77. *CEM* 2 (1801): 107.
78. *ABMMI* 4 (1823): 189.
79. *CEM* 3 (1803): 278.
80. *RI* 1 (1816): 349; *MBMMI* 1 (1807): 336; *MBMMI* 2 (1808): 35; *MBMMI* 3 (1813): 309; and *MBMMI* 2 (1804): 281–82.
81. Carroll Smith-Rosenberg, "Hearing Women's Words: A Feminist Reconstruction of History," in her *Disorderly Conduct: Visions of Gender in Victorian America* (New York, 1985), p. 45.

moral agency which is the core of this experience. While women were being silenced for their "disorderly" and "dissimulating" speech in church discipline meetings, their right to speak was being at least symbolically restored in the literature of religious conversion.

"Left to eat the fruit of my own ways":
The Male Experience of Grace

The moral problem posed by salvation for men was of the opposite order. Not a lack, but an excess, of self-awareness hindered their search for God. Consequently, men found that they had to seek out the assistance of others in their quest for grace. Only by reestablishing relationships on earth could men prepare their hearts for reunion with God.

Whereas women were usually awakened by the loss of family and friends, men were more often brought under conviction by the conversion of people close to them—most frequently, their wives. A similar dynamic is actually at work in both cases; while the sudden void left by the dissolution of a close relationship led women to seek a substitute "other" to whom they could become reattached, the fear of being left behind while others attained salvation inspired in men a change of heart. In both cases, it was the experience of aloneness which prompted male and female sinners to attend to their souls. Women, however, were responding to the positive desire to reestablish a comforting relationship; men, on the other hand, seem to have been reacting against the negative prospect of losing ground in a competitive race to God. An account of a revival in Lebanon chronicled the experience of a man "who was struck under sudden conviction. His wife having before obtained a hope, proposed joining the church. He was then led to reflect on his own state and situation. The idea of being left to go down to hell, while numbers of his neighbours and even his wife had set out for heaven, caused him to tremble."[82] Another man accused the minister in his town of being "a snake in the grass" for "trying to separate him from his wife. 'He wants to take her to heaven, he says, and send me to hell.'"[83] After reflecting on "the thought of his wife's being a Christian and going to heaven, while he was left behind," a middle-aged man was struck by this biblical passage: "'Two shall be in the field, the one shall be taken, and the other left.' This he could not

82. *CEM* 4 (1803): 182.
83. *RI* 9 (1824): 419.

endure."[84] A youth in Killington lamented, "I should, forever, be left to eat the fruit of my own ways."[85]

The fear of being "left" is pervasive in the men's accounts. To understand the depth of men's anxiety, we must keep in mind the rapidly changing economic and social conditions of the early nineteenth century. Several factors combined to produce a sense of rootlessness and unrestrained competition among American males in particular: the rapid economic and geographic dislocations occasioned by the spread of the market economy into all regions of the country, the instability of unregulated and proliferating financial institutions and the cycle of boom and bust created by fluctuating credit terms, the growth of mass political parties and mass social reform movements which offered the ordinary citizen unprecedented opportunities for political action, the migration of thousands of men and women westward in search of greater economic and personal freedom, and the disestablishment of the Congregational church in New England and the resultant scramble among denominations for members and money. Moreover, the cultural ethos of individualism which emerged later in Jacksonian America helped to institutionalize and celebrate competition as a supreme social good. It is no wonder that male fears of being left behind should find their way into narratives of spiritual upheaval.

Men under conviction often presented encounters with others as frightening or disturbing. Unlike their female counterparts, who reluctantly relinquished their earthly attachments only when it appeared necessary, men initially recoiled from the attempts of well-meaning friends to help them, turning to others only when the failure of their own efforts became obvious. A forty-seven-year-old man, described as "a vagabond upon earth . . . [who] had no associates, but seemed a solitary being, almost shut out of society," avoided all conversation with Christian friends. Only when he became seriously ill did he seek help: "With a bible in his hand, he used to go from one to another, begging them to read to him, for he could scarcely, if at all, read himself, and entreating them to pray with him. He often said, that he was afraid, that he should be so lost."[86] Some men went so far as to cut off all communication with family and friends in a last-ditch attempt to evade the requirements of God's law: "I finally determined to turn my wife out of doors, and put out my children or turn them upon the world, and make as

---

84. *CEM* 7 (1806): 57.
85. Ibid., 5 (1804): 33.
86. *CEMRI* 8 (1815): 437.

great a slaughter and destruction of everything I had, as I could; and then go
into the wilderness where never man had been, if I could find such a place,
and then die and go to hell!"[87] The kind of utter isolation this man longed
for could not in the end offer release from the arrows of conviction; another
man found relief only when his "voice" had failed: "In his last agony of soul,
he was heard in the woods more than half a mile; his distressing cries
brought the neighbours to the place, to know the cause. They did not
approach him until they perceived his voice to fail him. Then they went to
him, and found him prostrate and helpless. They carried him home."[88]

For several men, the realization that they could not reach God alone was a
belated discovery; their words elucidate the problem of moral agency they
faced and speak to the failure of self-sufficiency. One man, who had attempted to hide his "feelings and exercises" when first convicted, was "fully
convinced that my conduct in this respect, was unwise and injurious. Had I
freely opened my mind to some person acquainted with the exercises of sinners under conviction, and the devices of Satan to destroy them, I might have
been much relieved under the despair and temptations I experienced."[89]
Another young man declaimed against "my sinful bashfulness, which kept
me from communicating my thoughts to any one, even to my most intimate
friends, who are still ignorant of them to this day." He, like the man quoted
above, concluded, "If I had taken counsel in my awakenings, it now appears,
as if I should have been saved the most of my anguish."[90] As we have seen,
this lesson was not easily accepted by male converts.

Once grace was bestowed, men felt enabled—not to face God alone—but
to return to those attachments which had before seemed so constricting.
Empowerment for men lay in the renewal of social ties rather than in the
freeing of self-expression. The Reverend John Sharp, who had once avoided
Christian conversation, "now sought the company of those pious people of
whom I had been ashamed."[91] The man who had attempted to flee into "the
wilderness where never man had been" recorded that when his burden of sin
was lifted "his wife was the first object that met my eye, and a lovelier one I
never saw. I wanted to fall at her feet, and beg her pardon."[92] Another man
"thought he loved his family before; but never did he have that affection for
them which then seemed to flow from his heart. And the people of God

87. *MMM* 2 (1804): 35.
88. *ABMMI* 2 (1820): 266.
89. *CEM* 1 (1801): 426.
90. Ibid., 5 (1804): 33.
91. *ABMMI* 6 (1826): 158.
92. *MMM* 2 (1804): 36.

appeared to him exceedingly precious; whereas before, he almost despised them."[93] Stephen Page, wrote his biographer, "lost sight of himself through the solicitude he had for others. His thoughts first turned upon a sick brother . . . and from his nearest connexions to his acquaintances, until finally he found but one family on earth, and all distinctions vanished."[94] Only by "losing sight of himself" could the male sinner recover his place in the nexus of familial and social relations which constituted the very condition of his salvation. Restored to family and friends, the male convert has become integrated into the Christian community he once rejected.

When we compare these stories of spiritual renewal to those of the mid-eighteenth century, some interesting parallels are apparent. Male saints of the early nineteenth century, like their brethren of the First Great Awakening, found in the experience of grace the means to reunite with a larger community of believers. Like Nathan Cole, who after his conversion had visions of the brotherhood of saints, John Sharp and Stephen Page were reintegrated into the religious community by the intercession of God's grace. Women saints of the 1800s, on the other hand, shared with such eighteenth-century converts as Hannah Heaton and Susanna Anthony the infusion of divine power and grace into their very beings. Both men and women of the early nineteenth century have been "empowered" in some sense through the conversion experience, but—as in the 1740s—such empowerment took very different forms. Texts of conversion from both periods celebrate, on the one hand, the individualism of women's spirituality and, on the other, men's place within the community.

The institutional context of the conversion experience, however, was very different in 1800 than in 1740. The evangelical community had undergone a tremendous transformation in the intervening years, as dissenting churches that once proudly proclaimed their indifference to structure joined common cause with the religious establishment. Women who turned their spiritual energies inward, as had their sisters before them, now found that such glorious individualism was no longer an asset but a liability in the tempered religious atmosphere of the early republican period. In contrast, in embracing an economy of religious experience which sacrificed individual expression to the needs of the larger community, male evangelicals of the early 1800s were strategically placed to lead the evangelical order toward secular respectability. Womens' religious individualism, which had heralded the

---

93. *RI* 2 (1818): 542.
94. *ABMMI* 3 (1821): 116.

emergence of a distinctive evangelical style of worship in the 1740s, was now perceived to be anachronistic at best and (as church discipline records indicate) subversive at worst. In retaining an older religious vocabulary of the personal, private, and sensual, female narratives of conversion reveal the extent to which women had been displaced from the center of church life in the evangelical community by 1800.

Yet despite their continued allegiance to a discredited language of religious experience, women evangelicals should have found some comfort in the conversion literature promoted by the evangelical press. For the drama of spiritual regeneration enacted by men and women evangelicals ultimately suggests an androgynous model of the conversion experience; while men were encouraged to cast off the excess baggage of self which had so encumbered their search for salvation, women were encouraged to reduce their dependence on friends and family and enlarge their sense of self so as to be able to approach the throne of grace. The language of enlightened rationalism and contractual social relations may have been more appropriate to the social and political pretensions of the evangelical churches in postrevolutionary New England, but male evangelicals had no choice but to discard it (at least temporarily) and embrace a more personal idiom if they hoped to be saved. As women matured under the experience of grace into responsible moral agents, so men responded to the biblical injunction to "become little children." "We must become as little children," wrote a converted Deist, "docile and humble, or we shall never feel entirely dependent, without which we can never ascribe all glory to God and the Lamb."[95] While women's tongues were liberated through conversion, men were "struck dumb" at the moment of grace; "I could not speak," declared P.R., "for it appeared to me I was a child. Helpless as an infant, weary and heavy laden, I sunk in the arms of Christ to be entirely at his disposal. . . . Here I found I rested sweetly as babes sleep in the arms of parents."[96] Patriarchal men thus became dependent children—a supreme irony. For women, the moral problem of conversion was more complicated; the evangelical demand for total submission had to be reconciled with the psychological necessity of assuming moral agency—one cannot give up what one does not possess. Presumably male and female converts reached a level of maturity and spiritual agency which lay somewhere between the enfeebling selflessness of women and the overbearing selfishness of men.

95. *CEMRI* 6 (1813): 256. Other accounts reaffirm the childlike nature of the regenerate state for men; see those in *MBMMI* 3 (1811): 75; *RI* 9 (1824): 443. A seventy-year-old man was "tamed" by the experience of grace: "Softness and gentleness had taken the place of his native ferocity." *CEM* 1 (1800): 221.

96. *MMM* 2 (1804): 281–82.

Two competing versions of the archetypal evangelical encounter with authority—the conversion experience—thus existed side by side in evangelical texts of the early nineteenth century and were reconciled, in the final analysis, in the figure of the androgynous saint. In one version, autonomous, self-interested, competitive (i.e., democratic) men abandoned, at least temporarily, the quest for self-fulfillment in order to reattach themselves to the larger community of saints. In the other version, women already deeply enmeshed in webs of personal dependence cut themselves off from family and friends in order to seek God alone, as autonomous moral agents. Which version represents the "true" narrative of the evangelical community's shifting relationship with authority in the postrevolutionary era? Should we consider the evangelical community as a whole to be metaphorically akin to the competitive, striving unregenerate men of the conversion tales? After all, the exigencies of political disestablishment and the voluntary system demanded that the evangelical churches compete in a national marketplace of religious ideas for both members and influence. Or should we consider the selfless, community-bound women of the conversion narratives to be the true figural representatives of an institution whose origins lay in the principle of *communitas*? The answer, it should be obvious, is both. The "androgynous" dimension to the regenerate state described in these stories of the self suggests that not only did conversion signify the blending of male and female qualities in the evangelical saint, but also the reintegration of the masculine and feminine qualities of the evangelical ethos as well. As I have attempted to show throughout this book, the tension between individual and community which was so central to the evangelical faith (and to the revolutionary reconstruction of political life in the late eighteenth century) was consistently expressed in gendered terms. The metaphor of androgyny for the state of grace connoted far more than a sexual middle ground: it signaled the ultimate compromise between two competing principles of social organization which had frayed the evangelical community from its inception.

What should we make of this apparent resurrection of the model of the genderless saint in the early nineteenth century? At the same time that the evangelical church was being transformed into a patriarchal household in which men ruled and women deferred, echoes of an earlier age of sexual egalitarianism resounded in the literature on religious conversion. On a superficial level, the androgynous saint of the nineteenth century resembles the Great Awakening convert who was physically transported by the power of grace to a transcendental realm existing above time and space. Yet we must never forget that the experience of conversion, however sublime, was an ephemeral one, a brief sojourn in a "Land of Light." The exalted state of grace inevitably gave way to the burdens of the contingent world in which evangelical men and women lived and carried out the social dictates of their faith. What awaited the female convert of the Second Great Awakening was a world profoundly structured by gender, a world in which patriarchal power was reinforced at every level of society from democratic politics to the bourgeois household. Women like Susanna Anthony and Sarah Osborn, on the other hand, had found in the 1740s that the act of conversion initiated them into a religious community that reaffirmed the liminality they had experienced through grace. However empowering the act of conversion was for evangelical women of the early republic, they inevitably returned to the fold of the church, where power was reserved for men.

CONCLUSION

TO SPEAK OF THE "GENDERING" OF EVANGELICALISM, as I have throughout this book, is to evoke an image that is perhaps too sociologically grounded. I have not meant to imply, indeed have taken pains to avoid implying, that the terms "masculine" and "feminine" bore a direct relationship to the experience of men and women within the evangelical community. Sin as a concept may have been metaphorically "feminized" in the turbulent aftermath of revolution, but individual women continued to worship side-by-side with men unreproached by the shadow of Eve. The public image that the evangelical church fashioned for itself as it stepped up to the task of civil and family government may have been "masculinized," but of course some individual men continued to defer to their strong-willed wives and daughters in the privacy of their own homes (and perhaps in the less public spaces of the meetinghouse as well). And for every Betsey Luther who challenged the new sexual politics of the church and paid the price of excommunication, there surely were other women (unremarked and unrecorded) who were satisfied with a reduced role in church governance or who voiced their opinions without such grave consequences. We can make only general inferences about the abilities and opportunities of individual Baptist women as they negotiated the demands and responsibilities of home and hearth, but we can conclude that the official discourse of evangelicalism was far less hospitable to women in 1800 than it had been in 1740, however shrouded the consequences for the sexual balance of power in any one congregation or family.

If our ability to make definitive conclusions about how individual men and women responded to the new gender politics of evangelicalism is limited, we can at least speculate on the role that languages of gender played in the various ideological reconstructions of postrevolutionary America. When we turn our attention from the lives of men and women situated in particular settings to the discourse of gender itself, we are often confronted with what appears to be a seismic shift in vision. The explosion of interest and scholarship in women's history in the last two decades has led to a radical departure from traditional ways of knowing and doing history. The whole, many of us now believe, is no longer equal to the sum of its parts. Adding gender to our master narratives of historical change has not meant simply adding a new chapter to the story but rewriting the story itself. Our entire framework for understanding the past—our sense of narrative, of causality, of periodization—has been challenged by the epistemological fractures introduced by feminist theory. Familiar truths no longer appear so familiar or so true when viewed through the lens of gender.[1]

Nowhere is this more apparent than in our reappraisal of the American Revolution as the first great act in the drama of democracy as it unfolded in the Western world in the late eighteenth century. Spreading like wildfire through the dry and brittle forms of the ancien regime, the democratic revolutions of America, France, Holland, and Belgium created the modern political culture we associate today with mature capitalist societies. Enshrined at the core of this transformation is the autonomous individual, disentangled from the web of vertical dependencies which had bound the premodern world together. All lines of inquiry into the political, economic, social, and cultural transformations wrought by the age of revolution converge in the figure of the autonomous individual: the story of political revolution is the story of how subjects enmeshed in various forms of patronage became independent citizens; the story of economic change is the story of how the "invisible hand" of the market freed men and women from the imperatives of the moral economy to act autonomously in their own self-interest; and the story of social evolution is the story of how an organic, corporate, hierarchical vision of society gave way to a mechanical, individualistic, horizontal model in which each American was, to quote Alexis de Tocqueville, "shut up in the solitude of his own heart."[2]

The celebrated individual—free, autonomous, self-sufficient—thus stands at the endpoint of all our narratives of the many revolutions of this topsy-turvy age. And this individual is, we now understand from the work of feminist historians, hardly the "genderless" subject of classical liberal theory. The master narrative of the age of revolution is a deeply gendered

---

1. Joan W. Scott, "Gender: A Useful Category of Historical Analysis," *American Historical Review* 91 (December 1986): 1053–75; Joan Kelly, "The Doubled Vision of Feminist Theory," in her *Women, History, and Theory: The Essays of Joan Kelly* (Chicago, 1984), 51–64.

2. Alexis de Tocqueville, *Democracy in America*, ed. J. P. Mayer (New York, 1969), 2:508. The clearest exposition of how these various transformations are related can be found in Gordon Wood, *The Radicalism of the American Revolution* (New York, 1992). See also Carroll Smith-Rosenberg, "Dis-covering the Subject of the 'Great Constitutional Discussion,' 1786–1789," *Journal of American History* 79 (1992):841–73.

one, and we have only begun to appreciate the extent to which the democratic promise of citizenship and independence was both implicitly and
explicitly construed as a male prerogative. The Revolution looks decidedly
less revolutionary when viewed from the perspective of women. If this
insight were simply a matter of adducing from the historical record women's
exclusion from the legal and political rights of citizenship, our task would be
finished. While there remains a good deal of dissension over the long-term
effects of the Revolution on women's legal, economic, and social status
within antebellum America, on the issue of citizenship itself—the right to
vote and serve in public life—there is no doubt that men alone constituted
the political nation in the early republic.

But the masculine bias of the revolutionary movement goes far deeper
than the political disenfranchisement of women who, after all, had always
occupied the margins of colonial political culture. More important, the very
language and ideology of the revolutionary movement cast the struggle
against monarchy and tyranny in gendered terms. A "manly" citizenry rose
up in arms against an effeminate imperial power whose danger lay precisely
in its ability to emasculate its colonial subjects. As feminist historians have
shown in the case of both the French and American revolutions, such political terms as "nation," "citizen," and "virtue" were not gender-neutral but
were in fact imbued with a deep sense of the opposition between masculine
and feminine. We cannot truly appreciate the rhetorical power these terms
held for eighteenth-century men and women without recognizing the degree to which sexual identity was implicated in political identity in this
revolutionary age. Lockean rhetoric aside, the great moment of the democratic revolution did not decisively sunder the personal from the political.
We have been misled by the triumph of the liberal vision in the early
nineteenth century into mistaking the rhetoric of "separate spheres" for
reality.[3]

As a colonial society, America itself was gendered female in a world in
which dependency of any kind (geopolitical, familial, social, sexual) was
denounced as feminine. To admit women into the rights of citizenship in
the new republic would thus have been to perpetuate the stigma of feminine
dependency which had inhered in the colonial subject.[4] If we can under-

3. Linda Kerber has made this point repeatedly, most forcefully in "Separate Spheres, Female
Worlds, Woman's Place: The Rhetoric of Women's History," *Journal of American History* 75 (1988):
9–39. See also the exchange among Ellen DuBois, Mari Jo Buhle, Temma Kaplan, Gerda Lerner,
and Carroll Smith-Rosenberg, "Politics and Culture in Women's History: A Symposium," *Feminist Studies* 6 (1980): 26–64.

4. The politically debilitating association of dependency with women was given renewed
vigor after the American Revolution, Joan Gundersen argues, as dependency itself lost the voli-

stand the "feminine" to be, as feminist scholars suggest, a heuristic category for the dispossessed, then colonial men who were the subjects of other subjects were doubly feminized. The fragile nature of male authority in a colonial society in which the central source of power lay beyond the grasp of would-be patriarchs made women a particularly vulnerable target for failed male ambitions. The misogynistic rage uncovered by Kenneth Lockridge in the private writings of two prominent Virginians, William Byrd II and Thomas Jefferson, derived from the unbearable gender tensions inherent in the colonial situation.[5] Unable to reproduce the patriarchal privileges they aspired to, colonial men (even those of enviable wealth and political status) raged at the suppressed female within.

The dilemma was even more acute for those Americans who, like evangelical Protestants, inhabited a subordinate position within colonial society itself. If colonial men in general were doubly feminized in a monarchical world, then male evangelicals were in an even more tenuous position. Each layer of subordination removed colonial men further and further from the patriarchal ideal that continued to burn brightly in the late eighteenth century. The triumph of liberalism freed some men from this dilemma, but as Carole Pateman has argued so effectively, it was an illusory triumph for women, because political theories of the state simply transferred patriarchal privilege from the father to the son. Rather than ungendering politics by sundering the theoretical link between the family and the state posited by patriarchalism, Lockean liberalism reified that link as "natural" and inscribed it in the figure of the bourgeois husband and father. A variant of liberalism we can identify as "feminist" did take shape later in the nineteenth century, one that sought to extend to women the same political rights and responsibilities that men (at least white men of property) had enjoyed since the Revolution, but nineteenth-century feminism remained ideologically rooted in a conception of power which was essentially patriarchal as Pateman uses the term. The first Anglo-American feminists did not (with few exceptions) question the separation of men and women into distinct spheres, nor did they dispute the notion that men had sexual dominion over women because of "natural" differences between the sexes. Rather, they laid claim to a political presence either by denying their femininity all together

---

tional aspect with which it was invested in early modern social theory and came increasingly to signify domination. Gundersen, "Independence, Citizenship, and the American Revolution," *Signs* 13 (1987): 59–77.

5. Kenneth Lockridge, *On the Sources of Patriarchal Rage: The Commonplace Books of William Byrd II and Thomas Jefferson and the Gendering of Power in the Eighteenth Century* (New York, 1992).

or by insisting that their peculiarly feminine virtues provided the necessary moral ballast to the male world of competitive democratic politics.[6]

This is not to say that "patriarchy" was a static concept in the age of revolution. Colonial sons vied with their royal father to secure home rule—and then with one another to decide who should rule at home. A new kind of paternalism, rooted more in the sympathetic ties of affection than in the coercive powers of property, is certainly evident in postrevolutionary discourse about the family and the state, but it was still a model of authority which subordinated women to men. The filial squabbles of the early republican period were not without effect, however; for in calling into question a certain type of paternal rule, revolutionary patriots implicitly questioned the equation of masculinity with unrestrained power. However successful the revolutionary generation was in reinstating the patriarchal model of authority it had usurped, for a moment at least masculinity was as precarious a commodity as republican virtue.

The gender anxieties evident in late-eighteenth-century evangelical discourse, as men made the difficult transition from "brides" to "soldiers" of Christ, reflect the broader crisis in gender norms which historians have discovered in a wide variety of eighteenth-century contexts. From science to politics to religion, the eighteenth century seems to have been an age in which there was no longer consensus on what the proper relations of men to women should look like, or indeed what it meant to be male or female. Thomas Laqueur's provocative study of medical theory suggests that a more fluid understanding of gender, in which masculinity and femininity were but two poles of a "one-sex" continuum, was replaced by a categorical representation of gender in the eighteenth century. In making sex an ontological rather than a social problem, Laqueur suggests, the groundwork was laid for the modern understanding of gender as a fixed biological reality rather than as a social construction. As the category of "woman" attained a new stability, discussion came more and more to center on how precisely to define that category.[7] The genesis of an essentialist understanding of gender

6. See, for instance, Barbara Taylor's discussion of Mary Wollstonecraft's feminism. As Taylor notes, "It was impossible for women to speak *as* citizens without speaking *against* their womanhood," so firmly identified was citizenship with the male sex. Thus Wollstonecraft was often forced to speak "against womanhood and for masculinity" in order to make a claim for women's political rights. Taylor, "Mary Wollstonecraft and the Wild Wish of Early Feminism," *History Workshop* 33 (1992): 206.

7. Thomas Laqueur, *Making Sex: Body and Gender from the Greeks to Freud* (Cambridge, Mass., 1990). Laqueur understates the degree to which the new epistemology of sexual incommensurability which took shape in the late eighteenth century was still one that hierarchically ranked

thus lay in the intellectual and cultural developments of the eighteenth century, an age that saw human reason reified in the manly form of the Enlightenment philosophe and the remnants of medieval backwardness (superstition, animality) relegated to various female forms, ranging from the "female monster" to the hysteric.[8]

On one level, this book narrates the progression of the evangelical community's understanding of gender from a rather porous one, in which men and women moved easily between the sexual identities they inhabited in their secular lives and the feminized demands of their faith, to a modern, essentialist construction of gender, in which masculinity was taken to be the normative condition and femininity the derived (and derided) other.[9] It is not difficult to see the resurgence of patriarchy in postrevolutionary New England as an emblematic episode of how the eighteenth century "made sex," to paraphrase Laqueur. Women were deemed unfit for the business of governing not because they lacked sufficient quantities of the abilities men possessed in abundance (rationality, moderation, self-interest), but because their entire natures betrayed a fundamental incapacity to govern. As we saw in the disciplining of male and female members in the postrevolutionary years, disorder was lodged firmly in the inner recesses of the female character rather than in the external realm of behavior. As Laqueur argues, the biology of sexual incommensurability offered political theorists across the

---

one sex above the other. Women may have been regarded as biologically incommensurable with men by the late eighteenth century, but—as Denise Riley shows—they still remained in political and social theory the derivative category. Difference was construed within an existing framework of hierarchy; that framework was not dismantled. Riley, *"Am I That Name?" Feminism and the Category of "Women" in History* (Minneapolis, 1988). For a reading of early modern medical theory which focuses on the enculturation of gender differences within the one-sex paradigm, see Gail Kern Paster, *The Body Embarrassed: Drama and the Disciplines of Shame in Early Modern England* (Ithaca, 1993).

8. For discussions of how the Enlightenment was constructed in masculine terms against a feminized medieval past, see Peter Wagner's unpublished essay "'The Female Creed': William Byrd as Ribald Satirist," Department of Modern Languages, University of Aston in Birmingham; and Lockridge, *On the Sources of Patriarchal Rage*, especially chap. 2, "'The Female Creed': Misogyny Enlightened?" See also Susan Gubar, "The Female Monster," *Signs* 3 (1977): 380–94.

9. It is interesting to note in this context that the evangelical ethos in the mid-eighteenth century evinced a more fluid understanding not only of gender but of all social and cultural boundaries; just as humoral medical theories envisioned the human body as a mass of permeable boundaries and orifices through which vital fluids were constantly exchanged, so evangelical religion envisioned the essence of faith as the eviscerating of all boundaries separating the soul from God. In early modern medical theory "*all* boundaries were threatened because they were—as a matter of physical definition and functional health—porous and permeable," Gail Paster writes. Paster, *The Body Embarrassed*, p. 13. The porous gender norms Laqueur identifies as the consequence of the "one-sex" model were thus one part of a larger epistemological framework in which boundaries were conceived of as permeable frontiers rather than as unbreachable fortresses.

revolutionary spectrum a way to explore the question of women's public role without challenging the central myth of bourgeois liberalism which envisioned a "genderless rational subject" at its core. Both feminist and antifeminist writers in postrevolutionary France, for instance, turned to the new epistemology of sexual difference in order to make claims for or against women's participation in the new "public sphere." Antifeminists claimed that women's essential difference from men precluded their participation in such masculine endeavors as politics; feminists claimed that, on the contrary, such difference demanded special participation by women whose interests men could not presume to represent.[10] Evangelical women in the 1830s and 1840s would make similar claims to a public role in the various reform movements of the Second Great Awakening on the grounds of their distinctive feminine sensibilities—the very grounds on which they had been denied a governing role in the 1790s and early 1800s.

But it is also possible to see echoes of an older epistemology in the elaboration of a feminized model of sin. Here women represented the normative category of transgression, but men were not immune from being construed as disorderly "women" because of their essential maleness. The persona of sin was gendered female regardless of the sex of the sinner in the late eighteenth century, just as the persona of the saint had been gendered female regardless of the sex of the convert in the earlier period. This flexibility was more apparent than real, however. Sin was always a temporary state—a momentary return to the feminine world of chaos and disorder. However often men found themselves "unmanned" in the exercise of church discipline, they were able to reassert their masculinity by the simple act of confession and restoration.[11] Most men who sinned did, in fact, find their way back to the church in relatively short order in the late eighteenth and early nineteenth centuries. Salvation, on the other hand, was—one hoped— an irreversible condition. Saints might backslide, but the occasional lapse of a fallible man or woman would not negate a genuine conversion. The feminized saint, in other words, was a far more trenchant figure than the feminized sinner, and far more subversive of notions of stable gender identity.

On the whole, late-eighteenth-century evangelicals evinced a markedly different sensibility toward sexual identity than had their counterparts in the

---

10. Laqueur, *Making Sex*, pp. 196–97.

11. In similar fashion, male novelists who wrote in a female voice in the eighteenth century ran no risk of "being trapped in the devalued female realm," as Madeleine Kahn notes; the "narrative transvestism" that is a striking feature of the first English novels owes much of its cultural power to the eclipsing of the "one-sex" model of human biology. Kahn, *Narrative Transvestism: Rhetoric and Gender in the Eighteenth-Century English Novel* (Ithaca, 1991), p. 6.

Great Awakening. Ministers through their consociations and didactic writings had succeeded in realigning the evangelical order as a whole along a more conventional male-female axis, one in line with contemporary developments in the Anglo-American world. The devaluation of the erotic element in the evangelical ethos—a devaluation we saw in nineteenth-century conversion narratives—paralleled the efforts of late-eighteenth-century medical theorists to reformulate womanhood as devoid of passion.[12] The seducing, carnal woman who plagued the imaginations of early modern thinkers gave way to the virtuous, chaste angel in the house so celebrated in Victorian literature. As the category of woman was emptied of its sensuality, so too was evangelicalism purged of its sexual overtones in the early nineteenth century. Yet, in a critical departure from mainstream cultural trends, evangelical women themselves did not share in this general deeroticizing of the category of femininity. Rather, they became the repository for all that the evangelical community wished to repudiate in its own past. Ironically, then, women became transformed into seducing, carnal creatures as the evangelical church itself shook off the residue of disreputable femininity. Not until the 1830s or 1840s would evangelicals feel secure enough in their reconstruction of a masculine self to allow images of women (now sanitized to reflect a pious and passionless nature) once again to represent the public face of religion.

It is important to note that in this particular scenario intellectual currents alone cannot explain the shift toward a more normative understanding of gender. It was, rather, *political* events—growing disillusionment with the paternal rule of the Crown, the desire for independence and "manly" autonomy, the final break with the "mother" country—that compelled Americans (including and perhaps especially evangelicals) to privilege the masculine over the feminine in their collective self-fashioning. Moments of intense political crisis are often fertile ground for misogynistic constructions of women as "other," as Hanna Pitkin, Kenneth Lockridge, and Joan Landes have shown in very different contexts. In republican Florence, colonial Virginia, and revolutionary France, an emerging ruling class insinuated itself into the crevices of power by claiming masculine prerogative over an effemi-

---

12. Nancy F. Cott, "Passionlessness: An Interpretation of Victorian Sexual Ideology, 1790–1850," *Signs* 4 (1978–79): 219–36. For a discussion of how religious discourse in general became deeroticized between the seventeenth and nineteenth centuries, see Susan Juster, "The Spirit and the Flesh: Gender, Language, and Sexuality in American Protestantism," paper prepared for the Wingspread Conference, "New Directions in American Religious History: The Protestant Experience," Racine, Wis., October 1993.

nate ancien regime.[13] In each case, the anxieties borne of peripheral status—anxieties that, at bottom, were rooted as much in sexual as in political insecurity—were resolved by a shrill assertion of manly valor among aspiring elites.

For all their insecurities, evangelical men never exhibited the hyper-masculinity characteristic of these other embattled elites. Rather, their patriarchalism was modulated by the knowledge that the feminized aspects of faith could not be entirely foresworn without damaging the vital core of evangelicalism—the traumatic experience of the "New Birth." Again and again, evangelical men reached for worldly glory only to be brought low by the demands of grace. The importance of the "New Birth" receded in the later nineteenth century, as the theological and moral dimensions of evangelicalism came to occupy greater space in devotional literature, but until 1830 or so no self-professed evangelical could escape the humbling experience of conversion in which the carnal self and all its desires were obliterated in a single stroke.[14] The men who ruled the evangelical church and governed the evangelical home knew that they served God, not their own secular ambitions—and if they forgot, the evangelical press reminded them through its stories of proud men who became "little children" in the eyes of God. Once "brides" of Christ, then manly "soldiers" who fought the good fight, and finally prudent "governors" of church and home, evangelical men were also and always "children of God." Such was the paradox of grace, and it continued to temper the patriarchal strivings of the evangelical community well into the nineteenth century. Like other self-made men in postrevolutionary America, the evangelical church balanced precariously on the precipice of manhood, all the while looking over its shoulder at the female self it had left behind.

13. Hanna F. Pitkin, *Fortune Is a Woman: Gender and Politics in the Thought of Niccolo Machiavelli* (Berkeley, Calif., 1984); Lockridge, *On the Sources of Patriarchal Rage*; and Joan Landes, *Women and the Public Sphere in the Age of the French Revolution* (Ithaca, 1988).

14. For a discerning and highly evocative description of this transition, see George Rawlyk, *The Canada Fire: Radical Evangelicalism in British North America from 1775 to 1812* (Kingston and Montreal, 1994), Introduction and passim.

INDEX